MARK TWAIN AND SHAKESPEARE

A Cultural Legacy

Anthony J. Berret, S.J.

UNIVERSITY
PRESS OF
AMERICA

Lanham • New York • London

Copyright © 1993 by
University Press of America®, Inc.
4720 Boston Way
Lanham, Maryland 20706

3 Henrietta Street
London WC2E 8LU England

Library of Congress Cataloging-in-Publication Data

Berret, Anthony J.
Mark Twain and Shakespeare : a cultural legacy /
Anthony J. Berret, S.J.
Includes bibliographical references and index.
1. Twain, Mark, 1835–1910—Knowledge—Literature.
2. Shakespeare, William, 1564–1616—Appreciation—United States.
3. Shakespeare, William, 1564–1616—Influence.   4. American
fiction—English influences.   I. Title.
PS1342.L5B47   1993   818'.409—dc20   93–25233 CIP

ISBN 0–8191–9220–1 (cloth : alk. paper)

The paper used in this publication meets the minimum requirements of
American National Standard for Information Sciences—Permanence
of Paper for Printed Library Materials, ANSI Z39.48–1984.

With gratitude to my father,
and in memory of my mother.

CONTENTS

ACKNOWLEDGMENTS

Those who have helped me most through the long and shifting process from thought to writing are, in the order of appearance, Garry Wills, Joseph Godfrey, S.J., Richard Fusco, Victor Doyno, and Dominic and Carole Roberti. The Jesuit communities at St. Peter's College, St. Joseph's University, and Robert Southwell House also gave me many kinds of support.

Part of the first chapter was published in *Mark Twain: Ritual Clown* (Siena Research Institute), and part of the fourth chapter was published in *American Literary Realism, 1870-1910*. Mark Twain's notes in *The Shakespeare Problem Restated* by George Greenwood are quoted with permission of the Henry W. and Albert A. Berg Collection, The New York Public Library, Astor, Lenox, and Tilden Foundations. Twain's unpublished "Autobiographical Dictations" and Joseph T. Goodman's "Hamlet's Brother" are quoted with permission of the Mark Twain Papers, University of California at Berkeley.

Introduction

By giving one of his books the title, *Mark Twain's America*, Bernard De Voto wanted to hail the new frontiers that Mark Twain scouted and claimed for literature: the West, the Mississippi Valley, and the political and industrial establishments of the late nineteenth century. Yet the title could also have a significance that reaches beyond the book. It could serve as a deed, or legal title, by which Mark Twain becomes an owner or trustee of the American literary estate, and rightly so, because he incorporated large tracts of the American experience into his writings and personality. Yet Mark Twain is not the only author who has been granted property in America through the title of a book. Other authors who share this honor include William Cullen Bryant, Charles Ives, Edmund Wilson, Norman Mailer, and John Updike. The most surprising holder of property in America by this norm, however, is William Shakespeare, especially since his claim is supported by two book titles instead of one.

In *Will Shakespeare and His America* Nancy and Jean Francis Webb ascribe to Shakespeare not only the territories that De Voto thought belonged to Mark Twain—the West, the Mississippi River, and the mansions and corporations of the Gilded Age—but other parts of America as well. According to the Webbs, Shakespeare's right to the West is based on the frequent productions and popularity of his plays there.   The stalwart American backwoodsmen, like their Elizabethan ancestors, found their lives reflected in the bloodshed, melodrama, broad comedy, "exaggerated and colorful speech" and "larger-than-life emotions" of Shakespeare's plays.   His tragedies helped them express and analyze the ambitions, crimes, booms and crashes generated by the Gold Rush.   His plays also drifted down the Ohio and Mississippi rivers on rafts and showboats, and they were staged in the palatial theaters of the Gilded Age, with renowned actors and actresses from England in the lead roles.[1]   Most recently, in *Shakespeare's America, America's Shakespeare*, Michael D. Bristol approaches the topic of Shakespeare's ownership with a stress on capital rather than real estate.   He describes the near monopoly that Shakespeare enjoys over American culture and how this monopoly is used in collecting, editing, teaching, and scholarly research to represent and support the vested interests of tradition, individualism, and a hierarchical social order.[2]

In a partly comic and partly serious way, Mark Twain viewed Shakespeare as a "claimant" of things which did not belong to him, although by *things* he meant the writings attributed to him, not property in America.   Twain thought that someone else was the author of Shakespeare's works, and he grouped Shakespeare with other false claimants: Satan, Louis XVII, Mary Baker Eddy, and Arthur Orton, an Australian butcher who claimed to be the long lost son of Lady Tichborne.[3]   Despite their false claims, however, Twain seemed to show more fascination than scorn for these people.   He had a friend save newspaper clippings of the Tichborne trial, and he built his novel *The American Claimant* around the story of Jesse Leathers, a distant cousin of his, who claimed to be the rightful Earl of Durham.   In fact, some of his most colorful characters are those who register fraudulent claims, Colonel Sellers in *The Gilded Age* and *The American Claimant*, and the King and the Duke in *Huckleberry Finn*.   If he is at all consistent, Twain would certainly admire Shakespeare for claiming some portion of the American turf, whether his claim were legal or not.

Believing that the name *Clemens* meant "claimant," Twain also included himself in this notorious crew. Like the buyers and collectors of his era who raided Europe for symbols of wealth, culture, and aristocracy, he imported carpets, furniture, woodwork, and sculpture to decorate his mansion in Hartford. He also appropriated foreign materials for his writing. He set six of his books in Europe, and he based two of them on European models, *The Innocents Abroad* on *Pilgrim's Progress* and *A Connecticut Yankee* on *Le Morte D'Arthur*. First and foremost among his thefts, purchases, or borrowings from Europe, however, are the works and person of Shakespeare. Not only did he write a book on Shakespeare—his only book about another author—but he integrated scenes, language, and characters of Shakespeare into many of his other writings. Although this could be interpreted as a typical pillaging of Europe to gain literary prestige, the fact that Shakespeare was already settled and naturalized in American culture made it rather a legitimate exploitation of his own country and background. Twain treated Shakespeare as an inheritance or legacy, something handed down to him, not directly, but through other authors and cultural activities. This gave him the right to use Shakespeare freely, but also respectfully, since Shakespeare was in fact a former possessor and developer of the property that Twain considered his own.

Other American authors created a tradition by incorporating Shakespeare into their works, perhaps because they wanted the pre-eminent author of the English Renaissance to signal and support a similar renaissance in their own country. Of the thirty-three chapters in James Fenimore Cooper's *The Last of the Mohicans*, twenty have epigraphs from Shakespeare, and the epigraph to the novel as a whole is also from Shakespeare. Although the epigraphs are taken from eleven different plays, there is a concentration on *The Merchant of Venice* for its themes of ethnic and racial conflict, justice and revenge, and on *A Midsummer-Night's Dream* for its tactics of disguise and impersonation. Cooper frequently used epigraphs to draw parallels between his own works and those of Shakespeare. Following a different strategy, Nathaniel Hawthorne scattered words and phrases from Shakespeare through *The Scarlet Letter* in order to reproduce the "boldness and rotundity of speech" characteristic of people living in the Elizabethan age and shortly after, and he included in his story a sufficient number of phrases and images from *Hamlet*—the hidden crime, the scholar's attempts at detection, the swearing to secrecy, the midnight watch on the platform, the ghosts and madness—to pay tribute to that play as a forerunner of his own study of evil, revenge, and retribution. Herman Melville commended Hawthorne for expressing a blackness and profundity worthy of Shakespeare, and he further prophesied, "Believe me, my friends, that men, not very much inferior to Shakespeare, are this day being born on the banks of the Ohio....The great mistake seems to be, that even with those Americans who look forward to the coming of a great literary genius among us, they somehow fancy he will come in the costume of Queen Elizabeth's day....[I]f Shakespeare has not been equalled, give the world time, and he is sure to be surpassed."[4] By clothing some of his own work in Elizabethan costume, Melville showed that he wanted at least to honor Shakespeare, if not equal or surpass him. Among the various prototypes that he assigned to Captain Ahab in *Moby-Dick*— Jonah, Job, Satan, Prometheus—are Shakespeare's tragic heroes. Like Hamlet, Ahab forces his crew to cross lances and swear to cooperate in his act of revenge, and he offers poor Pip the shelter of his cabin during a storm, as Lear did to the Fool. The whale itself is compared to Richard III because of its hump and savage nature. Melville used Shakespeare, therefore, to reinforce his own drama of fate, brutality, madness, and elemental fury. Although Ralph Waldo Emerson complained that the poetry of his time was too "Shakespearized" and not original, he also believed that Shakespeare was a "representative man," and thus a model for the writer in a democratic society, because he absorbed and reflected the thoughts and aspirations of his contemporaries.[5]

In a collection of essays about Shakespeare's influence on writers of the American South, which includes studies of William Gilmore Simms, Sidney Lanier, and William Faulkner, Thomas J. Richardson has a chapter on Mark Twain: "Is

Shakespeare Dead? Mark Twain's Irreverent Question." After establishing Twain's familiarity with Shakespeare's works through reading, attending plays, and directing private theatricals, Richardson focuses his study on four pieces by Twain which fit loosely into the category of Shakespeare burlesques: a modern newspaper report of Caesar's assassination called "The Killing of Julius Caesar—*Localized*"; an unfinished burlesque of *Hamlet*; the burlesque of Hamlet's "To be, or not to be" soliloquy which appears in *Huckleberry Finn*; and *Is Shakespeare Dead?*, a pseudo-critical study of the Shakespeare-Bacon controversy. Richardson finds that Twain's general approach to Shakespeare is one of burlesque, one that stresses the incongruity between Shakespeare's plays and nineteenth-century American society, thereby exposing both to deflation, laughter, and criticism. This use of Shakespeare's works as both objects and agents of satire exemplifies Twain's "ambivalent attitude toward Shakespeare and his works, as part of his characteristic ambivalence toward established civilization, traditional standards, and classic literature." Richardson notes the dilemma between reverence and irreverence that Twain felt when deciding how freely he could handle Shakespeare's text in composing his burlesque *Hamlet*.[6]

In his brief study Richardson points out two of the main characteristics of Twain's reaction to Shakespeare—burlesque and ambivalence. In my longer study I shall, on the one hand, add further illustrations of these characteristics. Not only did Twain write eight pieces that would qualify formally as Shakespeare burlesques, but he also quoted or referred to Shakespeare in numerous other instances to produce the same comic and satirical effects as the burlesques. I shall also amplify and examine Twain's ambivalent attitude toward Shakespeare, and give more emphasis than Richardson does to one side of that ambivalence, Twain's reverence for Shakespeare. Besides representing classic literature, which Twain certainly aspired to, Shakespeare also represented, for Twain, colorful and realistic language, broad comedy, and the robust life-style of the English Renaissance. Twain consulted Shakespeare for examples of these qualities, and he put what he learned from him into *The Prince and the Pauper* and other historical novels. He was also profoundly affected by Shakespeare's exhaustive treatment of evil, fate, deceit, violence and suffering, and of the gracious or menacing effects of nature on humanity. In his own handling of these themes Twain left subtle allusions to Shakespeare as signs of his influence and affinity. It was not just Shakespeare's status, therefore, that caused Twain to revere him, but also the many excellences which he found in his works and the solidarity with him which he felt when he thought that he and Shakespeare were expressing similar ideas and sentiments.

Another important aspect of Shakespeare's influence on Twain which I shall add to Richardson's study is the extensive and varied treatments of Shakespeare in American culture. Twain was licensed and inspired by these to rummage through Shakespeare for journalistic humor and arty burlesque, as well as historical backgrounds and tragic spectacle. The fact that Shakespeare was already established at all levels of American society, not just among the educated and refined, gave Twain the liberty to cite him as a representative American instead of a foreigner or member of an exclusive class, and it encouraged a free and versatile handling of his works.

Following the spirit of their time, critics in the later nineteenth century used terms of Charles Darwin and Herbert Spencer to describe an evolution in the works of Shakespeare from the dreams, tricks, and romances of the Comedies, through the facts and patriotic ideals of the Histories, to the fully developed passions and enlightenment of the Tragedies.[7] Although this has been proved inaccurate as a description of Shakespeare's artistic progress, it happens to express very well the progression in Mark Twain's use of Shakespeare. Following this scheme, therefore, I shall divide my study into four parts. After a chapter on Twain's comic-serious interest in Shakespeare's life and person, focusing mainly on the Shakespeare-Bacon controversy, I shall devote a chapter to the predominantly comic treatment that Twain gave to Shakespeare's works during his early journalistic career in the West. Although this comic treatment of Shakespeare persisted throughout Twain's writing career, it was complemented by a serious investigation of Shakespeare's works for historical data and antique forms of speech when Twain was preparing to write a novel set during the English Renaissance. His move to a professional and cultivated community in Hartford, Connecticut, and his lengthy stays in Europe, increased his taste for culture and tradition, and inspired him to write a novel that would appeal to high class readers. He found that Shakespeare's works provided him with useful models for these pursuits, just as they had been perfect foils for his comic exercises. Finally, the political and economic problems of his day, of which he was himself to become a victim, and the enduring social injustices, which seemed to nullify the effects of the Civil War and return America to an era of profit and leisure supported by slavery, caused Twain to reconsider Shakespeare's tragedies and imagine scenes and characters from them looming in the backgrounds of his own stories. Progressing, therefore, through stages of comedy, history, and tragedy, and usually retaining the former stages even after achieving the latter, Twain's use of Shakespeare is multi-layered and many-faceted, yet it reaches its fulfillment, I think, not in irony or ambivalence, but in respect and aspiration.

A writer like Mark Twain, however, who insisted so adamantly on deriving his material from direct experience, might object to any form of dependence on another author. When he was told that the dedication which he wrote for his first book duplicated one in a book by Oliver Wendell Holmes, he immediately wrote Holmes a letter of apology in which he explained that reading and rereading Holmes's book must have filled his mind with ideas that he later thought were his own. Holmes agreed. In his answer to Twain's letter he admitted that "we all unconsciously worked over ideas gathered in reading and hearing, imagining they were original with ourselves." About ten years after this, in 1879, Twain told the story to guests at a dinner celebrating Holmes's seventieth birthday, and labeled the phenomenon "unconscious plagiarism." He claimed that "pride protects a man from deliberately stealing other people's ideas."[8] Despite the unconscious, and therefore blameless, nature of this theft, however, Twain still felt uneasy, and what must have aggravated this feeling was the eminent stature of Holmes. Twain cherished Holmes's early letter as the first one that he had ever received from a famous person, and his dinner speech, delivered to a gathering of writers for the prestigious *Atlantic Monthly*, occurred at a time when he was trying to be recognized as a serious writer by the literary establishment. He must have been extra-sensitive to any suspicions of stealing from the great in order to become one of them.

Around the same time as his speech on "unconscious plagiarism," Twain coined another term to explain the origin of similar ideas that come from different authors who are thinking or writing separately but contemporaneously. His term was "mental telegraphy," and he used it to explain several kinds of seemingly accidental occurrences—crossing letters, simultaneous inventions, coincidental meetings—but especially literary composition, or plagiarism. He related incidents about Samuel Johnson and Voltaire, Louisa May Alcott, William Dean Howells, and himself.[9] Of course these are cases of writers who were working at the same time, so they do not apply to influences coming from authors of the past. However, Twain's thoughts and essays reveal his persistent concern about the issue of influence.

One important aspect of this issue is the stature of the author from whom the influence is coming. If it is a minor author, or one whose stature is equal or inferior to that of the author being influenced, the content of the influence may conceivably be elevated or improved by the second author, and that at least would constitute some originality. However, if the influence is coming from a major or superior author, one whose material would presumably not be improved upon, questions might arise concerning originality and plagiarism. Around the time that he was writing on plagiarism and telegraphy, Twain was reading and taking notes in Henry H. Breen's *Modern English Literature: Its Blemishes and Defects*, which has a section on plagiarism. Breen deplored Alexandre Dumas' statement that "a man of genius does not steal; he conquers: and what he conquers, he annexes to his empire." Yet Breen could refute this only by claiming that Dumas was not a genius like Shakespeare or Moliere. Twain seemed to agree with Dumas. In his copy of Breen's book, he noted, "Shakespeare took other people's quartz and extracted gold from it."[10] Twain certainly practiced this himself on lesser literary figures—journalists, showpeople, writers of children's books, and so forth—but he would not have described his use of Shakespeare in these terms since he saw Shakespeare as his superior.

The "anxiety of influence" analyzed recently by Harold Bloom applies with some validity to Mark Twain, even though he was not a poet and Shakespeare was not his major literary precursor. In order to escape the charge of dependence or imitation, Twain could have felt the need to revise or misinterpret Shakespeare's works when he made use of them. The two categories of Bloom that fit Twain's use of Shakespeare are "tessara" and "askesis." In the former, writers treat a precursor's work as incomplete, and try to complete it in their own work. Bloom finds this a frequent practice of American writers who are influenced by the British. Americans often consider the works of the British too idealized, and feel that they have to make them rougher and more down-to-earth like the speech of ordinary people.[11] This could be what Twain and other Americans did in their Shakespeare burlesques and in their use of Shakespeare analogues for realistic stories. In another strategy, "askesis," writers intentionally limit the influence of their precursor to certain minor factors, reducing thereby the overall achievement of the precursor to just those factors and thus decreasing the precursor's intimidating power over them.[12] Twain's recourse to Shakespeare for historical fact, antique language, and ribaldry confines Shakespeare's art to these limited categories and thus renders his influence less significant.

Another way to lighten the burden of influence is to realize that all writing is influenced by previous texts. Although Twain did not have the benefit of recent critical theories concerning intertextuality, he seemed to understand that what he wrote was usually a response to several other texts. This could have come from his background in journalism, where he frequently responded to editorials by other reporters or newspapers, or it could have come from his humorous exercises, many of which were burlesques of other works. Whatever its origin, it did not stop after his early writings. It continued into the major phases of his career. There is a photograph of Twain writing at a desk in his outdoor octagonal study on a mountain top which overlooks Elmira and the hills beyond. On his desk is a pile of books which he is presumably using as sources for his writing. He referred and alluded to numerous books in his classics, *Huckleberry Finn* and *A Connecticut Yankee*.

Although Shakespeare is only one among many of the authors whom Twain used as sources, his uses of Shakespeare are especially significant because of their frequency and their variety. They show the influence of Shakespeare's works themselves, and that of the other authors—journalists, politicians, and showpeople, as well as classic writers—who also used Shakespeare for similar or different purposes. A study of these uses, therefore, describes many levels and sectors of American culture, and reveals the many threads, both popular and classic, that are woven into Twain's richly constructed passages. It proves that Twain, through his inclusion of such varied sources into his work, was trying to become an author who was valued for classical stature as well as popular appeal.

To write with powerful effect, he *must*
write out *the life he has led*—as did
Bacon when he wrote Shakspeare.[1]

Biography

In May 1835 a limited edition of the fifty-page monograph, *New Facts Regarding The Life of Shakespeare*, was published in London as a letter to Thomas Amyot of the Society of Antiquaries. Its author, John Payne Collier, a lawyer and former newspaper reporter, had gained a scholarly reputation and memberships in learned societies as a result of his 1831 book, *The History of English Dramatic Poetry to the Time of Shakespeare*. He also gained access to the library at Bridgewater House, which contained the records and manuscripts of Lord Ellesmere, Queen Elizabeth I's Keeper of the Great Seal and King James I's Lord Chancellor. There he claimed to have found four documents that added "new facts" to the life of Shakespeare and that formed the basis of his new book. In actuality, however, he had not found the documents but forged them, hoping by fraud to increase his own scholarly prestige and elevate the social status of Shakespeare.

Collier began *New Facts* with a quotation from his earlier book: "on looking back to the life of Shakespeare the first observation that must be made is, that so few facts are extant regarding him." Although neoclassical critics recognized Shakespeare's artistic mastery, they attributed it to his "genius," his original and direct contact with nature through intuition and imagination. It did not matter how extensive or noteworthy the facts of his life were because with this gift of genius he was able to see profound and universal truths in the most commonplace experiences. During the eighteenth century, however, history and biography became important resources for the study of literature, and critics began to look for detailed experiences in Shakespeare's life—education, travel, professions, acquaintances—that would account for the emergence of his most illustrious works. Unable to find such experiences in a near vacuum of biographical data, they often resorted to making inferences, accepting legends, and searching the works themselves for facts about his life. Collier idolized Shakespeare as the "Poet who above all others, ancient or modern, native or foreign, has been the object of admiration," and he tried to extend this pre-eminence to Shakespeare's life and person by fabricating documents.[2]

Biographers were disturbed that Shakespeare seemed to have been a penniless vagabond when he first came up to London from Stratford around 1587. To correct this disparaging image of the great poet, Collier created a document that listed Shakespeare's name among the shareholders of the Blackfriars Theater in 1589. This contradicted, he said, the idle story of Shakespeare's making a humble start in London by holding horses at a playhouse door. Collier created another document to suggest that Shakespeare had known the actor, Richard Burbage, while living in Stratford and might have avoided menial jobs on his arrival in London by joining the theater company of Burbage's father. This document was a letter to Lord Ellesmere from one H.S. Collier guessed that H.S. was Henry, Earl of Southampton, a noble patron of Shakespeare. In the letter, H.S. calls Shakespeare his "especial friend" and even quotes *Hamlet* anachronistically in describing how Burbage "fitteth the action to the word." Collier added other special effects to this find by having it occur on April 23, the accepted anniversary of Shakespeare's birth and death. The other two documents discussed Shakespeare's high income and his possibly being considered for a distinguished position in the education of child actors. It is clear that all four documents reflect the desperate attempts of Collier to extol Shakespeare's life and person.[3]

Before his crimes were finally exposed in the late 1850s, Collier had formed a Shakespeare society and written several other books on Shakespeare, forging letters, records, poems, and manuscript corrections to document them. But his attempts represent only one extreme in the quest for biographical data about Shakespeare. At the very time when his forgeries were being exposed, the Shakespeare-Bacon controversy began to stir. Certain scholars expounded the theory that Francis Bacon must be the real author of the works attributed to Shakespeare because Bacon's formal education and broad life experiences seemed more plausible sources of such eminent works than anything found in the life of Shakespeare. With this new turn in the plot, the study of Shakespeare's life and works acquired the materials and atmosphere of a popular mystery or detective story. Scholars inspected old manuscripts with candles and magnifying glasses for clues of forgery or signatures in secret codes that might disprove traditional assumptions about authorship.

It was probably this note of mystery that first attracted Samuel Clemens to the study of Shakespeare's life. He recalled that he followed and discussed the Shakespeare-Bacon controversy at its beginning in the late 1850s when he was a pilot apprentice on the Mississippi, before he became the professional writer and humorist, Mark Twain. Yet he did not produce a book on the controversy until the end of his writing career. I shall first skip ahead to this book, *Is Shakespeare Dead?*, because it represents Twain's most sustained treatment of Shakespeare's life and the Shakespeare-Bacon controversy, and because it contains the only references to his early interest in these issues. I shall then return to the 1850s and try to reconstruct his acquaintance with the controversy in its early stages.

Is Shakespeare Dead?

Off and on since the 1870s Mark Twain had been writing or dictating pieces about his life, but not until 1904 did he finally "hit upon the right way to do an Autobiography." With his purpose and method clear, he began in January 1906 to work daily on his project. Sitting in bed in his New York house on Fifth Avenue or pacing the veranda floor at Stormfield, his new mansion in Redding, Connecticut, he dictated his memories and impressions before an audience of two, a stenographer who took them down in shorthand, and Albert Bigelow Paine, the person whom he chose to be his official biographer. He told Paine to build his biography out of passages selected from the finished or unfinished manuscript of his autobiographical dictations.

Twain understood from the start that writing a complete and true autobiography was an impossible task. It would have to include, along with his words and deeds and the things that happened to him, the very thoughts that passed through his mind. These thoughts were his true history, but to record them, even if he could remember them, would take a whole volume for each day of his life. He might, however, link present thoughts with past actions and events by making his book a combined diary and autobiography. In this way he would make history more vivid and fascinating by adding to it the immediacy of "news." Past and present would be "constantly brought face to face, resulting in contrasts which newly fire up the interest all along like contact of flint with steel." Instead of blocking out the events of his life in chronological order, therefore, he began each morning of dictation in diary form, talking about the thing that happened to interest him at the moment and wandering freely through different episodes of his life.[4]

What interested Mark Twain in January 1909 was the Shakespeare-Bacon controversy. Critic John Macy visited him in Stormfield and discussed a book about to be published that disclosed hidden signatures of Francis Bacon in Shakespeare's works. Twain added mystery and suspense to this news by binding himself to secrecy and divulging the matter only to his autobiography "for distant future revealment." He kept even Paine ignorant of the particulars, although he argued with him on the subject of Shakespeare's authorship. Paine wanted to believe "the romance of the boy, Will Shakespeare, who had come up to London and began by holding horses outside of the theater, and ended by winning the proudest place in the world of letters," but Twain warned him of a bombshell which might "unhorse Shakespear permanently and put Bacon in the saddle."[5]

The expected bombshell was William Stone Booth's *Some Acrostic Signatures of Francis Bacon*. Aware that Bacon and other Elizabethans often concealed messages and signatures in a text by acrostics, Booth examined several Quarto editions and the First Folio edition of Shakespeare's works and found evidence of Bacon's signatures. He looked mainly in the first and last pages of a play, since he thought that these would be the logical places to put a signature. For example, on the last page of the First Folio edition of *The Tempest*, which is also presumed to be Shakespeare's last play, Booth found evidence of Bacon's signature in Latin—Francisco Bacono—in the epilogue spoken by Prospero, from "Now my charmes are all oro-throwne" to "Let your indulgence set me free." Beginning with the first letter *f* of the last word *free* and moving line by line up the page first to the left and then to the right, Booth deciphered the name *Francisco* spelled out in the initial letters of words from the *f* of *free* to the *o* of *oro-throwne*. Similarly, he saw *Bacono* spelled out from the *b* of *be* in the second-last line to the *o* of *oro-throwne*.[6]

Booth's book was not published until late in 1909, but Twain got an early peek at the proof sheets. After studying some of the acrostics, he looked forward with anxious anticipation to the book that would discrown Shakespeare and enthrone Bacon. When the book appeared, however, he was disappointed. "The ciphers were ingenious," he said, "but not wholly convincing. Their publication caused hardly a ripple & made few converts for the Baconians."[7] Booth's study revived Twain's interest in the Shakespeare controversy, but did not contribute any ideas or methods to his book on the topic.

The title of Twain's book, *Is Shakespeare Dead?*, has a history. When touring Europe and the Holy Land in 1867, Twain and his fellow travelers, or "innocents abroad," would bait tour guides by asking, "Is—is he dead?" when Leonardo da Vinci or Michelangelo was mentioned. As bold and free Americans, they felt the urge to put down an Old Master and ridicule the guides and guidebooks that idolized him. "Is he dead?" became their private joke and motto. Twain used the expression again in an 1893 short story, "Is He Living or Is He Dead?" Here the master was Jean Francois Millet, who languished in poverty because he could not sell his paintings. As a publicity stunt, he announced his own death and got his friends to arrange a state funeral. This fraud resulted in big sales and finally brought him fame and fortune. When Twain, therefore, gave his book the title *Is Shakespeare Dead?*, he was toying once again with the urge to put down a cult figure and expose a sham.

Is Shakespeare Dead? is essentially a creative response to George Greenwood's *The Shakespeare Problem Restated* (1908). Both Twain and Greenwood declare themselves heretics against the orthodox belief that Shakespeare of Stratford wrote the poems and plays attributed to him. They argue their point by removing all the myths and superstitions about Shakespeare's life and finding in the few known facts that remain no sign or promise of a distinguished literary career. Stratford, according to Greenwood, was a squalid provincial town most of whose citizens, including Shakespeare's parents, were illiterate. After leaving school "at an exceptionally early age," Shakespeare became apprenticed to a butcher and then to a draper, and in 1582 was forced into an "improvident and uncongenial marriage" to Anne Hathaway when she was three months pregnant. In 1587 he "deserted" his family, moved to London, and became one of the common players who in that day were classified under the law as vagabonds, beggars, and rogues. He later joined a theater company and accumulated enough money as an actor, manager, and shareholder to buy New Place, the biggest house in Stratford, where he returned to live in 1610 or 1611, occupying himself with trading, lending, suing and being sued until his death. His will mentioned lands, houses, dishes, and furniture, but no books or manuscripts. In his copy of Greenwood's book Mark Twain scored the passages which recounted these meagre details about Shakespeare's life, and he included their contents in chapters III and IV of his own book.[8] He applauded Greenwood's careful separation of these bare facts from all the conjectures and assumptions that turned Shakespeare into a scholar, a traveler, a soldier, a poet, a classicist, and an aristocrat. Greenwood's book is filled with satirical references to the word *doubtless*, so often used in Sidney Lee's *A Life of Shakespeare*. Twain used this device as well, resorting to such phrases as "we are warrented in assuming" and "we have every right to believe" when he could not provide historical evidence. In his writings he often tried to expose the humble facts that lay beneath romantic pretensions, especially when prominent figures were involved. He did it in 1869 with Abelard and Petrarch, and in 1894 with Shelley. Now Shakespeare was his victim.[9]

Greenwood also aroused Twain's interest in the relation between an artist's life and works. The life should match the works because it was a necessary source for them. Many of the notes that Twain made in his copy of Greenwood express this relation: "Men are developed by their *environment*—trained by it. Consider Shakspere's;" "It is environment, & environment alone, that develops genius or strangles it;" "To write with powerful effect, a [he] *must* write out *the life he has led*—as did Bacon when he wrote Shakspere."[10] Greenwood argued that great artists were developed by reading and living, not by miraculous inspiration. Citing Marlowe, Jonson, Burns, Keats, and Leonardo as examples, he quoted John Addington Symonds on the necessary combination of schooling and living in Jonson's apprenticeship:

> This raw observant boy, his head crammed with Tacitus and Livy, Aristophanes and Thucydides, sallied forth from the class-room, when the hours of study were over, into the slums of suburban London, lounged around the waterstairs of the Thames, threaded the purlieus of Cheapside and

Smithfield, and drank with 'prentices and boxed with por-
ters, learned the story of the streets, and picked up insensi-
bly that inexhaustible repertory of contemporary manners
which makes his comedies our most prolific sources of information on the life of London in the sixteenth century.

Greenwood concluded, "Thus Westminster and London made
him what he was." Twain underlined this. He also wrote the
names of the artists in the margins where Greenwood treated
them. Beside the above passage he wrote "Ben Jonson" and
strangely enough "Huck Finn."[11] What does Huck have in
common with these persons? His street education? Surely not
his reading. Perhaps in looking back twenty-five years Twain
recalled that he created Huck both from his reading and his life
experience. Both were necessary.

For Twain, however, life experience was much more important than book learning as a source for good writing. In the
margin of Greenwood's book he noted, "Did ever a man move
the world by writing solely out of what he learned from schools
and books, and leaving out what he had *lived* and *felt*?"[12]
Scholars tried to prove that Shakespeare acquired a solid classical education in Stratford's Free School, but even if they had
succeeded in proving this, Twain would not have been satis-
fied. He had left school early himself, and although he read
voraciously during his life, he worried when his reading became a source for his writing. He always feared "unconscious
plagiarism" and "mental telegraphy," the terms he used to
describe influences from other writers. Rather, the sources
that he considered crucial for an author were technical training and skill in the tools and terms of a trade.

Having learned and practiced the trades of printing and
piloting, and having added some expertise at different types of
mining, Twain boasts in Chapter VII of his book that he knows
the dialect of each trade and can "catch any writer who tries to
use it without having learned it by the sweat of his brow and
the labor of his hands." Bret Harte, for example, did not learn
mining by experience—"with pick and shovel and drill and
fuse"—but by listening and reading. On the contrary, Richard

Henry Dana proved in *Two Years Before the Mast* that he "didn't learn his trade out of a book, he has *been* there." Twain quotes a few lines from *The Tempest* to show that Shakespeare obviously had no first-hand knowledge of seamanship. He admits, however, that Shakespeare's works contain copious and exact references to the law, and he accepts the "expert testimony" compiled by Greenwood as proof of this. Of course, since there is no compelling evidence that Shakespeare ever studied or practiced law, Twain sees the legal terms in the works as one more reason to believe that Shakespeare was not their author.

To demonstrate the improbability of Shakespeare's authorship in a humorous way, Twain recalls an incident that occurred when he was a cub pilot on the Mississippi. His pilot mentor, George Ealer, idolized Shakespeare, and used to read him passages from Shakespeare hour after hour. The young cub Clemens thought that his education was being impaired because the Shakespeare passages that Ealer read to him were constantly interrupted by commands to the crew. A passage from *Macbeth* that should have been read as follows,

> What man dare, I dare.
> Approach thou like the rugged Russian bear,
> The armed rhinoceros, or the Hyrcan tiger.
>
> *(III, iv, 99-101)*

ended up sounding this way:

> What man dare, *I* dare! Approach thou *what* are you laying in the leads for? what a hell of an idea! like the rugged *ease* her off a little, ease her off! rugged Russian bear, the armed rhinoceros or the *there* she goes! meet her, meet her!...

This prompted Clemens to play a trick on Ealer, who of course was an ardent believer in Shakespeare's authorship. Clemens wrote out a passage from Shakespeare like the one above with piloting instructions included and had Ealer read it as though the whole thing came directly from Shakespeare's text. Then, after persuading Ealer that no one could pick up piloting terms and use them correctly unless he had been a pilot, Clemens argued that Shakespeare, never a pilot, could not have written the passage.[13]

This practical joke has an element of seriousness. Whether Twain was deeply concerned or not about Shakespeare's authorship, he certainly insisted that writers know the technical terms of the subjects they are writing about. The fact that he places this early discussion about Shakespeare's authorship in the setting of his own apprenticeship in piloting, a skill which he was most proud of and often used as a metaphor of his literary training, indicates that for him Shakespeare's text, whoever wrote it, displayed the kind of liveliness and craftsmanship that come from experience and careful training. When Ealer read the passage that was doctored-up with piloting instructions, he "read it as it will never be read again; for *he* knew how to put the right music into those thunderous interlardings and make them seem a part of the text, make them sound as if they were bursting from Shakespeare's own soul, each one of them a golden inspiration and not to be left out without damage to the massed and magnificent whole."[14] Indeed Shakespeare's text harmonized well with the technical jargon and excited commands of a pilot during a dangerous crossing. Besides being just a comic argument against Shakespeare's authorship, therefore, this exercise in burlesque is really an appreciation of the power of Shakespeare's poetry.

In fact, Twain's book itself can be considered an artistic appreciation of the Shakespeare problem. Twain is not mainly a biographer or literary critic, but a creative reader, a humorist, and an artist. What fascinates him about Shakespeare is not the discovery of a fraud or the mysteries clouding the life of a great poet. Rather, he wants to relish all the facts and nonfacts surrounding Shakespeare, and the common note of these, the quality that gives them mystery and richness, is duplicity. Greenwood tried to prove that Shakespeare's works were not composed by the man from Stratford, whose name he spelled "Shakspere," but by someone well educated and much traveled whose life is reflected in the works and who wrote under the pseudonym of "Shakespeare," perhaps Francis Bacon. Twain also portrays two Shakespeares, but he contrasts them in ways more complex than merely poet versus imposter. For artistic purposes he mixes Greenwood's two Shakespeares into one many-sided personality. Shakespeare is a country bumpkin and a town celebrity, a minor player and a major poet, a businessman and an artist, a rogue and a prophet, a penniless vagabond who later buys the biggest house in Stratford. In these qualities he resembles many of Twain's heroes who were big schemers and confidence men, "claimants" who laid claim to titles, fortunes, talents, and legacies that did not belong to them or did not even exist. Some choice specimens include Colonel Sellers of *The Gilded Age* and *The American Claimant*, and the King and the Duke, those phony noblemen and tragedians in *Huckleberry Finn*. Frauds though they were, Twain still found the rudiments of art in their poses, plots, and persuasive style of talk. He was as much exhilarated as he was disgusted at the big bonanzas and shady deals engineered by the moguls of his time, and he created characters that evoked both of these reactions. The Shakespeare of his book fits right in with the rest of them.

Finally, it is clear that Twain wants to compare Shakespeare's life with his own. His subtitle for the original edition of *Is Shakespeare Dead?* is "From My Autobiography," and he calls the book part of "This formidable Autobiography and Diary of mine." Unlike other authors, who use their autobiographies as open windows from which to view and discuss famous persons who passed through their lives, Twain compares his book to a mirror: "This autobiography of mine is a mirror, and I am looking at myself in it all the time. Incidentally I notice the people that pass along at my back—I get glimpses of them in the mirror—and whenever they say or do anything that can help advertise me and flatter me and raise me in my own estimation, I set these things down in my autobiography."[15]

Scattered through his autobiography were several chapters dealing with "claimants"—Satan, Shakespeare, Louis XVII,

Arthur Orton, Mary Baker Eddy, and others. The word *claim-ants* sounds enough like Clemens that Twain certainly in-cluded himself in this group. He played on the word when discussing whether one of his ancestors sat in judgment against Charles I. He said he was not sure of it, but "the other Clemenses claim that they have made the examination and that it stood the test."[16] Comparing himself to Shakespeare as claimant, therefore, he marvelled that no one in the village of Stratford remembered much about Shakespeare, while in his own case, after living a little over fifteen years in Hannibal—raised in straitened circumstances, poorly educated, and fi-nally running away just like Shakespeare—he became a cel-ebrated person and "benefactor of the human race," and the hometown folks could recount several incidents of his early life.[17] Not only did he rise from Hannibal to Hartford, but he also became an artist and a businessman, and wrote under a pseudonym like the author of Shakespeare. So just as there is a Shakspere and a Shakespeare, or a Bacon and a Shakespeare, there is a Samuel Clemens and a Mark Twain. All through his career Twain exploited artistically the many duplicities con-nected with his authorship, his personality, and his background. He turned the Shakespeare of Greenwood into a reflection of his own complex literary persona.[18]

In *Is Shakespeare Dead?*, therefore, Mark Twain uses the Shakespeare controversy to express ideas that have recurred often in his own life and works: the exposure of fraud and pretense, the importance of experience and training in the formation of a good writer, and the power and attraction of the many-sided person—mysterious, contradictory, and encompass-ing. Moreover, in this, his last book, written at the very end of his career, he provides information about his early interest in the Shakespeare controversy. Relying on his power of recall, then, I shall turn back to the late 1850s, when the controversy began and Samuel Clemens was a pilot apprentice learning the Mississippi.

Delia Bacon and Ignatius Donnelly

Mark Twain said that Greenwood's book revived his "fifty years' interest" in the Shakespeare controversy, an interest which "was born of Delia Bacon's book—away back in that ancient day—1857, or maybe 1856." He recalled that about a year after Bacon's book appeared, George Ealer of the *Pennsylvania* became his instructor in piloting—and in Shakespeare, reading to him continually from Shakespeare's works and discussing with him all the literature of the Shakespeare controversy.[19] Twain's memory of these dates was correct. Delia Bacon's book was published in 1857, and Ealer was his instructor for November 1857 and from February to June 1858.[20] There is, however, no mention of the Shakespeare controversy in his notebooks and letters of this early period. Almost twenty-five years later, in *Life on the Mississippi*, he referred to Ealer's reading of Shakespeare, but not to any discussion of the controversy.[21] From what Twain recalled in his last book, therefore, it would seem that he first encountered the controversy by either reading, reading about, or hearing about Bacon's book, then by debating the issues of the controversy with Ealer. Was he aware of Bacon's book at that time? and did he discuss the controversy with Ealer? or was he just remembering something that never happened, as he said he did often in his old age? Since he sometimes denied having read books that he really did read, perhaps he should be believed when he claims to have read one, especially if he could recall its author and date of publication so long afterward. Greenwood's book, by the way, makes no mention of Delia Bacon. I proceed then, with some trust and some caution, to review Bacon's book and imagine what Twain might have gained from it.

Born in Ohio in 1811, Delia Bacon attended private schools in Connecticut and New York, including Catherine and Mary Beecher's school in Hartford. She then supported herself by teaching, writing fiction, and giving public lectures in New York and New England. A prevalent theme in her studies was the historical context of literary works. Around 1845 she began to examine Shakespeare's works in relation to his life and to the lives and writings of his contemporaries, and this led her to doubt his authorship. With funds from a New York banker and a letter of introduction from Ralph Waldo Emerson, she sailed for England in 1853 and spent four years there reading Elizabethan literature and writing her book. After suffering from sickness, financial problems, and editors' rejections, she finally saw her book published in April 1857, mainly because of the moral and financial support of Nathaniel Hawthorne, then United States consul in England, who also wrote the preface to her book.[22]

While working on her book, Bacon sent articles on her research to *Putnam's Monthly* in New York, and one of these, "William Shakespeare and his Plays: an Inquiry concerning them," was published in January 1856. This was the first article of the Shakespeare controversy. In it Bacon cited the "monstrous incongruities" between Shakespeare's illustrious works and his ordinary life as evidence against his authorship.[23] This would become the main argument of the controversy. As we have seen, it is the argument of Greenwood's book. Excited by this introductory statement, the editor of *Putnam's* requested more essays, but when they came he found them deficient in factual evidence and was advised to reject them.[24] Actually, after her first essay on the topic Bacon changed her tactics. Instead of concentrating on biographical evidence to challenge Shakespeare's authorship, she began to analyze his plays thematically and compare them to the works of his contemporaries. Her acquaintances, notably Hawthorne, encouraged her to continue in this vein, but to drop her theory about authorship.[25] She did continue her work of analysis and comparison, but she still intended it to be used as evidence against the authorship.

The title of Bacon's book, *The Philosophy of the Plays of Shakspere Unfolded,* reveals an ideological approach rather than a biographical one. Bacon discovered a unifying theme of social reform running through the plays. Her theory was that a group of intellectuals became impatient with the tyrranous practices of Queen Elizabeth and King James. They planned to liberate the English people from the bonds of slavery and ignorance. Enlightened by the methods of inductive and practical philosophy, the forerunner of modern science, they rejected the magic, miracles, and fables which were used to support the unjust social systems of the Dark Ages, and they tried to carry their message to the common people. If, however, they spoke clearly and directly, they would be accused of treason by the authorities and would probably not be understood or accepted by the uneducated populace. Instead of speaking openly or philosophically, therefore, they concealed their revolutionary ideas in the allegories, poses, and jests of dramatic poetry. They created a method of speaking and writing in which a conflict existed between depth and surface, truth and disguise.[26]

Bacon names several intellectuals or "wits" who cooperated in this endeavor. Although Montaigne was not a member of the London circle, Bacon believes that his essays created the style which the English wits used in their writing and conversation. His habit of burying the secrets of philosophy in seemingly careless forms of vulgar discourse, his loose, shifty, enigmatic sentences which hide truth in beauty, mirth, repartee and digression, gave reformers the strategy that they needed. Bacon compares Montaigne's style with the circumlocutions and postures that Hamlet resorted to in denouncing the regime of Denmark.[27]

An Englishman who adopted this style and made himself the leader of the reforming faction was Sir Walter Raleigh. As explorer, philosopher, politician and poet, he founded a new "Round Table" to emancipate the English people from despotism. Like Hamlet and Prospero, however, he had to speak in the person of a magician, a jester, or a madman to appeal to the rabble and to avoid suspicion. Bacon suspects that the author of Shakespeare's works acquired his ideology and method from conversing in Raleigh's circle.[28] She includes Edmund Spenser in the same circle because he addressed the preface for the first three books of *The Faerie Queene* to Raleigh and adopted the new style for his poem. Although he meant his book to educate a gentleman of his own time, he chose the story of King Arthur for its delight, variety, and examples, and because it was removed enough from current politics to arouse no suspicion.[29]

Francis Bacon, the principal philosopher of the circle, contributed his inductive method of learning, in which general truths
are reached only by a slow and careful examination of particular instances. His notion of progression in learning from
memory, to imagination, to reason, led to his use of history and
poetry in both the development and expression of philosophy.
Delia Bacon thinks that he wrote Shakespeare's plays in order
to lead an ignorant populace to abstract truth through the
concrete images of history and poetry.[30]

Throughout her book Bacon investigates the theme of reform and the use of the new style in Shakespeare's plays. She
refers often to those comedies which describe holiday excur-
sions away from a corrupt court to an enchanted forest or
tropical island. *Love's Labors Lost*, *As You Like It*, and *The
Tempest* satirize the unjust and superficial practices of society,
yet hide and soften this satire by comedy and romance.[31] The
history plays portray the fears and guilty consciences of weak
and oppressive kings, and clearly sanction their overthrow.
Bacon attributes Henry IV's insomnia to the guilty conscience
of a usurper, and she stresses Henry V's realization, when
disguised as a foot soldier he traversed the camp on the night
before the battle of Agincourt, that only the "idol ceremony"
separates a king from a commoner.[32] These plays may be
interpreted as propaganda against monarchy, but their message is deflected by exciting deeds, colorful characters, and by
their setting in the relatively distant past.

In a series of chapters Bacon discusses the world of *King
Lear*, where institutions are no longer in accord with natural
conditions. The play exposes flattery and artificiality, in the
person of Lear, to the brutal realities of nature, symbolized by
the heath, the storm, and Edgar in his disguise as Tom o'Bedlam.
Lear learns his lesson when he exclaims, "Take physic, pomp; /
Expose thyself to feel what wretches feel" (III, iv, 33-34). Bacon explains why Lear refuses at first to enter the hovel of poor
Tom:

> Because the great lesson of state has entered his soul: with
> the sharpness of its illustration it has *pierced* him: he is

thinking of 'the Many,' he has forgotten 'the One,'—the many, all whose senses have like conditions, whose affections stoop with the like wing. He will not enter, because he thinks it unregal, inhuman, mean, selfish to engross the luxury of the hovel's shelter, and the warmth of the 'precious' straw, while he knows that he has subjects still abroad with senses like his own, capable of the like misery, still exposed to its merciless cruelties.

♦ ♦ ♦

For in that ideal revolution—in that exact turn of the wheel of fortune—in that experimental 'change of places,' which the Poet recommends to those who occupy the upper ones in the social structure, as a means of a more particular and practical acquaintance with the conditions of those for whom they legislate, new views of the common natural human relations, new views of the ends of social combinations are perpetually flashing on him;

♦ ♦ ♦

In that school of the tempest; in that one night's personal experience of the misery that underlies the pompous social structure, with all its stately splendors and divine pretensions; at that New School of the Experimental Science, the king has been taking lessons in the art of majesty. The alchemy of it has robbed him of the external adjuncts and 'additions of a king,' but the sovereignty of MERCY, the divine right of PITY, the majesty of the HUMAN KINDNESS, the grandeur of the COMMON WEAL, 'breathes through his lips' from the Poet's heart 'like man new made.'

When Lear finally enters the hovel and adopts Tom as his philosopher, he bows to natural forces and begins to respect the common people. According to Bacon, this scene represents a social and political revolution. The philosopher-poet, or Bacon-Shakespeare, who wrote it calls for a new adjustment of reason to sense, art to nature, and social institutions to basic humanity.[33]

Several aspects of Bacon's book could have contributed to Twain's development. As he recalled late in his life, it was the book that first interested him in the Shakespeare controversy. The image that it gave of the real Shakespeare—a person of broad knowledge, reading, travel, formal training, and social conscience—must have appealed to him as a cub pilot. He took great pride in the rigorous apprenticeship that he had to serve in order to learn the intricacies of the river. But even when he was obliged to follow the beck and call of his pilot instructors and submit to their ridicule, he argued vehemently against pilot George Ealer on the topic of Shakespeare's authorship, and shortly after this he actually struck pilot William Brown with a stool for calling his brother a liar.[34] So Bacon's book gave him the opportunity to put down a would-be master, the Stratfordian Shakespeare, and it might have inspired him to take sides with the real Shakespeare, a brilliant and clever individual who could match wits with the likes of Raleigh and Spenser, plot the downfall of monarchs, and assume the disguise of a poet or comedian in order to gain popular support for his cause.

It is also interesting to wonder if Bacon's book had any influence on Twain's later novels of social criticism and reform. Through most of his writing career he believed in the same liberal ideas that Bacon saw illustrated in Shakespeare's plays: the parallel progress of science and freedom, the return to nature when laws and institutions become unjust or coercive, and identification with the sufferings and hopes of the common people. Twain filled his major works with these values, and he used a technique similar to the one that Bacon found in her Elizabethan reformers: he criticized society indirectly through comedy, history, and romance. This technique is evident in *The Gilded Age, The Prince and the Pauper, Adventures of Huckleberry Finn*, and *A Connecticut Yankee in King Arthur's Court*, all socially conscious novels. Of course, Twain did not have to consult Bacon for examples of this technique. The literary tradition holds numerous examples of it. But one factor that makes Twain's use of it suggest the influence of Bacon is the number of references and allusions to Shakespeare in these novels. The scene in which King Lear wanders across the heath, permits the rude elements to purge him of his vanity, and gains through this ordeal a deep compassion for humanity, a scene to which Bacon devotes a large portion of her book, reappears in the plots and imagery of *The Prince and the Pauper, Huckleberry Finn,* and *A Connecticut Yankee.* I shall later analyze these and other references to Shakespeare in Twain's works, but here I will just imagine that Delia Bacon could have contributed to them from afar by her concepts of Shakespeare as a social reformer and the style of indirection that he used.

Despite the affinities in thought and technique between Bacon's book and Twain's later works, the question of whether Twain actually read her book still remains unanswered. Another way of establishing some familiarity with her book on Twain's part, besides just discussions with George Ealer, is to find reviews or summaries of her book in periodicals that Twain was known to have read. The New Orleans *Daily Picayune* for June 11, 1857 announced the publication of her book in a humorous way, quoting an old farce, *High Life Below Stairs:* "Shickspur! Shickspur! Who wrote Shickspur?" "Who? Why, Ben Jonson, to be sure! I thought everybody knew who wrote Shickspur!" The rest of the newspaper piece is serious, however, although the author admits that he has not seen Bacon's book and is relying on a review of it in the Boston *Post.* He mentions Bacon's early article in *Putnam's,* and summarizes the essential points of her book: "Miss Bacon makes a careful and close examination into the life and writings of the great men of that time—Lord Bacon, Sir Walter Raleigh, and others. She appears to consider them as a band of reformers, for whom the world was not prepared, and who were compelled to conceal their plans of reform; and that they are the real authors of the plays which were brought out in the name of Shakespeare."[35] There were more reports in the *Picayune* of reviews, mostly unfavorable, published in other periodicals. One, for instance, calls the book a "dull dry dreary speculation in pursuit of a chimera buzzing in a vacuum."[36] These pieces and others could have informed Clemens about the existence and content of Bacon's book around the time of its publication.

Even if Twain did not remember Bacon's book after the twenty-five or more years that passed between his supposedly reading it and his use of its ideas and technique in his social novels, he was reminded of the Shakespeare controversy by another book which appeared just before *A Connecticut Yankee* and which also portrayed Shakespeare as a social reformer, Ignatius Donnelly's *The Great Cryptogram*. Apparently Twain considered having his own company publish this book. In a letter to one of his associates in July 1887 he wrote and then crossed out, "Couldn't we get Ignatius Donnelly's Shakespeare-cipher book? No—we don't want it." Then in September he wrote to Orion, his brother, that Charles Webster turned down the book, and with it $50,000 in profit, because he knew nothing of the Bacon controversy.[37]

Born and educated in Philadelphia, Ignatius Donnelly entered politics in the 1850s and promoted a variety of reform causes for the next forty years. He began by founding a new city in Minnesota for European immigrants. Before and during the Civil War he campaigned for the emancipation of slaves, and afterwards, as a Radical Republican, he supported Reconstruction and Negro suffrage. Later, he joined the Populists against railroad monopolies, the Liberal Republicans for civil-service reform, and the Granger movement. His books include *Atlantis*, a popular history of the world which incorporates history, science, and legend, and *Caesar's Column*, a science-fiction dystopia about life in New York in the year 1988. When he became interested in the Shakespeare controversy, he pored through Shakespeare's plays in search of internal evidence about their authorship. After finding the necessary clue, he began to write his book, which was published in 1888 after being advertised in the press for almost three years.[38]

In the first section of his book Donnelly repeats the argument that the uneducated Shakespeare of Stratford could not have written such distinguished plays. The more likely author was Francis Bacon who, besides being well educated and much traveled, moved in the powerful circle of Raleigh and Essex and collaborated with them to free the English people from the tyranny of the Tudors. Bacon expressed his philosophy through plays in order to train the common people in virtue, and he concealed his identity because his philosophy was rebellious and because playwrights had a low reputation in his time. As further evidence of Bacon's authorship, Donnelly compiles nearly two hundred pages of parallels—words, metaphors, errors, and literary references—between the works of Bacon and those of Shakespeare. Donnelly's application of a reform philosophy to Shakespeare's plays comes very close to Delia Bacon's theory and could have been derived from it. He includes a brief chapter on her life and theory toward the end of his book and quotes her occasionally in the course of his argument.

Donnelly's main focus, however, is the presence of ciphers, or secret messages, in the plays. Noting that Elizabethans often identified themselves by ciphers, he finds hidden signatures in all words of the plays that relate to Bacon or Shakespeare: *Francis, Francisco, William, shake, spear, peer, bacon, beckon*, etc.[39] Then, establishing a number system based on page numbers of the 1623 Folio edition of Shakespeare's plays, on the number of words in a column and their ordinal places in the text, and on the number of hyphenated, bracketed, and italicized words, he connects a word on one page with a word on another to form a "cipher narrative." This narrative is hidden in the first and second parts of *King Henry the Fourth* and tells how *King Richard the Second* was performed in 1597 and 1598 to popularize the Essex rebellion. Queen Elizabeth recognizes herself in the weak and pompous Richard who is deposed and murdered, and she seeks the treasonous author. The Essex party, with Bacon, pay Shakespeare of Stratford to pose as the author in order to divert suspicion, but they fear his capture and confession. After a brief summary of the narrative, Donnelly spells it out over two hundred pages with one word at the end of each line representing the end product of his numerical computations on the rest of the line.[40] Donnelly's narrative also gives the most uncomplimentary picture of Shakespeare found in all the Baconian literature. Shakespeare is a glutton and a drunkard, uneducated, gross, and vulgar, and bothered constantly by gout, consumption, and syphilis.

After getting Ann Hathaway pregnant, he fled the region, but then returned, was arrested, and was forced to marry her. He made his fortune by inheritance, playhouse proceeds, and usury. Because of these qualities and his sense of humor, Bacon used him as a model for Falstaff and Sir Toby Belch, and Ann was the model for Mistress Quickly.[41]

During the fall of 1887, when he was deciding whether to publish Donnelly's book, Twain outlined a study of his own that would prove John Milton to be the author of *Pilgrim's Progress*. He believed that Milton was involved in the Shakespeare fraud with Bacon and Jonson, since his poem "On Shakespear. 1630" was included with their tributes in the 1632 Folio. Milton borrowed the tactic of the Shakespeare editors, using another person's name but hiding his own in a cipher.[42] Twain's argument in this piece was the relation of biography to literature. *Pilgrim's Progress* must have been written by someone who traveled abroad, and since Bunyan never did so, Milton must have been the author. He visited Paris and Rome, and probably used them to describe the Delectable City and the Eternal City of his dream.[43]

Twain's proposed Milton study, or burlesque, suggests a possible influence of the Shakespeare controversy on *A Connecticut Yankee*. Noting that Milton planned in his "*Epitaphium Damonis*" to write a British epic about Arthur and Merlin, Twain argued that the Arthurian material was only a cover for what was really to be an epic on English religion and politics. Although Twain was planning his novel as early as December 1884 and had the first chapter written by November 1886, his concept of it as a satire on his own time did not mature until later, so the strategy of hiding satire in an Arthurian tale could have come from his reading of Donnelly on Shakespeare and his own exercise on Milton. Hank Morgan, the Connecticut Yankee, resembles in many ways the members of Donnelly's and Delia Bacon's circle of Elizabethan reformers. He is a man ahead of his time who must hide his factories and schools and use his imagination to impress the rabble of medieval England. He even uses a cipher in one of his telegrams to Clarence. Like Raleigh, he founds a new Round Table to emancipate mankind from ignorance and slavery. Moreover, allusions to *King Lear* and *The Tempest* in *A Connecticut Yankee* further suggest the influence on Twain's novel of the reform motif discussed in the Shakespeare controversy.

Reading these books that portray Shakespeare as a social reformer who appealed to the masses by thrills and jests of the theater could have inspired Mark Twain to use the same technique. He could criticize his society through history, romance, and humor, and still maintain his reputation as a popular showman, and he could cite Shakespeare, the author par excellence, as his authority and model in this. Among the many duplicities that Twain cultivated in his literary persona was the critic-culprit. When he criticized his society, he knew that he was also criticizing himself, for he too participated wholeheartedly in the wild schemes and visions of profit that characterized his time. Instead of being accused of hypocrisy, however, or losing his credibility because of complicity in these ventures, he should be appreciated for his ability to mix prophecy with popularity, to judge even though he is himself judged.

The High and the Low

When the outbreak of the Civil War halted commerce on the Mississippi, Samuel Clemens, after two years of apprenticeship and two years of employment as a pilot, had to look for another job. He spent a couple weeks training in a state militia in preparation for war, but the militia was quickly routed by Union troops. Meanwhile, his brother Orion was appointed Secretary to the Governor of the Nevada Territory, so Sam accompanied him on the stagecoach west to Carson City in the summer of 1861. He worked for a while as secretary to Orion, but soon grew tired of that:

> So I became a silver-miner in Nevada; next, a gold-miner in California; next, a reporter in San Francisco; next, a special correspondent in Europe and the East; next, an instructional torchbearer on the lecture platform; and, finally, I became a scribbler of books, and an immovable fixture among the other rocks of New England.[44]

In Virginia City, Nevada, Sam Clemens became a full-time reporter for the *Territorial Enterprise* and began to use the pen-name Mark Twain. The spirit and style of this silver-mining boom town—the big talk, the quick fortunes, the blind leads, and the frenzied buying and selling—helped him create the hoaxes and tall tales of his early newspaper sketches, and Shakespeare's plays helped him during this time in the same way, as I shall demonstrate in my next chapter. But there is one incident from these newspaper days that might show his continued interest in the problem of Shakespeare's life and a possible influence of Shakespeare's life on his own. I must proceed again with caution, however, because he did not relate this incident until 1906, more than forty years after it happened—if indeed it did happen.

Joseph Goodman, editor of the *Enterprise*, was away on vacation in San Francisco, and Mark Twain, as acting editor, had to fill one column of editorial each day. Since the first editorial would appear on April 23, 1864, Shakespeare's birthday and three-hundredth anniversary, Twain decided to write about Shakespeare. He "borrowed" from the Cyclopaedia all that Shakespeare had done, then added what he had not done, "which in many respects was more important and striking and readable than the handsomest things he had really accomplished."[45] This could be an early instance of Twain's recognition that facts about Shakespeare's life were scarce and needed embellishment to make interesting copy, but the circumstances surrounding this editorial are also significant. In this passage of autobiographical dictation, Twain used his brief tenure as editor to explain his eventual departure from Virginia City. Searching constantly for things to say in his editorials, he resorted often to insults and libel of a rival editor. These led to challenges and almost to a duel, and he was finally advised by authorities to leave the territory.[46] In *Roughing It*, however, he gave a slightly different version of his reasons for leaving the territory, and one much closer in time (1872) to the actual occurrence. After two years of reporting for the *Enterprise*, he wrote, "I began to get tired of staying in one place so long....I wanted to see San Francisco. I wanted to go somewhere....I wanted a change." While filling in for Goodman, he found it harder and harder to produce an editorial every day, and when Goodman returned, he chose not to become a reporter again: "I could not serve in the ranks after being general of the army. So I thought I would depart and go abroad into the world somewhere."[47] Here he expresses more than the need to escape from an editors' feud in Virginia City. He wants to advance, to go to San Francisco, to see the world, and evidently to find something better than journalism. Although Twain does not mention the Shakespeare editorial in this version of his departure, his later recollection of it as part of the incident suggests that the mere thought of Shakespeare, especially of the meagre facts about Shakespeare's life, could have caused him to feel confined by his own limited experiences and newspaper work and to seek broader horizons and nobler outlets for his literary talents, ones that might raise him to the stature of a classical author.

After leaving Virginia City, Twain did "go abroad into the world." He went from San Francisco, to Hawaii, to New York, to Europe, to the Near East, to Washington, to Buffalo, and to Hartford, Connecticut. In 1870 he married Olivia Langdon, the daughter of an Elmira coal merchant, and in 1871 he moved to Nook Farm, a community of professionals in suburban Hartford. He thus "became a scribbler of books, and an immovable fixture among the other rocks of New England."

Late in the summer of 1872 Twain traveled to England to arrange for publication of his books there and to gather material for a satirical book on English manners and customs. Although he never wrote the book on England—perhaps because he liked the people and their country too much to satirize them—he took many notes for it, and he completed one sketch, about his visit to Westminster Abbey.[48] He tells in it how he is summoned at night, just as he is about to retire, and driven through the streets of London under an overcast and threatening sky, then ushered through gates and tunnels until he reaches "the tomb of the great dead of England." There he finds his way silently through the dark with his hat reverently removed, and comes upon the Poet's Corner where the lantern of his guide reveals the names of Spenser, Shakespeare, Milton, Johnson, and Dickens. On Shakespeare's monument he reads the lines of Prospero's speech from *The Tempest*:

> The cloud-capt towers, the gorgeous palaces,
> The solemn temples, the great globe itself,
> Yea, all which it inherit shall dissolve,
> And, like the basic fabric of a vision,
> Leave not a wrack behind.
>
> *(IV, i, 152-156)*

A kitten follows him through the crypt, accenting the contrast between living and dead, noble and common. It curls up to sleep at the feet of Queen Elizabeth's effigy, providing a "most eloquent sermon upon the vanity of human pride and human grandeur." When the Parliament House clock tolls midnight, it is "a derisive reminder that we were a part of this present sordid, plodding, commonplace time, and not august relics of a bygone age and the comrades of kings."[49] Despite the commonplace images—the kitten and the clock—this sketch fosters a reverential awe for antiquity and nobility, and Shakespeare is enshrined with the most distinguished authors. But this expresses only one side of Twain's conception of Shakespeare.

The other side appeared a year later when Twain was in England again, this time for a lecture tour. His wife, Livy, was with him, and he decided to play a trick on her. He asked her to accompany him on a trip to visit some friends, but their real destination, to her surprise, was Shakespeare's tomb in the church at Stratford-on-Avon. Twain's notes on this occasion emphasize the doubts and suspicions concerning Shakespeare: if he was a celebrated writer, why did he not keep a diary or have a biographer like Boswell? the only piece of writing that proves his existence is a letter of someone asking to borrow money from him; Samuel Pepys, the famous diarist, must have met some people who were living in Shakespeare's time and knew him personally—why does he fail to mention him? why was there no monument erected in his memory? is it that he was not appreciated in his time or that true genius is its own monument? Another item that Twain notices at Stratford is commercialism. Venders sell as relics splinters of a mulberry tree that is supposed to have grown in Shakespeare's garden and been chopped down in the eighteenth century. Tourists also fight to see Sir Walter Scott's signature scribbled on a window of Shakespeare's birthplace.[50] Twain wrote to his friend Mary Fairbanks, "We'll dig up Shakespeare and cart him over to our side a spell." He was probably referring to P. T. Barnum's attempt to buy Shakespeare's birthplace and transport it to New York for a tourist attraction. In a letter to the New York *Times* in April 1875 Twain asked Americans to subscribe to the Shakespeare Memorial Theater in Stratford. He claimed that it took an American, Barnum, to revive England's dead interest in the place.[51]

In these two visits Twain shows his conflicting reactions to Shakespeare. Memory and reverence clash with suspicion and neglect. Later he would contrast the noble lines of Prospero carved in Westminster Abbey with the plain verses on the tomb in Stratford to argue that the man of Stratford could not have been the great poet. But here he seems to allow the conflicting sides to coexist. Instead of choosing one and rejecting the other, or letting them cancel each other out, he combines them in such a way that they support and enhance one another, revealing the mysterious and complex character of Shakespeare.

Twain's most comical expression of this mixture occurs in *1601: Conversation as it was by the Social Fireside in the Time of the Tudors*, which describes a conversation of Queen Elizabeth and ladies of her court with certain poets and playwrights of the time. The narrator of this piece, a squeamish cup-bearer to the queen, despises the "canaille" whom she chooses to entertain, and "feels his nobility defiled by contact with Shakespeare, etc." Yet he must stay and witness this "right strange mingling of mightie blood with meane," and "behold rank forgot, & ye high hold converse with ye low as upon equal termes." In the course of the conversation someone "breakes wynde," and the queen asks the "author" to "confess the offspring" (Notice that this is a question of authorship). When his turn comes, "Master Shaxpur" testifies:

In ye greate hande of God, I stand & proclaim my innocence. Tho' ye sinlesse hostess of Heaven hadde foretold ye
coming of this most desolating breathe, proclaiming it a
worke of uninspired man; its quaking thunders, its firma-
ment-clogging rottenness his own achievement in due course
of nature, yet hadde I not believed it; but hadde said, "ye
Pit itself hath furnished forth ye stinke and Heaven's artillery hath shook ye globe in admiration of it."[52]

Although Shakespeare is classed here among the canaille,
his eloquence rings with alliteration and assonance, and soars
from hell to heaven, even as he disavows the authorship of a
fart. What Twain found most attractive in Shakespeare was
this fusion of contradictory elements. In it he saw reflections of
his own style and personality. It is significant that he wrote
1601 during the same summer in which he began his classic,
Huckleberry Finn. Some critics interpret this as a deplorable
waste of time and talent, but without such diverse projects
Twain could probably not have worked such richness into his
classic.

With this complex image of Shakespeare before him, therefore, reaching as it did from grandeur to meanness, Mark
Twain could be inspired not only to attempt the higher forms of
literature, but also to incorporate and preserve in these his
early writings and varied life experiences. Twain did not let
his printing, piloting, mining, and journalism disappear from
his major works, just as he did not let his living on the Mississippi and in the West be forgotten after he moved to New
England. In the speech that he gave at a dinner celebrating
John Greenleaf Whittier's seventieth birthday and the twenti-
eth anniversary of the prestigious *Atlantic Monthly*, he portrayed New England's literary brahmins—Longfellow, Emerson,
and Holmes—as tramps sponging food and whiskey from a
California prospector. He later wrote to Mary Fairbanks, "I
could as easily have substituted the names of Shakespeare,
Beaumont & Ben Jonson."[53] Although Shakespeare was part
of the literary establishment like the New England brahmins,

it was easier to link him to the rowdy elements of the frontier because of his divergent characteristics.

But this complex view of Shakespeare was not limited to Mark Twain. Major scholars and critics of the nineteenth century considered diversity to be the special mark of Shakespeare's genius. Samuel Taylor Coleridge, for example, objected to certain neoclassical critics who referred to Shakespeare in a patronizing way as a delightful monster or inspired idiot because his plays, sublime as they were, did not follow the rules of Greek tragedy. Coleridge believed that the so-called irregularities of Shakespeare were the very source of his magnificence. Drawing a distinction between Greek and English drama, Coleridge explained that Greek dramatists sought unity and simplicity by separation of heterogeneous elements, such as comedy and tragedy, while English dramatists tried to fuse heterogeneous elements, mixing comic with serious, noble with common. He found historical precedent for this English trait of fusion. It reached back to medieval times when dramatists had to fill mystery plays with comedy and spectacle in order to instruct an ignorant populace. But he also found in it enduring values and advantages: "greater assimilation to nature; greater scope of power (more truths, more feelings); effects of contrast, Lear and the Fool; and that the true language of passion becomes sufficiently elevated, by having before heard the lighter conversation of men, in the same piece, under no strong emotion."[54] Coleridge's approach to Shakespeare and English drama was not unique. It was widespread among English romantic critics, and heavily influenced by German studies of Shakespeare.[55]

Of course Coleridge's ideas are focused on the writings rather than the person of Shakespeare, although romantics tended to see the writings as reflections of the person. But a similar mingling of contraries appears in Sir Walter Scott's portrayal of Shakespeare the person in *Kenilworth*. The Earl of Leicester addresses Shakespeare affectionately as "wild Will" and "mad wag," and the Earl of Sussex, who thinks that bearbaiting is more realistic than theater, praises Shakespeare's pugnacity: "He is a stout man at quarter-staff, and single falchion, though, as I am told, a halting fellow; and he stood, they say, a tough fight with the rangers of old Sir Thomas Lucy of Charlecot, when he broke his deer-park and kissed his keeper's daughter." Sussex was not embarrassed by Shakespeare's legendary deer stealing. Even Queen Elizabeth quotes from *Troilus and Cressida* to make a point: "Think of what that archknave Shakespeare says—a plague on him, his toys come into my head when I should think of other matters."[56] While condescending to Shakespeare, these nobles nonetheless admire him personally and quote from his works.

Nineteenth-century biographers often cited various mixtures of diverse elements to account for Shakespeare's distinctive artistic talents. Charles Knight argued that the period of broad transition during which Shakespeare lived occasioned the blending of ancient and modern values found in his works, and since the division of labors had not yet occurred, Shakespeare could engage in both town and country pursuits and use what he learned from them to enrich his writing.[57] This variety of occupations gave him practical experiences which, when combined with imaginative associations, helped make him a "poetical naturalist," and enabled him to apply his artistic genius to productions that were popular and financially successful.[58] Richard Grant White, an American Shakespeare scholar and biographer, also attributed Shakespeare's profusion and versatility to the English Renaissance, a period when the rudeness of the Middle Ages coexisted with the cultivation of modern times. Shakespeare's genius evolved from his own race and time, but it was also universal and for all time.[59] And to this genius he added skills that made him practical and thrifty. White emphasized the social and economic realities behind Shakespeare's dropping out of school and leaving his hometown to try his fortunes in London. When he became a playwright, Shakespeare selected subjects and reworked old plays that he knew would draw audiences, and he furthered his interests by careful investments and applications for patronage. "He knew the full worth of money," White wrote, "and he saw that pecuniary independence is absolutely necessary to him who is seeking, as he sought, a social position higher than that to which he was born. Therefore he looked after his material interests more carefully than after his literary reputation."[60] This is a typical nineteenth-century combination of art and practicality, with a realistic stress on the latter. Henry N. Hudson, another American scholar, also based Shakespeare's diverse powers on the radical changes of his era. His ability to mix genius and study, imitation and originality, Latin and Saxon styles, and tragedy and comedy, resulted in profundity and universality: "with him the pitiful and the ludicrous, the sublime and the droll, are like the greatness and littleness of human life: for these qualities not only coexist in our being, but, which is more, they coexist under a mysterious law of interdependence and reciprocity; insomuch that our life may in some sense be said to be great because little, and little because great."[61] Finally, he enjoyed a "smooth and happy marriage....of the highest poetry and art with systematic and successful prudence in business affairs."[62]

These constant praises of Shakespeare's diversity that filled nineteenth-century literary criticism and biography must have encouraged Mark Twain to take conflicting stances toward him and to see him as a model for the checkered, multi-faceted, and contradictory persona that he was developing for himself. Furthermore, they could have inspired and confirmed the variety of treatments that Shakespeare and his works received in all types of popular literature and culture during the century. These treatments ranged from the idolatrous to the snobbish, the banal, the obscene, the rustic, and the sublime. It is to these that I now turn in the next chapter.

When I wish to write a great poem, I just take
a few lines from Tom, Dick, and Harry, Shakespeare,
and other poets, and by patching them together
so as to make them rhyme occasionally, I have
accomplished my object....By this wonderful method,
any body can be a poet—or a bard—
which sounds better, you know.[1]

COMEDY

Frances Trollope arrived in the United States at the beginning of the Jacksonian Era. In fact, she met President-elect Andrew Jackson when he visited Cincinnati in February 1829 on his journey east to his inauguration. Her motives for bringing her family over from England and her activities during her stay in the States reflect two main pursuits of the era, democratic idealism and business enterprise. She first tried to live at Nashoba, Fanny Wright's utopian community in Tennessee. When this experiment showed little promise of development and looked as though it could become a health hazard, she moved to Cincinnati, where she conducted two business ventures: the Western Museum, a gallery of fossils, Indian artifacts, wax figures, and a display of the "Infernal Regions"; and the Bazaar, an Alhambra-style palace with shops, a coffee house, a bar, galleries, and a ballroom. When the Bazaar went bankrupt, Mrs. Trollope left Cincinnati, toured in Washington, Philadelphia and New York, and returned to England. She turned her trip into a financial success when she published her reflections on it in *Domestic Manners of the Americans*.

Mrs. Trollope announced in the preface to her book that she would describe the effects of democratic government on daily life, and that these would show the advantage of being "governed by the few, instead of the many," and "encourage her countrymen to hold fast by a constitution that ensures all the blessings which flow from established habits and solid principles." Placing all power in the hands of the people, she thought, led to "jarring tumult" and "universal degradation." She complained later in her book that the leveling effects of democracy on manners and sensations produced a culture where there was no refinement, polish, elegance, or beauty.[2] She used one night at a Cincinnati theater, where Edwin Forrest was playing Hamlet, to illustrate her point. Although she disliked Forrest's style of acting, it was the behavior of the audience that caused her to leave early. Men, without coats, and with their shirt sleeves rolled up, chewing and spitting tobacco and smelling of onions and whiskey, sat with their feet up on the railings, or worse, sat on the railings and blocked the view of those behind them, or stretched out lengthwise on long benches. Instead of applauding, they cried out or stamped their feet, and bellowed a chorus of "Yankee Doodle" when seized by a patriotic fit. She experienced the same behavior at a Philadelphia performance of *King Lear*, and was shocked when she saw a woman in a New York theater breast-feeding her baby.[3]

These theater scenes, and numerous others like them, have been used more recently by Lawrence Levine to illustrate, not the lack of refinement, but the heterogeneous nature of American audiences. Through most of the nineteenth century, theaters in America were patronized by a mixture of social and economic classes—the higher class in the boxes, the middle in the pit, and the lower in the gallery—and these classes reacted to performances in a variety of ways, from polite applause to whistles, yells, and stamping of feet. Moreover, a diverse audience necessitated a diverse program. Often a Shakespeare play was followed by a farce, an Irish jig, plantation melodies, or a gymnastic act, and this mixed program even affected the performance of the main feature. An audience might demand an encore for Hamlet's soliloquy, or want Hamlet's soliloquy recited in the midst of another play. When Shakespeare's plays and other classics were presented in such lively demo-

cratic settings, they acquired the characteristics of these settings.[4] Furthermore, the writers and humorists of the time
utilized these settings to celebrate and explore the different
characters, points of view, and styles of speech among the
various classes. Shakespeare's plays especially, however they
were treated, provided open exhibitions of diversity in American society.

Mark Twain referred often to Mrs. Trollope's book in *Life
on the Mississippi* to assess whether American culture had
improved or declined over the fifty years separating the two
books. Although he quoted at length her description of the
Cincinnati audience, commenting either happily or sadly that
the America represented in it was a thing of the past, he did
not include this passage in his book. Another passage meant
for the book but finally left out of it demonstrates how a setting
or an audience can affect the performance of a play:

> An English dramatic troupe played Hamlet there [in Pitts-
> burgh] one night, in the regulation way, and played a
> burlesque of it the next night; but they didn't *tell* the
> audience it was a burlesque; so the women-folk went on
> crying whilst the roaring, gigantic Ophelia cavorted hither
> and thither, scattering her carrots and cabbages around in
> lieu of rosemary and rue; but they, and the men, too,
> complained, next day, that the performance, taken by and
> large, was bad—yes, and here and there extravagant, even![5]

Numerous accounts of similar Shakespeare performances
were given by American writers to accent, for humorous purposes, the contrast between cultures and classes, to celebrate
refinement and ridicule vulgarity—or vice versa, and to distinguish American expression from, or incorporate it into, a long
tradition of classical culture. This chapter will illustrate and
interpret the comic use of Shakespeare by Mark Twain and his
contemporaries, showing how it articulated the ideas and ten-
sions generated by the democratic spirit of the times. I shall
treat the comic use of Shakespeare under two headings. By
"rhetorical buffoonery" I mean the use of isolated quotes and

references to Shakespeare outside the context of a Shakespeare speech or performance; by "literary burlesque" I mean the comic handling of an entire speech, scene, play, or performance of Shakespeare.

Rhetorical Buffoonery

Mark Twain's earliest contact with the comic use of Shakespeare came probably from the newspaper rather than the theater, but the newspaper had to appeal in format and subject matter to the same heterogeneous population as the theater. Into its few pages it crowded accounts of current events, public speeches, chapters from recent novels, poetry, letters from traveling correspondents, advertisements, and humorous fillers, and sometimes these categories got mixed and confused, so that it became difficult to distinguish between fact and fiction, comedy and seriousness.

In his early teens Samuel Clemens ended his schooling and became a printer's apprentice. He was setting type for his brother Orion's Hannibal *Journal* during the summer of 1852 when a controversy broke out with a rival paper, the Hannibal *Tri-weekly Messenger*. Someone in town expressed concern about the danger and disturbance of barking mad dogs and wrote notices in the *Journal* signed "A Dog-bedeviled Citizen" calling for licenses and collars. Another correspondent suggested that all dogs be exterminated. The local editor of the *Messenger* joined the fight by defending dogs in an article, "Two 'Richmonds in the Field!'—any chance for a 'Richard?'" He complained, "To men of such extreme sensibility as the writer in question, barks-canine naturally prove annoying, but to those composed of firmer materials they only prove a source of solace…" He argued that "faithful watchdogs deter miscreants from making inroads upon the property of our citizens."[6] It is obvious from his overwrought style—the reference to Shakespeare's *Richard the Third*, "I think there be six Richmonds in the field" (V, iv, 11), and the diction, *barks-canine* and *miscreants*—that the local editor was satirizing the dog issue by exaggeration. He made the issue seem trivial by

discussing it in stately terms that were wholly disproportion-
ate to it. Using the same tactic two days later, he advised Dog-
bedeviled to quit his "comedy of errors" lest he be "transformed
into a beast," referring of course to Shakespeare's play and to a
line in *As You Like It* (II, vii, 1).[7] In September young Samuel
Clemens decided to enter the fray, probably because Orion was
out of town. He happened to know that the contentious and
posturing reporter for the *Messenger* had been recently jilted in
romance, so imagining that this gallant gentleman would doubtless resort to suicide, Clemens sketched a cartoon of him, with
the head of a dog (a *dog*-gerytype) because of his espousal of
animals, timidly feeling his way into a pond to drown himself.
Clemens called the piece "'Local' Resolves to commit Suicide"
and signed it "A Dog-be-deviled Citizen."[8] Although Clemens
used exaggeration here by assuming the suicidal intent, his
main humorous tactic is really the opposite. He ridiculed the
reporter not by exaggerated sentiment but by gross reduction.
The crude sketch of "Local" as part-man-part-beast with a
bottle of whiskey in his pocket, and the slangy and ungram-
matical style of the caption—he "resolves to 'extinguish his
chunk' by feeding his carcass to the fishes....Ain't he pretty?
and don't he step along through the mud with an air? 'Peace to
his *re*-manes!'"—and the puns, "*dog*-gerytype" and "*re*-manes,"
are all examples of vernacular reduction. I shall continually
distinguish this from exaggerated gentility in my analysis of
the comic use of Shakespeare. Although opposite in characteristics, both types of humor often achieve the same effect. Here
Clemens trivialized an incident by cheapening it (reduction),
while his rival did the same by overly appraising it (exaggeration).[9]

The *Messenger* reporter, who has recently been identified
as J. T. Hinton, a new resident in Hannibal that summer from
Quincy, Illinois, understood Clemens's vernacular methods.
He insisted that anyone who would stoop to caricature to make
a point had neither "the decency of a gentleman nor the honor
of a blackguard," that such people "depend upon gross and
insipid personalities to gain that which they could not do in a
respectable or decent manner." He challenged him to prolong

the feud with an allusion to *Macbeth* (V, viii, 33-34): "Lay on, Mad Fool,/ And d___d be he who first cries hold enough."[10] Hinton's appeal to honor, decency, and respect combines with his Shakespeare references and urbane style to create the pose of a cultivated gentleman socially superior to his uncouth rival on the *Journal*. Time and again references to Shakespeare express a similar contrast in social standing. They improvise on the theme of heterogeneity in American society. Through the energy and bravado of a newspaper feud between two opposite social types and their different techniques, this heterogeneity is turned into lively competition.

Throughout this controversy, Clemens remained only a reader of Shakespeare quotations. Instead of replying to the *Messenger* in kind—by quoting Shakespeare—he used low-comedy devices to shoot down his pretentious rival. It was not long, however, before he became a quoter himself. In November 1852, two months after the *Messenger* feud, he composed a piece for the *Journal* entitled "Connubial Bliss," which describes an Irishman returning home drunk to his family, smashing the kitchen stove, and chasing his wife about with a ten-foot pole. Clemens meant this to be a burlesque of temperance literature. Preachers usually went to extremes in depicting a "bloated, reeling drunkard who sleeps in the gutter at night,…a fugitive from the post given him by God in this life, a hastener to his grave, flying to 'the ills we know not of.'"[11] The final quote from *Hamlet* (III, i, 82) occurs in a context of florid language used for burlesque. Although Clemens treats class here in his satire on the stereotypical Irishman, he seems more intent on exposing the exaggerated rhetoric of moral reformers. Shelley Fisher Fishkin has shown how Clemens and other journalists often used extravagant happenings and inflated language to give readers practice in distinguishing between truth and prevarication in public discourse.[12]

There were many more comic treatments of Shakespeare in Hannibal newspapers, especially in the *Messenger*, where Clemens's rival proclaimed his "local" column "a chronicle and abstract of the times" (see *Hamlet* II, ii, 512) giving each event "a local habitation and a name" (*A Midsummer Night's Dream*

V, i, 17). Since 1852 was a presidential election year, burlesques of campaign speeches were plentiful. "Dick Daley's
Great Stump Speech" bristles with vernacular dialect and mis-
applied Shakespeare quotations. Describing the nation as a
canal boat without a rudder and a wigwam torn to pieces,
Daley asks, "Are such things to be did?...'O, answer me!/ Let
me not burst ignorance,' as Shakapeel says" (see *Hamlet* I, iv,
46). He can match the "hifaluting words" of his opponent: "'Go
it porkey-root hog or d-i-e-' as Shakapeel said when Caesar
stabbed him in the House of Representatives" (see *Richard the
Third* I, iii, 227). In his peroration he cries, "On, then! onward
to the polls! 'gallop apace, fiery footed steeds,' and make the
welking tremble with antispasmodic yells for Daily" (see *Romeo
and Juliet* III, ii, 1 and *Twelfth Night* II, iii, 54). After the
election this Whig paper mourned its party's loss in a letter
from Sam. Smith: "Its all over—the rase is run—the jig is up,
and Peerce is 'lected by gosh! But as Shakespear says, 'it's no
use crying over spilt milk,' which bein simplerfide means, grin
and bear it...."[13] The constant appeal to Shakespeare for
authority and prestige, coupled with the patent divergence of
styles between Shakespeare and street slang, exposes the con-
trivances behind all oratory and alerts listeners for possible
discrepancies between not just styles of speech but speech and
reality. Can words that so clash with each other in tone be
trusted to give a coherent account of reality?

Clemens received his earliest instruction in the comic use
of Shakespeare, therefore, from his hometown newspapers,
and these papers show the extent of Shakespeare comedy by
the number of pieces that they reprinted from papers of other
towns. One comic paper which stands out in its use of
Shakespeare is the *Carpet-bag*, a Boston weekly which first
appeared in March 1851. In early 1852, Clemens was copying
pieces from this paper into the *Journal*, and his first short
story, "The Dandy Frightening the Squatter," was published in
the *Carpet-bag* in May of that year.[14]

In Volume I of the *Carpet-bag*, one column that often contained Shakespeare quotations was "Funny Sayings," by Jethro
Smiley. In Number 34 (November 22, 1851) Smiley describes

an officer in the Florida war musing on how he might gain "the bubble reputation/ Even in the cannon's mouth" (see *As You Like It* II, vii, 152-153). In Number 35 (November 29) Smiley complains that an old maid is after him, and whether it is for his sayings or his affections, he confesses, "'Alas: the day, I know not,' as Mrs. Othello so pathetically expresses it." A sketch on butchers in Number 41 (January 10, 1852) signed by Yorick, argues that a butcher looks at the material world "Shylocklike, the pound of flesh is nearest his heart." Number 44 (January 31) contains an article entitled "Men of Weight" which proves that most Massachusetts state senators are men of weight because they are fat. It notes that Caesar "was fond of fat men, and of having such men about him" (*Julius Caesar* I, ii, 192). The issue in which Clemens's "Dandy" was published, Volume II, Number 5 (May 1, 1852), contains three Shakespeare pieces: a literary burlesque, a cartoon, and a political speech in which a Mr. Batkins claims that doughnuts are unconstitutional because they are brought to the House floor before adjournment and prevent that "consumation devotedly to be wished, as the player man says" (see *Hamlet* III, i, 63-64).[15] All of these sketches put Shakespeare's lofty phrases into local and homely settings. Do they stress the contrast between the two, or the similarity, or give equal value to both? Perhaps they try to hold together in comic tension both America's belief in the nobility of the common person and her constant urge toward self improvement and upward mobility.

Mobility and improvement are important aspects of Mark Twain's career, and both receive vivid and perceptive treatment in his works, especially in his travel writings. Five of his major books are travelogues. Even as a young printer Samuel Clemens felt the urge to move and progress. In 1853 and 1854 he made his first *grand tour*, visiting St. Louis, Philadelphia, New York, and Washington, and sending letters back home to his brother's newspaper. As part of this cultural tour or sentimental journey, he saw *Othello* in Washington and *The Merchant of Venice* in St. Louis. He did not practice his humor on Shakespeare, however, until he wrote some letters to the Keokuk *Post* in 1856 and 1857, signed Thomas Jefferson Snodgrass.

One is a literary burlesque of a St. Louis production of *Julius Caesar* and will be treated in the second part of this chapter. The other re-introduces Snodgrass after a lapse of four months since his previous letter: "It mought be that some people think your umble servant has 'shuffled off this mortal quile' and bid eternal adoo to this subloonary atmosphere—nary time. He aint dead, but sleepeth."[16] The *Hamlet* quotation and puffed-up diction are qualified here by local dialect—*quile* and *nary*—perhaps to show that Snodgrass, or Clemens, is still a local boy despite his living among the hoity-toity in St. Louis. The name *Snodgrass* might come from Augustus Snodgrass, the poet and secretary who travels with the Pickwickians. Although he is not a compulsive Shakespeare quoter, his verbose commentary adds humor to the group's itineraries. Clemens often used such a character in his travel books.

If Clemens's travels continued in the direction of culture and tradition, they should have taken him to Boston and then to Europe, and they eventually did, but before this happened, he learned another trade—piloting on the Mississippi—trained briefly in a state militia in preparation for war, and then traveled in the opposite direction, to the American West. When he grew bored there from doing nothing and tired from the drudgery and failure of silver mining, he finally took a job as local reporter for the Virginia City *Territorial Enterprise* in August 1862. In 1863 he began using the pen-name, Mark Twain.

Virginia City, Nevada Territory, was the perfect spot for rhetorical buffoonery. The boasts and bluffs used to describe mining claims, the fantasies of lucky strikes and big bonanzas, the arguments and insults caused by stiff competition and leading often to gunplay, contributed to Twain's humorous experiments with language. One incident which demonstrates the original vitality of Nevada mining slang, "the richest and the most infinitely varied and copious that had ever existed anywhere in the world," is the conversation between Scotty Briggs—a "stalwart rough," miner and gambler—and the town minister, "a fragile, gentle, spiritual new fledgling from an Eastern theological seminary." Scotty needs a "gospel-sharp"

or "clerk of the doxology works" to arrange a funeral for Buck
Fanshaw, who "passed in his checks," "throwed up the sponge,"
"kicked the bucket." When the minister finally understands
that Scotty wants a clergyman to "assist at the obsequies" of
one who "has departed to that mysterious country from whose
bourne no traveler returns" (see *Hamlet* III, i, 79-80), he agrees
to preach at the funeral.[17] In this instance, the vivid Nevada
slang clashes with an anemic Eastern parlance, the Shakespeare
quotation occurring in the latter. The stark contrast between
the two styles not only plays comically with diversity, but also
questions whether any communication is possible between persons so different in manner. Moreover, in the middle of the
nineteenth century, American speech and manners were still
in the process of formation, and this was most evident in the
new settlements of the West. Writers like Twain exulted in the
august privilege of witnessing and helping to originate a new
culture out of the diverse materials that came together in
Virginia City and similar boomtowns.

When Dan De Quille, the local editor whose place Twain
was hired to take, left Virginia City to visit his family in Iowa,
Twain wrote a burlesque epitaph, "The Illustrious Departed,"
in which De Quille "said '*Et tu Brute*,' and gave us his pen"
(*Enterprise*, December 28, 1862). Twain also managed to stir
up controversy with a reporter for the Virginia City *Union*,
Clement T. Rice, whom he called "Unreliable." In "Advice to
the Unreliable on Church-Going," Twain chided him about his
grooming: "you saturate yourself with cologne and bergamot,
until you make a sort of Hamlet's Ghost of yourself, and no
man can decide, with the first whiff, whether you bring with
you air from Heaven or from Hell" (*Enterprise*, April 12, 1863).
On a visit to San Francisco, Twain noticed with envy the way a
naval officer impressed young mothers with his knowledge of
unusual remedies for diseases, so he devised one himself for
brain fever: remove the brains; this was "originated by the
lamented J. W. Macbeth, Thane of Cawdor, Scotland, who
refers to it thus: 'Time was, that when the brains were out, the
man would die; but under different circumstances, I think not;
and, all things being equal, I believe you, my boy.' Those were

his last words" (see *Macbeth* III, iv, 79).[18] In these instances Shakespeare's lines are used to satirize overstatements in journalism, but they also seem to welcome some assimilation to local and domestic settings.

When Nevada was about to become a State, Twain was sent to Carson City to cover the constitutional convention, and he found in the speeches of the occasion, or perhaps put into them, many examples of rhetorical buffoonery, and Shakespeare seemed to dominate the performance. One delegate, a Mr. Sterns, insisted that his speeches be reported verbatim, without any reduction or paraphrasing of his stately, adorned, and embellished sentences. So Twain concocted the following speech for the *Enterprise* (December 1863):

> Mr. Sterns said—Mr. President, I am opposed, I am hostile, I am uncompromisingly against this proposition to tax mines. I will openly assert, sir, that I am not in favor of this proposition....In the language (of my colleague), I entreat you, sir, and gentlemen, inflict not this mighty iniquity upon generations yet unborn: Heed the prayers of the people and be merciful: Ah, sir, the quality of mercy is not strained, so to speak (as has been aptly suggested heretofore), but droppeth like the gentle dew from Heaven, as it were. The gentleman from Douglas has said this law would be unconstitutional, and I cordially agree with him. Therefore, let its corse to the ramparts be hurried—let the flames that shook the battle's wreck, shine round it o'er the dead— let it go hence to that undiscovered country from whose bourne no traveler returns (as has been remarked by the gentleman from Washoe, Mr. Shamp), and in thus guarding and protecting the poor miner, let us endeavor to do unto others as we would that others should do unto us (as was very justly and properly observed by Jesus Christ upon a former occasion).[19]

In its jumble of quotes and misquotes from *Julius Caesar* ("generations yet unborn," III, i, 113), *The Merchant of Venice* ("the quality of mercy," IV, i, 182-183), *Hamlet* (again "that undiscovered country"), the Bible, and "The Burial of Sir John Moore," in its total nearsightedness as to the sources of these quotes, and in its pretensions to spontaneity, this exercise exposes the bombast and sham of a political speech. The lines from Shakespeare, scattered among banal repetitions, show the extent of the speaker's presumptuousness. Even with the sham and presumption, however, Shakespeare is nonetheless integrated splendidly into a democratic setting. This mixing of effects shows again the richness that Shakespeare brought to popular discourse in America.

In a spirit of humor that exemplifies the blend of fact and fiction, Carson City held a burlesque convention of the "Third House" in which the speeches and personalities of the regular convention were mimicked and satirized. In December 1863, Twain presided at this convention, and in his opening address he exclaimed, "This is the proudest moment of my life. I shall always think so. I think so still. I shall ponder over it with unspeakable emotion down to the latest syllable of recorded time." Again, the empty repetition, the jumbled tenses, and the misquote from *Macbeth* (*latest* for *last*, V, v, 21) fit the parody of the occasion. During the mock debate one delegate shouted, "Mr. President: To be or not to be—that is the question."[20]

Just as other newspapers in Hannibal and the *Carpet-bag* from Boston influenced Twain's early use of Shakespeare, the writings and lectures of Artemus Ward were probably an important influence on him during his stay in the West. Charles F. Browne, who created Artemus Ward as a pen-name and comic persona, aspired at one time to an acting career, but failing in that, he resorted to journalism and later to lecturing. The theatrical ambitions lingered, however, in his many humorous references to Shakespeare.

In 1852, after various jobs in journalism, Browne was hired as a compositor for the *Carpet-bag*. Along with his printing and editorial work, he found time to write several sketches for the paper. One published in February 1853 and called "Paul Pryism" illustrates his early use of Shakespeare. Arguing against those who pass judgment on others, he quotes *Othello*

(III, iii, 322-324): "Trifles light as air are confirmations strong as proofs of holy writ." He continues: "Hamlet once, perhaps oftener, said, 'Be thou as chaste as ice, as pure as snow, thou shalt not escape calumny.' I believe him. Did Hamlet now live I should go to him, take him by the hand, and say, 'Hamlet, you're a brick; a truer thing was never said.'"[21] Here is the journalist's typical humorous mixture of Shakespearean language with colloquial jargon.

Browne moved west in 1856 to work as compositor, reporter, and editor for the Toledo *Commercial* and later for the Cleveland *Plain Dealer*. Around 1858 he invented the persona Artemus Ward, and sketches with that signature appeared in the *Plain Dealer*, as well as in other newspapers which copied them according to the custom of the time.[22] In 1860 Browne began sending articles to New York's Bohemian journal, *Vanity Fair*, and in 1861 he became its editor. He collected many of his early newspaper and magazine sketches and published them in *Artemus Ward, His Book*, in 1862.

Besides the Elizabethan-type genitive in the title of his book, Browne used Shakespeare in several ways, including the isolated references and quotations that I have called "rhetorical buffoonery." In one sketch, for instance, Ward complains that the public is neglecting his wax-figure and wild-animal show to attend popular lectures. He says, "Gents, it greeves my hart in my old age, when I'm in 'the Sheer & yeller leef' (to cote frum my Irish frend Mister McBeth) to see that the Show biznis is pritty much plade out" (see *Macbeth* V, iii, 23). Ward uses the same *Macbeth* quote in a patriotic piece entitled, "The Crisis": "Feller Sitterzens, I am in the Sheer & Yeller leaf. I shall peg out 1 of these dase. But while I do stop here I shall stay in the Union." While he was lecturing in the South, the Civil War broke out and Browne had to leave quickly. As Ward says in "Thrilling Scenes in Dixie:" "I had a narrer scape from the sonny South. 'The swings and arrers of outrajus fortin,' alluded to by Hamlick, warn't nothin in comparison to my trubles" (see *Hamlet* III, i, 58). Asked by a Confederate if he favors the war, he pretends that he does: "'Blud, Eargo, blud!' sed I,...Them words was rit by Shakespeare, who is ded." When his wife gave birth to twins, he stayed up all night celebrating "Joy in the House of Ward": "We sot there talkin & larfin until 'the switchin hour of nite, when grave yards yawn & Josts troop 4th' as old Bill Shakespire aptlee obsarves in his dramy of John Sheppard, esq., or the Moral House Breaker..." (see *Hamlet* III, ii, 373-374). In a burlesque tale called "Moses, The Sassy; or, the Disguised Duke," the heroine, Elizy, tries to convince Moses, who has just come from a fireman's brawl, that he is really a duke: "How hast the battle gonest? Thou didst excellent well. And, Moses, dost know I sumtimes think thou isest of noble birth?" Moses replies, "If it is so, then thus it must be! 2 B or not 2 B! Which? Sow, sow! But enuff. O Life! life!—*you're too many for me!*"[23]

These sketches have the same techniques that Mark Twain used in his recording of Mr. Sterns's speech at the Nevada convention. There is the quote taken out of context, misquoted or misspelled, and attributed to Shakespeare or one of his characters as if they were nineteenth-century contemporaries. In this way Shakespeare is acclimated to an American setting. His lines appear alongside colloquial idioms, are spoken with a local accent, and cover topics from war to family celebration and popular entertainment. When used by Ward, they seem to foster rather than satirize a feeling of local pride with their classical authority.

Edward P. Hingston, an Englishman who traveled through America as Browne's bookseller and press agent, describes some interesting features in the life of a showman. When the San Francisco *Golden Era* wanted a tantalizing ad for Ward's first California lecture, perhaps something that related Shakespeare to spiritualism, Hingston ploughed through Mary Cowden Clarke's *Concordance to Shakespeare*, a book which he found in many a newspaper office, and managed to turn up enough quotes to create a sketch called "Shakespeare an Agent for Artemus Ward." Hingston summons Shakespeare from the dead and proves by quotes that Shakespeare knew Ward three hundred years before and acted as his advance agent. Among Shakespeare's rave reviews are: "Thou knowest my old *Ward*" (*The First Part of King Henry the Fourth*), "The best *Ward* of mine honour" (*Love's Labors Lost*), and "They will have me go to *Ward*" (*The Second Part of King Henry the Sixth*).[24] Besides linking Shakespeare to journalism, show business, and advertising, this sketch reveals how reporters could muster Shakespeare quotes for any occasion.

Mark Twain was probably influenced by Artemus Ward in several ways, including his use of Shakespeare. He read the *Carpet-bag* and other papers that printed Ward's sketches, and he might have read Ward's 1862 book. During a lecture tour of the West in late 1863, Ward visited Virginia City, lectured there, and spent long hours at the office of the *Enterprise* with Twain and his associates. Just prior to this visit, Twain published an advance letter, supposedly by Ward but more probably by Twain himself, which exemplifies Ward's rambling style of story-telling. Twain did write a parody of Ward in "First Interview With Artemus Ward," and his rendition of Simon Wheeler's "Jumping Frog" story also resembles Ward's techniques.[25] The "Jumping Frog" story is sometimes printed as a letter to Ward, and it was meant to appear in Ward's 1865 book, *His Travels*, but missed the printer's deadline. Like Ward, too, Twain later became a comic lecturer. Although the passages that have been pieced together to form the probable texts of his lectures show no use of Shakespeare, there were references to Shakespeare in the advertisements and blurbs for these lectures. A poster for one of his Sacramento lectures blared, "RICHARD III, replete with thrilling incidents and startling situations," and "America's Great Tragedian, EDWIN FORREST;" but with the small print between the headlines the poster read: "RICHARD III...would have been produced on this occasion but for the much regretted absence of...EDWIN FORREST." In publicizing this lecture on the Sandwich Islands the Sacramento *Union* assured patrons that the lecturer's "toils and sufferings as a missionary have not...sicklied him over with the pale cast of thought..." (see *Hamlet* III, i, 85).[26]

Just before he left Virginia City for San Francisco in May 1864, Twain engaged in an editorial feud with James Laird of the Virginia City *Union*. When Laird refused to apologize for an insult, Twain challenged him to a duel. An editorial in a third newspaper, the Gold Hill *Evening News*, cried "Horrible oh horrible," a reference to *Hamlet*'s "O, horrible! O, horrible! most horrible!" (I, v, 80), and it warned that so trivial an issue could lead to bloodshed or maiming by saying, "there is a divinity that *unshapes* our *ends*" (see *Hamlet* V, ii, 10).[27] The editorial also referred to the empty threats of the feud as Falstaffian. This is not Twain's writing, but it reflects the style of journalism which he read and wrote, the atmosphere of competition and speculation that he lived in, and the use of Shakespeare both to endorse and ridicule that atmosphere.

Literary Burlesque

Parallel in time with the isolated references to Shakespeare that I have called "rhetorical buffoonery" were longer pieces, comic plot summaries and reviews, and parodies of speeches, scenes, performances, and whole plays. These I shall call "literary burlesques." They contain one or both of the same comic devices—exaggeration and reduction—that were found in the buffoonery. They exaggerate when they carry the style and sentiment of the work that is parodied to absurd extremes, and they reduce when they translate the original style of the work into contemporary jargon and replace its original setting and characters with ones that are comically realistic and familiar. "Literary" signifies that the burlesque is based on a definite work of literature, in this case, one by Shakespeare.

There were literary burlesques of Shakespeare in the same newspapers and magazines that carried the buffoonery, and that Mark Twain read and wrote for in his early career. In the Hannibal *Tri-weekly Messenger*, for example, a sketch with the title "Playing Possum" described a performance of *Romeo and Juliet* in "one of the Western theatres." As Romeo, believing Juliet to be dead, is about to take poison, a stalwart countryman leaps onto the stage, knocks the vial from Romeo's hand, and yells:

"Why, yer gal ain't dead, I tell yer! The way it was they wanted to make Juliet marry that chap thar," pointing to

Paris,..."but I tell you Juliet war spunk—she got her back right up, and vowed she wouldn't do even if, while she were lyin' in the vault, the ghost of the other feller whom you kilt should dash her brains out with the bones of some of her dead cousins. Wall, her spunk war up, and she took the stuff the parson fixed, so she could play possum till you got hum."[28]

This is a typical instance of the burlesque "performance," an account of some odd happening during a regular play, which may or may not interrupt or change the play.

The *Carpet-bag* also contained several Shakespeare burlesques. One issue (January 3, 1852) describes a performance of *Julius Caesar* in Cleveland during which a loud-mouthed lakeman shouted a greeting to one of his friends. The dead Caesar raised himself and said, "Turn those men out....Proceed." A piece entitled "Shakespeare Improved" in another issue (November 15, 1851) tells of a performance of *Macbeth* in Buffalo in which a local comic actor had to play Macbeth due to the drunkenness of the regular actor. In the banquet scene, when the ghost of Banquo appeared, the local actor was supposed to deliver the following speech:

> Avaunt! And quit my sight! Let the earth hide thee!
> Thy bones are marrowless, thy blood is cold,
> Thou hast no speculation in those eyes
> Which thou dost glare with.
> *(III, iv, 93-96)*

Instead, he blurted out:

> You git eout: Go hide yerself—yer ain't got no marrer in yer bones—no warm in yer blood—yer ain't got no speckerlation in yer eyes—you *git* eout!

This is an example of a burlesque "speech," since Shakespeare's lines are translated into a vernacular accent and grammar. In the issue for May 1, 1852, the one in which Clemens's "Dandy"

was published, C. B. B. (perhaps Artemus Ward) tells of his
first and last appearance as Richard the Third, when his wig
came off during the duel with Richmond. Finally, on August
14, 1852, an editor tells of his receiving "A Black Tragedy" from
some Freesoil playwright with the *nom de plume*, Shakespeare.
Othello, a negro slave, falls in love with the daughter of a white
U. S. Senator. The editor thinks Iago's "O, you are well tuned
now!" refers to the fact that Othello and Desdemona play ban-
jos in a minstrel show. This is a burlesque "review" or reaction.[29]

All of these burlesques draw a contrast between
Shakespeare's great work and the humble circumstances—
setting, actors, audience, reader—of its presentation, and they
may be interpreted in ways that are varied, but not all mutu-
ally exclusive. Most obvious is the sheer contrast between
Shakespeare and the local setting or idiom. This produces
excitement, as any contrast would, but it also expresses the
diversity present in the new American society. On the one
hand, it could just assert this diversity, relativizing and equal-
izing its various components, while on the other, it could be
taking sides for and against the different components. For
instance, it could ridicule the cultural deprivation in certain
levels of American society, or it could express anti-British or
anti-elitist sentiment by pulling the lion's tail or cutting high
culture down to size and extolling the values of regional pride
and egalitarianism. The exhilaration which these burlesques
show in placing Shakespeare in a homely setting and translat-
ing his lines into local dialect seems to indicate a celebration of
the common people. Perhaps the conflict of pressures between
high cultural aspirations and merry self-sufficiency expresses
a fundamental polarity in the American experience. All of
these burlesques fit somewhere on the scale of these pressures,
some favoring one side, some another, and some resting pre-
cariously in the center.

There are eight pieces by Mark Twain that qualify as literary burlesques of Shakespeare, and they fall into four different
categories: a review, two plot summaries, four speeches, and
an unfinished play.

Many qualities of the best Shakespeare burlesques occur in a letter that Clemens wrote under the pen-name of Thomas Jefferson Snodgrass to the Keokuk *Post* in October 1856. It describes a visit of Snodgrass and his Dutch friend to a St. Louis production of *Julius Caesar*. Although Snodgrass avoids both the pit and the gallery and joins the fashionable in the dress circle, his uncouth behavior draws laughter, ridicule, and finally ejection. Introducing himself as "a peaceable stranger from Keokuk," he flaunts his rural accent—*drammer*, *demercratic*, *natur*—plays "Auld Lang Syne" on a comb, and refuses to take his feet off the railing. His provincialism is further shown by his reactions to the play. He is surprised that Roman streets have no fire plugs. He refers to the characters as Mr. Cesar, Mr. Cashus, and Mr. Brutus. The soldiers and "gals" remind him of Free Masons and Daughters of Temperance, and the conspirators who want to remove Caesar from office fight like "Buchaneers and Freemonsters," an allusion to the current presidential campaign. When a young lady exclaims, "Thar's Brutus—oh, what a mien he has," Snodgrass responds with a pun: "Madam, beggin yoor pardon, them other fellers is a consarned sight meaner'n him."

Despite his accent, uncouth behavior, and low comedy devices, however, Snodgrass seems to have a more accurate understanding of the play than the supposedly refined city audience. He is disturbed that the audience sympathizes with Brutus and the conspirators. He finds it "curus that they should kick up sich a noise every time anybody raved around and ripped out something hifalutin, but went half asleep when anybody was tellin about poor Cesar's virtues." The conspirators wanted to "make sausage meat of Cesar" because they couldn't be kings themselves, while Brutus wanted to "kill him like a Christian"—that is, for the sake of Rome. They fell upon Caesar "like Irish on a sick nigger." When a girl in the audience flinches and grunts a sympathetic "ugh" at the killing, everyone laughs.[30] In an ironic way, therefore, the city audience becomes a wild American mob rebelling against monarchy to pursue either its own self-interests or some artful platitude, while Snodgrass, the small-town bumpkin, emerges as a perceptive and sympathetic viewer.

The Snodgrass sketch illustrates what David Sloane has called "literary comedy." Unlike "southwestern humor," which tends to treat rural folks like Snodgrass with reportorial aloofness and aristocratic scorn, literary comedy tries to appreciate their humanity because it is interested in them more as individual persons than as regional types. It believes in the value of persons from all classes and backgrounds, and wants to observe how they handle the complexities of modern urban life by using their basic human resources. The main conflict that it sees is one between individual persons and the social institutions, organizations, and conventions which threaten to control or inhibit them. That is why it often chooses an unlettered rustic like Snodgrass to proclaim virtue and truth to those who have traded in their individuality for social status and esteem. It is comedy with a serious moral purpose and a generally democratic outlook.[31]

Given the ethical values of literary comedy, one can understand why burlesque was its principal vehicle. The exaggerated elegance of the burlesque style, and the irreverent treatment of some literary work or form of public discourse, aptly expose for ridicule social snobbishness and hypocrisy. Likewise, the presumptuous use of some classic as a paradigm for a comparatively trivial situation reflects the bold and often foolhardy ambitions of an upwardly mobile society. On the other hand, imitating a literary classic also demonstrates the cultural advancement of authors and their readers, and it helps them transcend regionalism by appeal to a work more universal in time and place, and thus more authoritative in expressing basic aspects of humanity. In his burlesque review or travel letter, Clemens derived his ethical values from Shakespeare as well as from Snodgrass, and perhaps from Dickens too, if he took the name of Snodgrass from *The Pickwick Papers*.

Sloane considers Artemus Ward a leading practitioner of literary comedy and an important influence on Mark Twain in that capacity. Ward's "Edwin Forrest as Othello," although published after the Snodgrass letter and therefore not a source for it, resembles the letter in theme and technique and shows a kinship between the two writers. Ward sent the sketch from Cleveland to the New York comic magazine *Vanity Fair* in late 1860. In the sketch Ward affects an uneducated village dialect to recount a trip to "Niblo's Garding" in New York to see "Ed Forrest" play "Otheller, More of Veniss." Since he usually goes to P. T. Barnum's "moral museum," he is shocked at the violence in the play, at how "Otheller smothers Desdemony to deth with a piller" and "cuts a small hole in Iago's stummick." Mike Cassio, an Irishman, "gits as drunk as a biled owl & allows that he can lick a yard full of the Veneshun fancy before breakfast, without sweatin a hair." Ward shows his ignorance when he says that the English think Forrest is better than their own actor, William Macready—it was just the opposite— but the "elitty" of New York seem uncultivated too. "Gothum's fairest darters" level their opera glasses at Ward, and one young man asks him if he ever saw Forrest dance the Essence of Old Virginny.[32] Like the Snodgrass sketch, this satirizes the pseudo-sophisticates of the city more than it does the country visitor. Ward, simpleton though he is, reacts with appropriate shock to the tragic action of the play, while the "elitty" are more concerned about the interlude and who is in the audience. There is an ironic, but genuine likeness between Ward's down-home simplicity and the basic human passions of Shakespeare's play.

Ward, however, was not the only influence on Twain's literary comedy. When Twain left Virginia City and moved to San Francisco, he joined one of the three most prominent circles of literary comedy in the United States, the others being in New York and Boston. Charles Henry Webb came to San Francisco from New York, where he had mixed with the Bohemians at Pfaff's tavern and contributed to *Vanity Fair*, the comic periodical to which Ward sent his *Othello* burlesque. Bret Harte arrived in San Francisco after doing printing and editing jobs in small California towns. Both Webb and Harte wrote columns for the San Francisco *Golden Era*, a weekly newspaper that catered to popular literary tastes and enjoyed a wide circulation in urban and rural California. In late 1863, dissatisfied with the provincialism and low tone of the *Golden Era*, Webb and Harte founded the *Californian*, a weekly literary magazine that was meant to serve a more cultivated, sophisticated, and urbane clientele. Aside from the reprints of contemporary novels and translations of foreign works that filled the magazine's pages, the most frequent original contributions were literary burlesques. Webb and Harte wrote several of these and later collected them into books entitled, respectively, *Parodies, Prose and Verse* and *Condensed Novels*. They used the burlesques to show off their versatility in elaborate imitations of various authors and to satirize popular trends. The target of their satire, however, was more the pioneer, the miner, or the local color story than the urban sophisticate. For them, burlesque represented a comic, but superior stance.[33]

Twain settled in San Francisco in May 1864, when the first edition of the *Californian* was published, but his everyday job that summer was local reporting for the *Daily Morning Call*, plus weekly articles for the *Golden Era*. In the fall, however, he was fired from the *Call*, quit the *Era*, and began writing weekly articles for the *Californian*. He explained this as a rise in artistic aspirations: "I have been engaged to write for the new literary paper—the 'Californian'—same pay I used to receive on the 'Golden Era'—one article a week, fifty dollars a month. I quit the 'Era,' long ago. It wasn't hightoned enough. The 'Californian' circulates among the highest class of the cummunity, and it is the best literary weekly paper in the United States."[34]

Twain followed the trend of other contributors to the *Californian* by writing several literary burlesques. "The Killing of Julius Caesar, *Localized*," a burlesque of Shakespeare, appeared in November 1864. Perhaps Twain took his cue for this piece from Artemus Ward's sketch on "Forts": "Shakspeer rote good plase, but he wouldn't hav succeeded as a Washington correspondent of a New York daily paper. He lackt the rekesit fancy and imagginashun."[35] Twain places Caesar's assassination in the context of a city election riot, and translates a contemporary account of it which he claims to have found in Latin in the Roman *Daily Evening Fasces*. He refers to Mr. J.

Caesar, the Emperor-elect, and to George W. Cassius, the "Nobby Boy of the Third Ward" and a bruiser in the pay of the opposition. He achieves the banality of journalism in his paraphrase of the following speech of Caesar:

> But I am constant as the Northern Star,
> Of whose true-fixed and resting quality
> There is no fellow in the firmament.
> The skies are painted with unnumbered sparks,
> They are all fire, and every one doth shine,
> But there's but one in all doth hold his place.
> So in the world. 'Tis furnished well with men,
> And men are flesh and blood, and apprehensive;
> Yet in the number I do know but one
> That unassailable holds on his rank,
> Unshaked of motion. And that I am he,
> Let me a little show it, even in this,
> That I was constant Cimber should be banished,
> And constant do remain to keep him so.
>
> *(III, i, 60-73)*

Twain renders it thus:

> He said he could not be moved; that he was as fixed as the North Star, and proceeded to speak in the most complimentary terms of the firmness of that star and its steady character. Then he said he was like it, and he believed he was the only man in the country that was; therefore, since he was "constant" that Cimber should be banished, he was also "constant" that he should stay banished, and he'd be hanged if he didn't keep him so![36]

While there is some cocky flaunting of journalese here, the piece rather satirizes local newspapers and city politics. Since the press thrives on violence, Twain envies the lucky Roman reporter who witnessed the killing and turned his account of all the bloody details into a "labor of love" and a "living delight" even though the reporter called it a "painful duty." The reporter, by the way, quoted Shakespeare as an eyewitness. Twain felt constrained in his job as local reporter for the *Call* not only because he had to seek out violence for news items, but also because his columns, especially those criticizing the San Francisco police force and court system, were often censored by his superiors on account of the paper's political connections, and this gave his writing the banal, watered-down quality of his burlesque paraphrase. Aspiring to literary artistry, Twain had become sensitive to the restrictions of newspaper work. The contrast between the two is brought out by setting journalism against the background of a Shakespeare play.

One other sign of Twain's higher aspirations is the disappearance of isolated Shakespeare quotes in his San Francisco writings. It seems that these were considered inferior in tone to the literary burlesques. Charles H. Webb, co-editor of the *Californian* and editor of Twain's first book, *The Celebrated Jumping Frog of Calaveras County* (1868), included "The Killing of Julius Caesar—*Localized*" in the book, and wrote in his advertisement: "Mark Twain never resorts to tricks of spelling nor rhetorical buffoonery for the purpose of provoking a laugh; the vein of his humor runs too rich and deep to make surface-gilding necessary."[37] Webb saw Twain's abandonment of constant literary quotations as progress toward refinement of style.

Twain wrote another satire on journalism in a burlesque plot summary of *Othello*. At the time, May 1870, he was part-owner, editor, and contributor to the Buffalo *Express*, and not very comfortable in these roles. His piece reports the tragedy of *Othello* as it might have appeared in the Cyprus *Morning Herald*, and it emphasizes the newspaper's cult of violence, especially in the headlines: "Fearful Domestic Tragedy—Shocking Result of Miscegenation and Jealousy—Two Attempted Assassinations—Three Horrible Murders, and One Suicide!!" It also exposes the phony moralism of a bloodthirsty reporter: "we feel it to be our duty as journalists to impress upon jealous husbands and gay Lotharios alike, the necessity of their being a little more prudent and circumspect in their mutual dealings." Again, prosaic paraphrase marks the journalist's style. Othello's final appeal, "Speak of me as I am, nothing extenuate,/ Nor set down aught in malice" (V, ii, 342-343), becomes: "Mr. O. requested that in our account...we should speak of him as he was, nothing extenuating, nor setting down aught in malice. At the close of a few well chosen remarks he suddenly stabbed himself."[38]

The "local" quality of the report is expressed by such names as Jefferson Davis Othello, Major Mike Cassio, Jim "Honest Iago" Crow, Senator George W. Brabantio, and Detective Lodovico. Satire is directed against the police force, the coroners, the insanity plea, juries, and ethnic relations. Othello is a native African who led the colored troops in the recent rebellion and, after the war, worked for the Freedman's Bureau. Brabantio disowns Desdemona for marrying "a nigger without a cent" and thus hurting his political ties with Tammany Hall. Iago, a segregationist, tries to destroy the interracial marriage. Twain's treatment of miscegenation during a period as tense on the topic of racial relations as the Reconstruction had to be very daring. Surely the universal themes and poetic fluency of Shakespeare's play helped him and his readers to view the contemporary issue with perspective, but also to appreciate the importance of these issues through their connection with a classic paradigm.

Reference to the issues of slavery, race, and Reconstruction suggests another probable source of Twain's Shakespeare burlesques, the minstrel show. In the middle decades of the nineteenth century, the minstrel show was one of the most popular forms of entertainment in America, and burlesques were a regular feature of the show. Minstrel burlesques, often those of Shakespeare, were a part of every minstrel show, but they also appeared as interludes during other plays, and they were printed up and sold in pamphlets for private theatricals. Mark Twain called the minstrel show "the show which to me had no peer and whose peer has not yet arrived in my experience." It represented "a standard and a summit to whose rarefied altitude the other forms of musical art may not hope to reach." He enjoyed the San Francisco Minstrels in San Francisco and New York, and before them, while growing up in Hannibal, he saw minstrels in Spalding and Rogers' Floating

Palace and Dan Rice's Circus. He brought his mother to see the Christy Minstrels in St. Louis.[39]

The minstrel show certainly provided a comic escape and release of tension from the most agonizing ethical and social problems of nineteenth-century America: slavery, and later, segregation and racism. By depicting black people as happy in their servile state, as innocuous to any form of advancement, and as dandified buffoons when they achieved any advancement, the minstrel show quieted its audience's fears of radical social change. However, it also responded to social issues more extensive than slavery and racism. A frequent source of humor in the minstrel show was social distinctions in general, especially as they were expressed through speech, dress, manners, education, and of course, race. Race, in fact, became the epitome and symbol of all social distinctions. Mark Twain noted the social contrasts portrayed by the minstrels. The clothing of the endman, or comedian, was "a loud and extravagant burlesque of the clothing worn by the plantation slave of the time"—not the rags and patches of the field hand, but the exotic livery of the house servant, with a standing collar "which engulfed and hid half of his head" and a coat with a "swallowtail that hung nearly to his heals," and he spoke in a broad Negro dialect. In contrast to him, the interlocutor, or straight man, wore the "faultless evening costume of the white society gentleman" and spoke in a "stilted, courtly, artificial, and painfully grammatical form of speech."[40] The minstrel show, therefore, was a satire on social distinctions and upward mobility, and this is brought out by minstrel burlesques, especially those of Shakespeare.

The majority of minstrel burlesques were set in the urban northeast. This was where the minstrels were most popular and prolific, and it was the scene of modern social complexity that the minstrels helped their audiences adapt to through laughter. The black people that the minstrels impersonated stood for all those who experienced difficulties living in a diverse society, yet also felt the freedom and urge to improve their social standing no matter what mistakes and embarrassments resulted from the attempt. In an *Othello* published by

Griffin and Christy's minstrels, Othello is a "nager, black as ink," but he is only one member of an ethnic conflict in which Iago is an Irishman and Brabantio a German who wants to make Desdemona fat "mit switzer kase and bread" so that P. T. Barnum will hire her as an exhibit. Othello and Desdemona enter singing the following lines to the tune of "Dixie":

> I love my Desdemona, away, away—
> And hand in hand, we'll take a stand,
> To spend Brabantio's money,—

This mixture of ethnic types is similar to that found in Ward's and Twain's burlesques of *Othello*. In *Shylock*, another Griffin and Christy burlesque, Shylock operates a New York clothing store and pawn shop, and speaks with a German-Jewish accent: "Aha! my frients; how's pishness dis cold day? / I brought you vun pair pants, and little veskit, eh!" Antonio sings "The Wearing of the Green" and puns with Shylock:

> Shylock: You asked for cash, but you'll not get *assent* from me.
> Antonio: Be *decent*, Jew! if you *dissent*,
> Why take my bond at ten per cent.;
> So now, good Shylock, how about the cash?
> To have it I'm *itching*.
> Shylock: Don't be rash![41]

Along with ethnic and class differences, attempts to climb the social ladder are frequent objects of satire in minstrel burlesques. In *Dar's De Money*, two dandies, Pete and Jake, in tattered frock coats and boots that don't match, try to put on the final scene from *Othello*. They fetch two chairs, a sheet and a pillow for a bed, and Jake puts soap into his mouth to show rage. He approaches the bed with Pete in it as "Darsdemoney," and bellows, "It is the caws! Yet I'll not shed her blood! Nor scar that whiter skin of hers than snoo, and smooth as monumental alabastrum." In *The Darkey Tragedian*, Mr. Brown, a stage manager, complains to Mr. Forrest, a would-be tragedian

dressed as Richard the Third, that all of his burnt-cork men
want to be tragedians. Forrest, trying out for "fust-class legitimate Hamlums, and Richard Number Two, and Skylark," recites passages from various plays of Shakespeare to illustrate
different emotions. Similar to this, *The Actor and the Singer*
presents two men trying out before stage managers. The singer
has a fake letter attesting that he has appeared in Europe, and
the actor, Edwin Forrest McKean Buchanan Bandman Daven-
port Booth, recites Macbeth's "What man dare I dare," mistakenly inserting Othello's "Speak of me as I am."[42] In all of these
burlesques, Shakespeare's plays, characters, and actors represent the high social and cultural standing that common people
aspire to, yet often make fools of themselves trying to achieve.
The minstrel shows gave them the opportunity to project their
aspirations and blunders onto comic actors disguised as people
far beneath them on the social scale, and they could thus laugh
at themselves from a position of detachment and superiority.
Of course, they could also identify with the comic actors and,
with more or less sincerity, mock their superiors and show a
happy contentment in a lower social position.   Popular art
forms like the minstrel shows usually foster a variety of different, even contrary, reactions.

Another probable influence on Twain's Shakespeare burlesques, one which combines theater with journalism, is the
writings of Sol Smith. Smith was an actor-manager who produced plays in towns on the Mississippi and Ohio rivers and
wrote newspaper sketches about the comical mishaps that resulted from staging these plays with makeshift properties before unpredictable audiences. His sketches were printed in St.
Louis and Hannibal papers in the 1840s and 1850s, and later
collected into books.[43]

Most of Smith's Shakespeare burlesques create humorous
contrast between high culture and local charm or naivete. In
one, for instance, a country girl, who had never been to the
theater, walks onto the stage during *Othello* just when Othello,
expecting Desdemona, says, "Here comes the lady." The audience and actors give her a round of applause. Another sketch
describes a performance of *As You Like It* in a crowded tavern

where the speech, "All the world's a stage," is appropriately interrupted by such comments as "Don't crowd me off," or "Now, pray, sit down," or "Waiter, bring me a julep." On another occasion, when Smith allows two amateurs to play the quarrel of Brutus and Cassius, one shows up dressed as a French "muscateer" and the other as a Turk or Scot. They dance a hornpipe, and Cassius delivers a death speech which is marred by many audible but necessary promptings. During one balcony scene from *Romeo and Juliet*, Juliet keeps asking a stage hand to use a swab (mop) on a lamp which is leaking flame. When Romeo remarks, "Her eye discourses; I will answer it," she calls again in an aside, "Will nobody get the swab? We shall all be burnt up!" but Romeo persists, "I am too bold; 'tis not to me she speaks," and Juliet agrees, "No, it is to somebody to bring the swab." Smith learned from his travels to capture the boastful language of river dandies. One of these, Spriggins, was on the *Scott* bragging about the famous actors whom he knew personally: "*Know* him? know BILL Macready? Well, I should rather think I *do*—intimately—intimately—spent most of my leisure time with him while he was in Orleans. It was by *my* advice he came out to the South...Ned Forrest? Have known him since he was a boy." After letting him go on for a while, Macready and Forrest introduce themselves to him.[44] This last is of course a typical satire on social aspiration and pretension.

Mark Twain wrote four single-speech burlesques of Shakespeare, all of which are to some degree integrated into larger works. Probably the least integrated is "Polonius' Advice to His Son—Paraphrased From Hamlet," which Twain sent to the Sacramento *Union* from the Sandwich Islands in July 1866. As part of a burlesque travel letter it fits Shakespeare's original, since Polonius is advising Laertes on how to behave in Paris, and since Shakespeare also intended the speech to be somewhat of a burlesque:

> Give every man thine ear, but few thy voice;
> Take each man's censure, but reserve thy judgment.

◆ ◆ ◆

Neither a borrower nor a lender be,
For loan oft loses both itself and friend,
And borrowing dulleth edge of husbandry.
This above all, to thine own self be true,
And it must follow as the night the day
Thou canst not then be false to any man.

(I, iii, 68-69, 75-80)

But Twain's version, though it seems more neatly crafted because of its rhyme and obvious metric form, is quite the opposite. It occurs just after a lyric description of moonlight on the
sea. Twain writes, "I turned to look down upon the sparkling
animalculae of the South Seas and watch the train of jeweled
fire they made in the wake of the vessel. I—", but then Brown,
his unsentimental traveling companion, interrupts him with
an "Oh my" because of seasickness. When neither pathetic
narratives, eloquent declamations, nor humorous anecdotes
make Brown forget his malady, Twain tries his version of
Shakespeare:

Give thine ear unto all that would seek it
But to few thy voice impart.
Receive and consider all censure,
But thy judgment seal in thy heart.

◆ ◆ ◆

Neither borrow nor lend—oft a loan
Both loseth itself and a friend,
And to borrow relaxeth the thrift
Whereby husbandry gaineth its end.

◆ ◆ ◆

But lo! above all set this law:
UNTO THYSELF BE THOU TRUE!
Then never toward any canst thou
The deed of a false heart do.

Twain recited these verses to help his companion forget his seasickness, but he was more successful. They brought every-thing up.[45]

Almost twenty years after this, Twain wrote a burlesque of Hamlet's most famous soliloquy for his classic *Huckleberry Finn*. As a hodgepodge of lines from different parts of *Hamlet*, *Macbeth*, and *Richard the Third*, the speech fits the hybrid nature of his novel as a whole, but especially the motley and inept performances of the King and the Duke:

> To be, or not to be; that is the bare bodkin
> That makes calamity of so long life;
> For who would fardels bear, till Birnam Wood do
>   come to Dunsinane,
> But that the fear of something after death
> Murders the innocent sleep,
> Great nature's second course,...[46]

Mixing lines from different plays of Shakespeare was one type of burlesque speech. The English comic magazine *Punch* pub-lished a speech from *Othello* which also contained lines from *Hamlet* and *Macbeth*. Othello enters with a lantern, a gun, and a bowie knife, and exclaims:

> To be, or not to be? Ay, there's the rub!
> I that am cruel, am yet merciful,
> I would not have her linger in her pain.
> 'Tis now the very witching hour of night,
> When churchyards yawn, and cats on tiles do fight.
> Is it a dagger that I see before me?
> I think it is. Yet I'll not shed her blood.
> If I quench thee, thou flaming minister,
> I can at will thy former light restore,
> If I've a lucifer...[47]

More will be said in Chapter IV about the integration of Twain's *Hamlet* soliloquy into the structure and themes of *Huckleberry Finn*. Many burlesque speeches came from longer plays and were often collected in anthologies.[48] It is important to note that Twain's burlesques were not confined to his early comic writing, but continued into the years of his most mature and serious works.

Two other burlesque speeches of Twain should be mentioned. One is the rendition of Macbeth's "What man dare I dare" interrupted by piloting instructions, which Twain wrote for his last book, *Is Shakespeare Dead?*, and which I have quoted and interpreted in Chapter I above. The other is a speech for the ghost of Hamlet's father which Twain apparently wrote for a longer play. It will be treated in connection with Twain's longer burlesque.

Besides the minstrel burlesques and others that were performed as parts of a variety show or as interludes during a longer play, there were full-play burlesques of Shakespeare. They had the slapstick, extravagant costuming, and inane puns of the minstrels, but as full-length plays they also had elaborate plots, sentimental songs with duets and choruses, and speeches that were humorous without being nonsensical. They often resembled Gilbert and Sullivan operattas, and W. S. Gilbert himself wrote a burlesque of *Hamlet* entitled *Rosencrantz and Guildenstern* which was published in *Fun* magazine for December 1874.

The first and most famous full-length burlesque of Shakespeare was John Poole's *Hamlet Travestie*. Published in London in 1810 and first performed there in 1811, it went through many printings and productions in England and America. As was usual with such burlesques, it often ran in a small theater while *Hamlet* was playing in a large one. For instance, in 1874 it ran in London opposite Henry Irving's famous *Hamlet* of two-hundred performances. Gilbert's burlesque was also published that year, and several burlesques ran opposite Edwin Booth's *Hamlet* in New York in the 1870s when Mark Twain saw the play and planned his own burlesque of it.[49]

Poole's *Hamlet Travestie* has three acts, and the dialogue is in heroic couplets. The soliloquies, narrations, and longer dialogues are sung to the tunes of popular songs. In Hamlet's

"To be, or not to be" soliloquy, "To sleep, perchance to dream,"
is sung as follows:

> But, perchance, in that sleep we may dream,
> For we dream in our beds very often —
> Now, however capricious't may seem,
> I've no notion of dreams in a coffin.[50]

Hamlet's advice to Ophelia and exchange with Laertes in the
grave are duets, and his speech to the players mimics several
actors of the time. Colloquialism (*mamma, dad*) and anachro-
nism (a chain watch) provide comic incongruity, and the play
ends with a boxing match and arsenic in a mug of ale. Poole
even supplies comic notes to burlesque critical and school editions of the play.

The most famous American full-length burlesque of
Shakespeare is George Edward Rice's *Hamlet, Prince of Denmark: An Old Play in a New Garb*, published in Boston in
1852. As in Poole's play, much of its humor is based on anach-
ronism. Hamlet and his friends are dandies sporting frock
coats and top hats, while the ghost appears in small clothes,
wig, and three-cornered hat. Laertes, with top hat and umbrella, leaves Elsinore on a steamboat. The guards smoke
"segars" on the battlements, Ophelia reads Byron and Moore,
and the gravedigger reads the Boston *Post*. Hamlet stabs
Polonius with a bowie knife and duels Laertes with a bow and
arrow. For his famous soliloquy, Hamlet enters in a dressing
gown with a revolver and speaks in couplets:

> To be or not to be, (that is the question)
> Relieved of an attack of indigestion.
> The fact is, I am sadly out of tune,
> And if some change don't take place very soon,
> I am determined (*takes out a revolver*) something
>   rash to do.
> And rid myself of this existence (*looks into
>   muzzle*) Whew!
> It don't look pleasant. (*puts it up*)

I guess not, just yet, —
A little longer I'll contrive to fret.

After enumerating the troubles which drive people to self-slaughter—the pangs of toothache, the mail's delay, buttonless shirts, stupid servants, a sulky wife—he concludes, "But as I said before, it is the dread / Of what comes after death that saves his head."[51] As in Poole's play, there are several songs based on popular melodies: Horatio's and the ghost's narrations, Laertes' advice to Ophelia, and others. Since Osric puts Russian Salve instead of poison on the arrows and Ophelia fakes death by chloroform, the play ends happily with the whole cast singing lines to the tune of "Oh Susannah." This play may provide an evening of carefree entertainment, but it also satirizes the activities and concerns of the nineteenth-century bourgeoisie, especially when they are compared with those in the original *Hamlet*.

Mark Twain is supposed to have first considered the idea of doing a burlesque *Hamlet* after seeing Edwin Booth play Hamlet in New York on November 3, 1873. Albert Bigelow Paine says that Twain went backstage after the performance and told Booth that he would add a comic character to the play.[52] In a letter to William Dean Howells on September 3, 1881, Twain says that he first—nine years before—tried to add a country cousin of Hamlet, but that a cousin could not be ignored by the other characters. So in the first three days of September 1881, Twain wrote about two acts of the play with the addition of Hamlet's foster brother, Basil Stockmar, a subscription book agent. Twain also used a technique that is not found in other burlesques. He kept Shakespeare's text intact, composing new lines only for Stockmar. Basil Stockmar resembles the characters in the other full-length burlesques of Shakespeare. He wears nineteenth-century clothes, carries a satchel and umbrella, speaks in slang, sits on the king's throne with his legs crossed and smoking a cigar, and finally gets drunk. He has, or thinks he has, some control over the action of the play. He will try to keep Hamlet in Denmark so he can sell him books and use his name as a plug. Later, when he realizes that Hamlet is the victim of a plot, he resolves to rescue him.

Like the other burlesques, this too is a language exercise. Stockmar uses the two speech techniques found in burlesques, parody and slang. He uses parody when he tries to imitate the "grandest kind of book-talk" in which the other characters speak. Even a servant, when ordering a carriage, will say it thus:

> Me lord hath given commandment, sirrah, that the vehicle wherein he doth, of ancient custom, his daily recreation take, shall unto the portal of the palace be straight conveyed; the which commandment, mark ye well, admitteth not of wasteful dalliance, like to the tranquil march of yon gilded moon athwart the dappled fields of space.[53]

Stockmar would prefer the slang, "Fetch the carriage, you duffer, and *hump* yourself!" Although functioning here as pure burlesque, the parody of Elizabethan speech foreshadows Twain's later use of archaic style for historical and more serious literary purposes.

Although he intended this burlesque to be a full-length play, Twain got no further with it than the second act. He apparently tried to rethink it, however. An undated newspaper clipping tells of an editor's having received advance sheets of a version of *Hamlet* by Twain. In a letter to the editor, Twain said that there was reason to believe that Hamlet had a younger brother who was sprightly and sunny in temperament. He proved this by a letter which he claimed to have discovered written by Claudius, Hamlet's uncle, to Tom Sayers, a nineteenth-century prize fighter, thanking him for the boxing gloves that he sent and promising to give them to Billy, since Billy's brother, Hamlet, was not interested in such things. Twain conjectured that Billy had once put a candle snuffer in Shakespeare's boot and so was left out of the play.[54] A letter that Twain received from Joseph T. Goodman, his former editor on the *Territorial Enterprise*, may help date this clipping. In October 1881, Goodman expressed interest in Twain's adding a brother to *Hamlet*, and in March 1883 Goodman sent the rough draught of a play, "Hamlet's Brother," for Twain to revise and complete. In it the brother's name is Bill, so the clipping may belong to this period.[55]

The clipping also contains another of Twain's burlesque speeches. Billy gets more involved in the play than Stockmar did. He disguises himself as the ghost, and tells Hamlet:

> I am thy father's spirit. Doomed to an everlasting swing around the circle. I could a tale unfold that would lift your hat to the ceiling. If there ever was a slick old fraud, your uncle is that man. The newspaper reports about my death were all wrong, although as near right as all newspaper reports. Mountain fever never got away with me. The man who is now in my political shoes dumped an ounce of prussic acid in my ear and that did the business. I can tell you, Hamlet, that for a good, quick, reliable poison, I consider prussic acid as unequaled. I am willing to furnish testimonials for the trade.[56]

Compare this to the ghost's speech in *Hamlet* (I, v, 9-10, 35-40, 59-70) to see how Twain comically modernized the speech by slang and by references to newspapers and advertising.

Twain's burlesque speech was definitely influenced by Goodman's play, "Hamlet's Brother." In both pieces the brother's name is Bill. Goodman's play is divided into seven "Rounds," each a burlesque scene from *Hamlet*. About three quarters of Goodman's play is the text of *Hamlet*, interrupted by comic additions. Recall that Twain put together his burlesque *Hamlet* in the same way. Goodman has Bill disguise as the ghost to fool Hamlet, and puts contemporary slang into his lines. Bill describes Hamlet's love for Ophelia thus: "He's sweet on Ophelia, sure—dead gone on her, I've sometimes thought; it never struck me, though, that he'd go daft about her; but he's such a spoon there's no telling what he might do."[57] Bill doctors up "The Murder of Gonzago" by having Gonzago awake in his orchard, spit a quid of tobacco, and take a drink of "Old Rye" with his impending murderer. Bill gets Polonius and Ophelia to play dead, have mock obsequies, and show up alive in the final scene. In general, Goodman has Billy play tricks on Hamlet to cure him of his morbid, dreamy, conceited, and verbose habits.

For his comic use of Shakespeare, then, Twain drew from a broad spectrum of sources in American culture. When he wished to satirize contemporary personalities, issues, or styles of communication, he matched them against Shakespeare, but he did not have to abandon popular and humorous writing to do this, since Shakespeare was already amalgamated with newspapers and show business. This extensive presence in popular culture gave Shakespeare's works the peculiar distinction of being simultaneously comic and serious, grand and familiar. Openness to such diverse reactions and uses made Shakespeare's works doubly rich and available for Twain's exploitation and imitation. The fact that he would devote long hours to a play-length burlesque of *Hamlet*, cutting passages out of the original and pasting them between his own comic additions, and furthermore, be doing this at the very height of his career, when he was writing the books that would become his classics, argues that he pursued Shakespeare for purposes that ranged from burlesque humor all the way to seriousness and profundity.

It had not seemed to me that the blushful passages
in Shakespeare were of a sort which Shakespeare
had actually heard people use, but were inventions
of his own, liberties which he had taken with the
facts under the protection of a poet's license.[1]

HISTORY

When Mary Mapes Dodge lost her husband in 1858, a
probable suicide due to depression over financial losses and the
sickness of their son, she moved with her two sons out of New
York City and back to a farmhouse in New Jersey with her
parents, sisters, and brother. A widow at the age of twenty-
eight, she looked for an occupation that would use her talents
and help support the extended family. In the privacy of an
attic "den" she began reading history and helping her father
write and edit a magazine for farmers and their families. She
also wrote short stories for children, and when some of them
appeared in Harper's *New Monthly Magazine*, an interested
publisher agreed to collect them and others into her first book,
Irvington Stories (1864), and then offered her a contract for an
annual children's book.[2]

Reflecting later on the proper standards for children's literature, Mary Dodge wrote that American magazines both
approach and fall short of the ideal: "We edit for the approval
of fathers and mothers, and endeavor to make the child's
monthly a milk-and-water variety of the adult's periodical.
But, in fact, the child's magazine needs to be stronger, truer,
bolder, more uncompromising than the other."[3] Apparently
she thought that children's magazines should treat topics im-

portant to adults, but should treat them plainly and simply, without protective screening, and without the nuances needed in adult journals. As she prepared to write her second book and classic, *Hans Brinker or, The Silver Skates* (1866), she seemed to follow this standard by blending facts about history and social customs into her story. In the preface to one edition of her book she wrote, "The story of Hans Brinker, or of any boy born and bred in Holland, cannot be fitly told without including something of the story of Holland itself,—of its history, its oddities, and the leading characteristics of its heroic and thrifty people....Therefore, necessary and careful descriptions of Dutch life and customs have been given in the narrative...."[4] Mary Dodge's interest in Holland had been sparked by a travel book, *The Rhine*, which her husband brought back from Europe after a brief business trip and tour in 1855. She also read John Lothrope Motley's recent works, *The Rise of the Dutch Republic* and *History of the United Netherlands*. To gather information on Dutch home life, she visited and talked with a family who had moved from Holland to New Jersey in the 1840s. Finally, after her book was published, she traveled to Europe herself and visited Holland to "see with my own eyes the land I had tried to picture for my readers....But, to my joy, every detail of the earlier picture of the country was verified."[5]

A large part of *Hans Brinker*, chapters X through XXXI, almost one half of the book, describes a St. Nicholas holiday trip through cities of Holland. The instructive purpose of this trip is emphasized by having an English student, Ben Dobbs, travel with the Dutch boys. Having read about the country's struggles, Ben "could scarcely tread a Holland town without mentally leaping, horror-stricken, over the bloody stepping-stones of its history." He learned to respond intelligently and appreciatively to each important site by remembering, admiring, and lamenting aspects of its past. His trip became a mental and emotional exercise, completing through personal experience the book knowledge which he had acquired in school. He even referred to literature where appropriate—the windmills reminded him of *Don Quixote*—and dutifully wrote his impressions down in a notebook.[6] His holiday trip resembles the culture tour or "sentimental journey" which a young adult was expected to take after completing college. Mary Dodge just extends this tour back into childhood. And following her standards for children's literature, she boldly depicts both the horrors and glories of Dutch history, just as she fills the other parts of her tale with poverty, accident, injury, sacrifice, and social conflict to balance the romantic dream prizes, buried treasure, and mystery jewel.

Mary Dodge promoted these same standards when Charles Scribner offered her the editorship of *St. Nicholas*, a new magazine for girls and boys. Practically every number contains a travel sketch or historical tale. In "Ready for Europe" (May 1876), Susan Coolidge expresses the general purpose of these travel sketches: "To travel anywhere, intelligently, has a great deal of education in it, and for an American to go to Europe, where [there] is so much we cannot as yet have in our own country, is education of the very best sort." But, she continues, in order to avoid bewilderment and confusion when visiting famous places, one should prepare in advance: "Every subject carefully looked into, every bit of history carefully tucked away into its proper place in your memory, every little interesting fact, every cell made ready for the reception of mental honey, will prove, when the right moment comes, a thing to be thankful for." Mrs. Oliphant's series on "Windsor Castle" (March to October 1876) recounts the stories of those who lived in the castle, from Richard II, Henry IV, and Henry V, known from Shakespeare's history plays, down to Queen Victoria, with emphasis on the child kings Henry VI and Edward VI. Several sketches and tales in *St. Nicholas* depict children in historical settings. "A Talk About Royal Children" (July 1879) discusses the childhood of kings and queens, princes and princesses. "A Child Queen" (November 1877) tells the story of Isabella, the daughter of Charles VI of France, who was given in marriage to Richard II when she was eight years old. After Richard's death, she received marriage proposals from Henry IV and his son, Prince Hal. This story is appropriately embellished with quotations from Shakespeare's history plays. Other sketches treat Joan of Arc—"The Little Maid of Domremy" (June 1876), little Louis XVII—"The Last Dauphin" (November 1879), "Lady Jane Grey" (March 1881), and Ferdinand and Isabella as children—"Borrowing Trouble" (May 1874). Mary Dodge herself wrote "The Princes in the Tower" (January 1874), describing the sad plight of princes Edward and Richard who were confined in London Tower and eventually murdered by Richard III. This piece illustrates her use of history and literature (although she does not mention Shakespeare), her candid inclusion of suffering and violence in a children's story, and her attempt to train the sentiments by an exercise of pity: "Not the Prince of Wales, nor the Duke of York, now, but two heart-sick terrified boys, who every moment dread—they hardly know what. If they only could feel their mother's arm about them once again! They have prayed and prayed, and they have cried till they can cry no more, and with breaking hearts they have straightened themselves proudly with the thought that they are the sons of a king, when suddenly they hear,..."[7]

Travel, history, literature, Europe, instruction, sentiment— these were considered the necessary qualities of serious writing for children, and Mark Twain, according to certain critics of his time, first became a serious writer by putting these qualities into a novel meant for children, *The Prince and the Pauper*. There was even a chance that this novel might be serialized in *St. Nicholas*, as his *Tom Sawyer Abroad* would later be, and as he sometimes imagined his *Joan of Arc* might be. Furthermore, two of his neighbors in Hartford, Charles Dudley Warner, with whom he co-authored *The Gilded Age*, and Lily Warner, Charles's sister-in-law, were contributors to *St. Nicholas* and friends of Mary Dodge. Naturally, this appeal to a different group of readers—boys and girls—and association with others who were writing for them, and the values that characterized this writing, modified Twain's approach to Shakespeare. He now used Shakespeare's authority for seriousness and instruction, and probed his works for facts about historical personages and authentic styles of speech.

The Prince and the Pauper

After mining in Nevada and California, and newspaper reporting in San Francisco, Mark Twain next became, in his own words, "a special correspondent in Europe and the East; next, an instructional torchbearer on the lecture platform; and, finally,...a scribbler of books, and an immovable fixture among the other rocks of New England."[8] He left California for New York in December 1866, and sent letters back to the San Francisco *Daily Alta California* about his trip south on the Pacific, across Panama, and north on the Atlantic, and about his sightseeing activities in New York City. While there he persuaded the *Alta* to pay his way on a tour of Europe and the Holy Land in exchange for travel letters, and he left New York on the steamship *Quaker City* in June 1867.

Twain referred to this trip as a Sunday school picnic and a "pilgrim's progress" because it was sponsored by Henry Ward Beecher's Congregational church in Brooklyn and had the Holy Land as its destination. But Europe was not just a Vanity Fair or tempting distraction between America and the Heavenly City. It too was sacred in a sense, culturally if not religiously, and the contemplation of its sites and monuments was supposed to purify the senses and enlarge the mind.

As Twain visited several hallowed spots in France and Italy, he often ridiculed them, admitting that he did not see the beauty or sublimity in them that he was supposed to see or that the guidebooks told him was there. But even this ridicule had a serious purpose. Twain wanted his reactions and descriptions to be honest, to represent exactly what he saw, not what he was supposed to see or was told to see. Because of his wry and irreverent reactions Twain often considered himself a "sinner" instead of a "pilgrim," yet he could rightly be called a "prophet," since he tried to expose hypocrisy and pretension and reveal the truth. Kenneth Lynn stresses Twain's frequent trips downward into crypts, morgues, catacombs, dungeons, and sepulchres.[9] To explore the very depths of reality Twain chose to undergo a symbolic death and decomposition. This is most evident in his visit to the Capuchin Convent in Rome,

where the bones of the departed brethren are divided according
to type among the various rooms. Although Twain imagined a
comic resurrection here when the final trumpet sounded—
"Some of the brethren might get hold of the wrong leg, in the
confusion, and the wrong skull"—he was horrified at the ghastly
sight. Just witnessing such a thing causes a kind of intellectual dismemberment. One of the monks began to identify
skulls by name: "Then he took a skull and held it in his hand,
and looked reflectively upon it, after the manner of the
gravedigger when he discourses of Yorick." Twain allowed his
mind to dwell on thoughts as profound and tragic as Hamlet's
graveyard reflections on mortality. He was moved enough to
rush his fellow sinners out of the room before someone could
ask the droll question, "Is—is he dead?"[10]

But Mark Twain's ventures into seriousness during the
tour were not confined to frank impressions and tragic explora-
tions. He also made honest attempts to appreciate the traditional splendors of Western Civilization. The trip was his
sentimental journey and grand tour. Although the poverty and
dilapidation of Venice at first disappointed him, reminding him
of a flooded Arkansas town, with gondolas seeming more like
hearses or canoes, he summoned all of his mental powers to
help him admire the ancient city properly. He recalled events
from its glorious history and contrasted them with its present
decline; he chose to view the city "from afar off as through a
tinted mist" or "under the mellow moonlight" where "the Venice
of poetry and romance stood revealed"; drawing upon the
literary images of Venice, he was able "to people these silent
canals with plumed gallants and fair ladies—with Shylocks in
gabardine and sandals, venturing loans upon the rich argosies
of Venetian commerce—with Othellos and Desdemonas, with
Iagos and Roderigos—with noble fleets and victorious legions
returning from the wars"; he was also reminded of Samuel
Rogers' verses beginning, "There is a glorious city in the sea."
Shakespeare is treated here as a classical author and part of
the cultural heritage. By associating his characters with Venice,
Twain was able to elicit an appropriate response to a significant place and thereby develop a refined and cultivated taste.
He did the same in Padua and Verona, with "their Montagues

and Capulets, their famous balconies and tombs of Juliet and Romeo *et al*...."[11] Like the tour in general, therefore, Shakespeare's works contributed to Twain's cultural development.

And the tour contributed in other ways. One of Twain's fellow pilgrims was Mary Mason Fairbanks, a writer, teacher, and wife of the publisher and part-owner of the Cleveland *Herald*. She became Twain's lifelong friend, correspondent, and cultural advisor. In his many letters to her he called her "Mother," and he tried to follow her principles on behavior and improvement. Another fellow pilgrim was Charles Langdon, on his grand tour between college and a position in his father's coal and iron business. At one point in the tour Charley showed Twain a miniature photograph of his sister, Olivia, and Twain fell in love with her at first sight. He met Livy and her family in New York City in December 1867, a little more than a month after the tour ended. When he visited her at her home in Elmira, New York, in August 1868, his proposal of marriage was rejected. He visited again in November and was privately accepted. In February 1869, their engagement was announced, and they were married a year later.

Parallel in time with his courtship, Twain was busy turning his travel letters to the *Alta* into a book. In the same month in which he met Livy, he received a letter from Elisha Bliss of the American Publishing Company in Hartford requesting a manuscript about the tour. Twain realized that having a book would raise his professional status and help make him a more worthy husband for an upper-middle-class woman. Some critics even accuse him of adding genteel passages to *Innocents Abroad* just to impress Livy, her family, or Mrs. Fairbanks. This is not true, at least, of his reactions to Venice. The night view, the references to Shakespeare, and the verses, all occur in his original *Alta* letter.[12] Writing a book for Bliss also brought Twain to Hartford, where he would soon move and join a highly cultured community of professionals. All of these factors—the European tour, the marriage, the book, and moving to Hartford—seemed to promise an advancement in social standing.

Twain's life and writing during the 1870s went through a

series of shifts between past and present, city and country, America and Europe, lectures, travel and fiction. Although established as a resident of Hartford and a participant in its social affairs, Twain spent much of the year on the road as a comic lecturer, and he did most of his writing during the summer at a farmhouse outside Elmira. He also managed three long stays in Europe in order to travel, lecture, and gather material for books. After *Innocents Abroad* (1869), his books ranged from stories of his western years—*Roughing It* (1872), to a satire on contemporary society, business, and politics—*The Gilded Age* (1873), which he co-authored with his Hartford neighbor Charles Dudley Warner, to autobiography and fiction about his piloting apprenticeship and early life on the Mississippi—"Old Times on the Mississippi" (1875) and *Tom Sawyer* (1876). His stature as a professional writer was rising—"Old Times" was published in the prestigious *Atlantic Monthly*—yet he was unable to shake off his predominant identity as a popular humorist, and, for his more respectable friends and colleagues, that made him a second-class writer. Even though *Tom Sawyer* provided a delightful mixture of humor and romance, it still gazed fondly backward at a less developed society, and Tom was a bad boy who had to escape constantly, if not wholeheartedly, from the responsibilities of adulthood.

Twain's literary friends and Hartford neighbors recognized his superior talents, however, and urged him to write a "first-class serious or sober work," something of "sober character and solid worth, & a permanent value." Mrs. Fairbanks wrote that she was eagerly awaiting his "best book" and "best contribution to American Literature," and Twain responded by describing for her the plans and work that he was putting into a new book: "it will appear without my name—such grave & stately work being considered by the world to be above my proper level. I have been studying for it, off & on, for a year & a half." When *The Prince and the Pauper* appeared in 1881, a reviewer found in it "other and higher merits than can possibly belong to the most artistic expression of mere humor." Many considered it to be Twain's first serious book.[13]

One mark of the book's seriousness was Twain's extensive

preparatory reading. He later recalled, "I had been diligently reading up for a story which I was minded to write, *The Prince and the Pauper*."[14] In notes at the end of his novel he identified some of the works that he consulted: Timbs's *Curiosities of London*, Hume's *History of England*, Trumbull's *Blue Laws, True and False*, and Jesse's *London, Its Celebrated Characters and Places*. Other sources, either mentioned in his working notes or clearly influential on his novel, were Holinshed's *Chronicles* and Hall's *Chronicle*, Froude's *History of England*, Craik and MacFarlane's *Pictorial History of England*, Head and Kirkman's *The English Rogue*, Lecky's *History of European Morals*, and Charlotte Yonge's *Young Folks' History of England* and *Cameos From English History*, as well as her historical romances, *The Prince and the Page* and *The Little Duke*.[15] While these books provided background material on history, geography, social customs, and moral philosophy, other books furnished models of archaic speech. Twain recalled, "I was reading ancient English books with the purpose of saturating myself with archaic English to a degree which would enable me to do plausible imitations of it in a fairly easy and unlabored way."[16] He compiled an eighteen-page list of "Middle-Age phrases for a historical story," the first two pages of which contain words and phrases taken mostly from Shakespeare, labeled *Shak*, especially from *The First Part of King Henry the Fourth*, labeled *K. Henry IV*. Subsequent pages contain words and phrases from *Ivanhoe* and *Kenilworth*, historical romances of Sir Walter Scott, with an occasional phrase from Shakespeare, labeled *Sh*.[17] Twain's seriousness is evident, therefore, from the number of books which he read and from the subject matter of these books: history, travel, philosophy, literature, and language. Such books were considered highly educational and cultivating, especially if they treated aristocratic societies of the European past. They represented a prestigious and sacred tradition.

Moreover, besides reading and taking notes, Twain did a practice exercise at imitating archaic English. In August 1876 he wrote *1601: Conversation as it was by the Social Fireside in the Time of the Tudors*. I have shown in Chapter I how this piece expresses the contrasts that Twain saw in the person of Shakespeare. Here I want to stress the study and training that he put into writing it. True, the piece was a practical joke. In 1906 a man seeking information on *1601* sent Twain some letters that were exchanged between John Hay and Alexander Gunn in June 1880. Hay jokingly called *1601* "a serious effort to bring back our literature and philosophy to the sober and chaste Elizabethan standard," but he thought "the taste of the present day...too corrupt for anything so classic." Twain replied in 1906 that *1601* was only "a supposititious conversation,...not, as John Hay mistakenly supposes, a serious effort to bring back our literature and philosophy to the sober and chaste Elizabeth's time: if there is a decent word findable in it, it is because I overlooked it."[18] Nevertheless, *1601* was an early product of Twain's "diligent reading" and "saturation with archaic English" in preparation for *The Prince and the Pauper*. The ancient English books mentioned in it add to the list of Twain's background sources: Samuel Pepys' *Diary*, the *Heptameron* of Marguerite of Navarre, Montaigne's *Essays*, Rabelais, Boccaccio, Cervantes, and finally, Shakespeare's "Kyng Henrie IV," from which many of Twain's "Middle-Age phrases" were taken.

Although none of the "Middle-Age phrases" from Shakespeare on Twain's list occur in *1601*—perhaps because Twain saturated himself in the archaic style so thoroughly that he could imitate it in an "easy and unlabored way" without having to copy individual words—many words and phrases in *1601* are common in Shakespeare: *dribbling, cod-piece, heaven's artillery, paltry, dalliance, drouth*. Many also come from *Henry the Fourth*, which "Shaxpur" reads during the conversation: *bulke, furnished, yesternight, break wind*. The last is used by Falstaff when he claims that he will lose his breath—"break my wind"—if he has to walk instead of ride to the site of a planned robbery, but Shakespeare certainly intended the pun (*I Henry IV*: II, ii, 13).[19] *Swaggering* appears often in *The Second Part of King Henry the Fourth* II, iv, to describe Ancient Pistol. This scene in the Boar's Head Tavern could have inspired *1601*. It has royalty (Prince Hal) associating with commoners, burlesque recitations of Pistol, and women (Nell Quickly and Doll Tearsheet)—not really gentlewomen, although Prince Hal calls them such—indulging in rough, bawdy talk filled with oaths and curses. The tavern scenes in general, from which most of the Shakespearean phrases in Twain's list are taken, provide a language and spirit akin to those described in *1601*. They mix the classes and the sexes, the gallant and the obscene, in vigorous, earthy, and figurative prose.

The results of Twain's reading, notes, and burlesque exercise can be found in *The Prince and the Pauper*. Items from *Henry the Fourth* which are listed on the first two pages of his "Middle-Age phrases" appear also in the dialogue of his novel: *way* (or *place*) *for the king, jumps with*, and *'Odsbody* (*Godsbody* in Shakespeare). Words in the novel which are common in other plays of Shakespeare include *palter*, *cozen*, *disproportioned, chafe, beguile, prating, throttle, madcap, wanton* (used as a noun and a verb), *anon*, *soft* (meaning *hush*), and *apace*. Other phrases found in Shakespeare include *box on the ear, customs and observances, bandying of words, airy nothings, say me nay*, and *perdition catch*. *An* is used for *if* and *be* for *are*, the pronoun *thou* is often omitted (*where dost live*), word order is changed (*good my lord*), and sentences are filled with curses, oaths (*S'blood, by these hilts*) and expressions of deference (*please you, I pray ye*). Sound patterns of alliteration and assonance, and a heavy stress on explosive Anglo-Saxon roots and monosyllables, add to the oral and primitive quality of the style. A concentration of these features can be found in two passages, one from *The First Part of King Henry the Fourth* and the other from *The Prince and the Pauper*. In *Henry the Fourth*, in a passage beginning with *God's body*, which Twain copied as *'Odsbody* on the first page of his "Middle-Age phrases," a carrier summons an ostler:

> God's body! the turkeys in my pannier are quite starved. What, ostler! A plague on thee! hast thou never an eye in thy head? Canst not hear? An 'twere not as good deed as drink to break the pate on thee, I am a very villain. Come, and be hanged! Hast no faith in thee?
>
> *(II, i, 25-29)*

Miles Hendon, perhaps the most vivid practitioner of Twain's "middle-age" style, assails John Canty, the pauper Tom Canty's father, with the following words:

> If thou do but touch him, thou animated offal, I will spit thee like a goose!...I took this lad under my protection when a mob of such as thou would have mishandled him, mayhap killed him; dost imagine I will desert him now to a worser fate? For whether thou art his father or no—and sooth to say, I think it is a lie—a decent swift death were better for such a lad than life in such brute hands as thine. So go thy ways, and set quick about it, for I like not much bandying of words, being not overpatient in my nature.[20]

It is quite evident too that Twain's debt to Shakespeare involved more than just diction and grammar. Just as the company and conversation in *1601* could have derived some of their spirit and style from the tavern scenes in *Henry the Fourth*, so the experiences of Prince Edward and Tom Canty reflect those of Prince Hal in the same plays. King Henry IV's wish that his real son might be the brave Hotspur instead of the dissolute Prince Harry, could have given Twain the idea for his plot:

> O that it could be proved
> That some night-tripping fairy had exchanged
> In cradle-clothes our children where they lay,
> And called mine Percy, his Plantagenet!
> Then would I have his Harry, and he mine.
> *(I Henry IV: I, i, 86-90)*

Although there are many sources from which Twain could have drawn this switching-places plot, his reliance on the Henry plays for features of style suggests that they too could have been influential. Just as Henry IV worries constantly about the wayward lifestyle of his son, Prince Hal, so Henry VIII worries about the seeming madness of Prince Edward.[21] Other scenes that invite comparison with Twain's novel are Prince

Hal's participation in and breakup of the robbery at Gadshill. Prince Hal seizes the stolen goods, is questioned by a sheriff who traces them to his tavern hangout, and is later arrested by a justice. Edward is forced to take part in a begging swindle, but exposes it in process to its victim. He also receives stolen goods during a robbery, is caught, is brought before a justice, and is put in jail.[22] The general theme of a prince's education toward more effective leadership by mixing with the lower classes permeates both Twain's novel and Shakespeare's Henry plays. Prince Edward learns mercy by suffering the harsh effects of English laws, and Prince Hal, as Henry V, has gained the respect and loyalty of the common soldiers at Agincourt by his previous dealings with their kind. He too shows mercy to those guilty of only minor offenses (see *Henry V*: II, ii).

In addition, Shakespeare's influence on *The Prince and the Pauper* involved more than just the Henry plays. While the first two pages of Twain's "Middle-Age phrases" quote exclusively from *Henry the Fourth*, subsequent pages contain items from other plays. For instance, *whey-faced, lily-livered* (p. 3), which is labeled *sh*, comes from *Macbeth*; *Beshrew my heart* (p. 5) is in *A Midsummer Night's Dream*; *flagon of Rhenish* (p. 5) appears in *Hamlet, shelled* (*shealed* in Shakespeare) *peascod* (p. 11) in *King Lear*, and *chop-logic* (p. 11) in *Romeo and Juliet*.[23] And like the quotes from the Henry plays, these too hint at more than stylistic influences.

The novel's epigraph from *The Merchant of Venice*, "The quality of mercy...is twice bless'd;...it becomes / The throned monarch better than his crown," introduces the lesson that Edward will learn from his ordeal as a pauper. This lesson is further illustrated by parallels in theme, plot, and character with *King Lear*. In "The Prince and the Pauper and King Lear," Robert L. Gale finds resemblances between the two works "numerous enough...to be notable but not sufficiently in the open to have been the result of any sustained intention on Twain's part." At this stage in his writing Twain had recourse to Shakespeare primarily for samples of archaic language, but in the process of gathering these, he also discovered material that would help him develop the scenes and characters of his story. According to Gale, the picture of Lear, stripped of his royal trappings and wandering across the open heath, contributed to Edward's experience as a pauper in the alleys of London and forest of Kent. Both Lear and Edward find shelter from wind, cold, and rain, one in a rude hovel and the other in a barn. Each learns from his trying ordeal to pity the poor and wretched. Lear comes to sympathize with Edgar and the Fool, and Edward later shows mercy toward those condemned to torture and death for petty offenses. Moreover, in their suspected madness, both Edward and Tom Canty are called "Tom o' Bedlam," just as Edgar is in his feigned madness. Finally, Miles Hendon resembles Kent by his service and loyalty to a rejected king. At one point he is confined in the stocks like Kent, and Edward views this as an insult to himself just as Lear does. After he is crowned king, Edward rewards Miles by making him the Earl of Kent.[24] If these probable influences of *King Lear* on *The Prince and the Pauper* are not explicit enough to qualify as intentional allusions, by which Twain would alert the reader to see *King Lear* as a literary paradigm for his novel, they at least represent, by their non-humorous use of Shakespeare, a middle stage between burlesque and paradigm. Twain would later be emphatically allusive in his use of Shakespeare, though not without the accompaniment of burlesque overtones.

Besides reading, note-taking, and practice exercises, Twain's travels also manifest a conscientious approach to his new novel. He had first visited England in the fall of 1872 both to arrange for a profitable publication of his books there and to gather material for a possible book on England. He returned the following May to continue his travels and to give comic lectures. Although he gathered more notes for a book, he was able to complete only a few essays, perhaps because he was so charmed by English life that he could not treat it comically or satirically in a major travel book. In the summer of 1879 he visited England again after a year's stay on the continent compiling material for *A Tramp Abroad*. This is when he familiarized himself with the locations in London that would figure in *The Prince and the Pauper*. It is interesting, there-

fore, that his first treatment of England is serious and affirma-
tive, both in the purpose of his novel and in the English literature which he consulted for its sources. The satire and criticism of England is mitigated through the novel's being set
three centuries in the past.

This turn toward seriousness in *The Prince and the Pauper*, marked as it has been by Twain's preparatory study of
history, language, and classic literature, and his investigative
travels, is further supported by his themes of education and
moral progress. The two main characters of the novel, Prince
Edward and Tom Canty, both undergo educational experiences,
one among his most needy and oppressed subjects, and the
other at court. Through these experiences, both gain moral
insights that change their behavior. By having to endure
poverty and the severity of English laws, Edward learns to pity
his subjects and pardon their minor offenses. Tom learns that
kingship is more than just a romantic dream, that it can be
used actively for social reform. And like the main characters,
the intended readers of the novel were educable youths. Twain
tested passages of his novel by reading them to his own and his
neighbors' children, and to the young ladies in his Saturday
Morning Club. He later presented it at his home as a play with
neighborhood children acting the parts. As mentioned above,
he even considered publishing it in *St. Nicholas*, a children's
magazine.

The themes of education, moral progress, and social reform, when related to Shakespeare, should remind us of Delia
Bacon's *Philosophy of the Plays of Shakspere Unfolded*, which
Twain claimed to have read in the late 1850s, twenty years
before he began work on *The Prince and the Pauper*. As I have
shown at length in my first chapter, Bacon traced the themes of
moral enlightenment and social reform through the plays of
Shakespeare, and more importantly, she stressed *King Lear*,
especially the scenes of Lear wandering on the heath, buffeted
by the storm, and seeking shelter in the rude hovel, the same
scenes that apparently affected Twain's novel. She also discussed the Henry plays, which Twain consulted for style, and
perhaps for plot and character. Critics have cited various

possible sources for the theme of moral education described in *The Prince and the Pauper*. I think that Delia Bacon deserves to be included among these sources, mainly because she unfolds this theme in the plays of Shakespeare.[25]

Twain's diligent study of history, language, and literature in preparation for writing *The Prince and the Pauper*, and the educational and moral purpose which he expressed in the novel's theme, raised his status as a writer in the eyes of his new genteel friends and colleagues, and evidently in his own mind too. His appeal to Shakespeare for examples of archaic style and historical drama, and the further effects of this on his plot, characters, and theme, establish Shakespeare as a guide and model whom he might approach to learn a higher form of writing. Previously in his burlesques he used Shakespeare mainly for contrast with his own milieu, and when there was similarity or integration between the two, it usually had an ironic or satiric effect. Now he was beginning to find elements in Shakespeare that he could imitate and integrate compatibly into his own work. But *The Prince and the Pauper* was a historical tale, far removed from his own generation and locale. It still remained for him to import Shakespeare into the setting that became his distinctive and predominant subject matter, the Mississippi Valley before the Civil War.

Scott and Howells

It has already been noted that several pages of Mark Twain's "Middle-Age phrases for a historical story" contain references to the works of Sir Walter Scott. Although Twain later blamed *Ivanhoe* for reviving in the American South the social divisions and romantic dreams of feudalism, to the point even of precipitating the Civil War, he nevertheless knew that Scott was a major writer of historical fiction, and since he was about to try his hand in that genre, he applied to Scott for assistance, beginning, naturally, with *Ivanhoe*.[26] He also found that Scott resorted to Shakespeare for help in language and history. So just as Twain had formerly received guidance and example in his comic use of Shakespeare from Artemus Ward, Sol Smith, and others, now he consulted authors who pursued Shakespeare for different reasons: history, language, and literary paradigms.

Howard Baetzhold has pointed out passages in Scott's "Introduction" and "Dedicatory Epistle" to *Ivanhoe* that might have prompted Twain to attempt a historical novel and given him a language strategy to use for it. In the "Introduction" Scott expresses his fear that "in confining himself to subjects purely Scottish [as he did in his previous books], he was not only likely to weary out the indulgence of his readers, but also greatly to limit his own power of affording them pleasure." That is why "the Author of the Scottish Novels...should be desirous to make an experiment on a subject purely English." If we substitute "American" for "Scottish," we may understand why Twain decided to try a different subject in *The Prince and the Pauper*. Also, in the "Dedicatory Epistle," Scott advises authors who set their stories in antiquity to avoid using many obsolete words. "He who would imitate an ancient language with success," he writes, "must attend rather to its grammatical character, turn of expression, and mode of arrangement, than labor to collect extraordinary and antiquated terms...." Twain seemed to follow this advice too. By "saturating" himself with archaic English he was able to absorb its grammar and syntax and did not have to rely merely on obsolete words for an antique effect.[27]

In *Ivanhoe* Scott distinguishes three styles of speech: Norman, Saxon, and a middle style between the two which mixes elements of both. Although Scott pretends to render these styles in translation, he tries to preserve the unique qualities of each. The expressions from *Ivanhoe* that Twain listed on pages 3 and 4 of his "Middle-Age phrases" come mainly from the Saxon style. *The curse of, I am no true man*, and *A murrain take thee* are all spoken by Gurth, a Saxon swineherd. Anxious to round up his hogs before dark and a storm, he exclaims, "The curse of St. Withold upon them and upon me! if the two-legged wolf snap not up some of them ere nightfall, I am no true man." Two other expressions on the list, *hath neither the fear of earth nor awe of heaven* and *broach the cask*, are spoken by Gurth's lord, Cedric, the leader of the Saxon cause. Although he calls Brian de Bois-Guilbert, the Norman, a "hard-hearted man, who knows neither the fear of earth nor awe of heaven," Cedric will welcome him at his table: "broach the oldest wine-cask; place the best mead, the mightiest ale, the richest morat, the most sparkling cider, the most odoriferous pigments upon the board; fill the largest horns." Aside from the presumed historical accuracy, or antique flavor, of these passages, there is a solid and lively aspect to them that gives them strength and excitement. The concrete one-syllable words of Angle-Saxon origin and the alliterative sound patterns ground the passages in direct sense impressions, while the curses, hyperboles, and superlatives lift them to grandeur. Cedric deplores the fashionable hunting terms of the Normans: "I care not for those over-sea refinements, without which I can well enough take my pleasure in the woods. I can wind my horn, though I call not the blast either a *recheat* or a *mort*; I can cheer my dogs on the prey, and I can flay and quarter the animal when it is brought down, without using the new-fangled jargon of *curee, arbor, nombles*, and all the babble of the fabulous Sir Tristrem."[28] Cedric and his compatriots—Gurth the swineherd, Locksley (Robin Hood), and the clerk-yeoman of Copmanhurst—represent the realistic side of romanticism. Twain seemed to record and copy their style for its earthy gusto as well as its antique flavor. One passage in *The Prince and the Pauper* which reflects this is Miles Hendon's words to a mad monk who claims to be an archangel:

> Marry, I do think there's not another archangel with so right a heart as thine. Wilt ride? Wilt take the wee donkey that's for my boy, or wilt thou fork thy holy legs over this ill-conditioned slave of a mule that I have provided for myself?—and had been cheated in, too, had he cost but the indifferent sum of a month's usury on a brass farthing let to a tinker out of work.[29]

Furthermore, *Ivanhoe*, like the plays of Shakespeare, contains other elements which Twain, while searching for examples of archaic style, could have found and used in developing plot, character, and theme for *The Prince and the Pauper*, including elements that relate to the plays of Shakespeare. The general aloofness and scorn which Norman leaders feel for their Saxon subjects is also reflected in the nobles and common people of Twain's novel. Cedric the Saxon resents the frenchiness of Richard Coeur-de-Lion, who has also been away from his subjects for several years fighting in the Crusades, and Cedric denounces his son, Ivanhoe, for collaborating with the Normans. Both Richard and Ivanhoe have been disinherited, one by his brother, Prince John, and the other by his father, and they must wander and fight in disguise until they win back their birthrights. Only when they join Robin Hood's foresters and a band of yeomen to defend the Saxon cause is wise and just leadership restored. The earthiness of the Saxon language symbolizes the closeness to the Saxon people and their problems that Richard and Ivanhoe have to experience in order to rehabilitate themselves for leadership. This resembles the moral education of Edward and Tom in Twain's novel.

It is also obvious that Scott uses Shakespeare's scenes and characters as paradigms for his own. Several chapters have epigraphs from Shakespeare. For example, chapters V, VI, and XXII have epigraphs from *The Merchant of Venice* which compare Scott's Isaac of York to Shylock. Both characters are Jewish, are money-lenders, and have daughters named Rebecca. Scott's comic portrayal of Isaac showing gratitude yet counting and checking money at the same time was definitely derived from Shakespeare. Isaac exclaims, "Seventy-one, seventy-two—thy master is a good youth—seventy-three—an excellent youth—seventy-four—that piece hath been clipt within the ring—seventy-five—and that looketh light of weight—seventy-six...." This recalls the speech of Shylock that Scott uses as an epigraph to Chapter XXII: "My daughter! O my ducats! O my daughter! /...O my Christian ducats! / Justice—the Law—my ducats and my daughter!"[30] To be fair, though, Isaac, unlike Shylock, who confuses his daughter with his ducats, bravely refuses money and offers his life for Rebecca. Scott also relates Cedric to King Lear, although there are no epigraphs from

Lear. Cedric has a fool who calls him "uncle" and a steward named Oswald, and he gives shelter to those caught in a storm, even though they are hostile Normans and a Jewish infidel. Several chapters have epigraphs from Shakespeare's History Plays, including Henry V's "Once more unto the breach," which stresses the collaboration of English nobles and commoners against the French. Scott clearly uses Shakespeare's plays as paradigms which lend authority and prestige to his own writing. I have supposed that Mark Twain's use of Shakespeare in *The Prince and the Pauper* was not explicit enough to qualify as paradigm, yet he drew material from the same plays as Scott— *King Lear* and the History Plays—and the epigraph to his novel was taken from *The Merchant of Venice*. Scott's explicit use of Shakespeare's works as paradigms could have stimulated Twain's use of them as sources in this novel and as paradigms in his later novels.

Another Scott novel that Twain consulted was *Kenilworth*, which was set during the English Renaissance, the same period as his own novel. *Kenilworth* furnished him with details and technical terms for items of clothing, weapons, and varieties of food and drink, all of which he listed in his working notes. He also listed words and phrases from Scott that seemed to capture the conversational style of the time. Many of these are taken from the brags, oaths, and curses spoken at the Black Bear tavern in Cumnor, mostly by Michael Lambourne, a tapster's boy turned pirate, gambler, cavalier, and soldier of fortune. Two of Lambourne's utterances, "I value Tony Foster's wrath no more than a shelled pea-cod" and "Wilt thou chop logic with me" are listed in Twain's notes and contain phrases from Shakespeare, *shelled pea-cod* appearing as *shealed peascod* in *King Lear* and *chop-logic* appearing as a noun in *Romeo and Juliet*. Although a minor detail, this illustrates how Twain and Scott were tapping Shakespeare for the same stylistic purposes.[31] Even Queen Elizabeth, who plays a major role in *Kenilworth*, spices her discourse with oaths and curses, and speaks in a vivid and earthy style. After knighting a man whose worthiness is doubtful, she admits, "while he sat on his knees before me, mopping and mowing as if he had scalding porridge in his mouth, I had much ado to forbear cutting him over the pate, instead of striking his shoulder."[32] In addition to its supposed historical accuracy, both Scott and Twain seemed to find a concrete and lively realism in the Renaissance style, and this caused them to view Shakespeare as a realist. Elizabeth cites a complaint voiced by the royal bear-keeper that ever since Will Shakespeare's plays became popular, "the manly amusement of bear-baiting is falling into comparative neglect; since men will rather throng to see these roguish players kill each other in jest, than to see our royal dogs and bears worry each other in bloody earnest." Although she frequents the bear-garden herself, Elizabeth sees a quality in Shakespeare's plays "worth twenty Bear-gardens."[33] This could mean that she appreciates Shakespeare's plays because they outdo bear-baiting in blood and violence, but whether it means this or not, it is realistic in its evaluation of the plays by comparing them to bear-baiting.

Like *Ivanhoe*, *Kenilworth* also provides Shakespeare paradigms for a number of its scenes. Chapter XIX, a scene in the Black Bear tavern, has an epigraph from a Boar's Head tavern scene in *Henry the Fourth*. The grand festivities at Kenilworth Castle (Chapter XXVI) are referred in the same way to the play put on by Peter Quince before the nobility in *A Midsummer Night's Dream*. Although the epigraph to Chapter XXXVI is taken from *The Winter's Tale* and supports the chapter's theme of adultery, the fact of Leicester's readily believing Varney's lies about Amy's infidelity parallels the action and emotions of Othello and Iago. Similarly, the guilty conscience that Leicester has for disowning Amy is related to that of Macbeth after the murder of Banquo (chapters XXI, XXXVII, and XXXVIII). Again, these clear paradigms could have inspired Twain to use Shakespeare as a source.

The Scott novel which Twain preferred to all the others because of its realism was *Quentin Durward*.[34] While in other novels Scott glorified the deeds and sentiments of chivalry, here he rang its death knell. Chivalry demanded brave and generous exploits done for love and honor, but what he found in fifteenth-century France was self-gratification, cold policy, and caustic wit. The two main historical figures whom he portrays, King Louis XI of France and Duke Charles the Bold of Burgundy, may be direct contrasts to one another in personal qualities, but neither can be considered virtuous or honorable. Louis pursues his own interests through secret and deceitful plotting and morally questionable compromises, while Charles asserts his will by violent and impetuous acts. Quentin Durward ventures into France, the fabled land of chivalry, to find a worthy leader and perform deeds of renown. When a silk merchant offers him employment, he turns it down for something more noble, but he later discovers that the merchant was King Louis in disguise, and that Louis's manner of proceeding as king does not differ much from that of a businessman. Still, through his uncle's influence, he joins Louis's bodyguard of Scottish archers, though he is constantly shocked by unchivalrous court practices, especially those regarding women and marriage. Louis forces a political marriage between his homely daughter and the Duke of Orleans, and he chooses Quentin to escort the Countess Isabelle to the reckless bandit William De la Marck for another political marriage, after she had already fled Burgundy to prevent a similar union. Quentin continues to be disillusioned by witnessing the acts of De la Marck and Duke Charles, and he even compromises his own integrity by testifying on behalf of Louis at a trial. He tells the truth, but not the whole truth, withholding his own unprovable but justified suspicions.

Twain's use of *Quentin Durward* as a source for *The Prince and the Pauper* suggests that he considered his novel a work of realism as well as history. Both Prince Edward and Tom Canty undergo ordeals of disillusionment. Whenever Tom fell asleep at his home in Offal Court, he moved in dreams "among great lords and ladies, in a blaze of light, breathing perfumes, drinking in delicious music," but then he awoke heartbroken in his wretched surroundings. When these romantic dreams came true, however, and he was mistaken for the prince, he became even more disillusioned. He felt like a captive in a gilded cage: "His old dreams had been so pleasant; but this reality was so dreary!" Now reigning as king in the palace he dreamt about his old life in Offal Court, and when he awoke, "the lying dream faded away—the poor boy recognized that he was still a captive and a king."[35] Edward, on the other hand, after he was locked out of the palace, thought that his life as a pauper was "the strangest dream," until he awoke and "realized that he was no longer a petted prince in a palace,...but a pauper, an outcast, clothed in rags, prisoner in a den fit only for beasts, and consorting with beggars and thieves." A further ironic twist to this contrast between dream and reality is added by Miles Hendon. Believing Edward mad, he found himself, as "knight of the Kingdom of Dreams and Shadows," in a "most odd and strange position, truly, for one so matter-of-fact." Yet he refused to laugh, because what was fantasy to him was real to Edward. Even the realist is fooled, therefore, and must be disillusioned.[36] In revealing the harsh details of both pauperism and the princely life, especially as they clash with romantic images of each, Mark Twain followed the example of *Quentin Durward*. Scott portrayed his paupers, the Bohemians, as well as his princes, as selfish, scheming, and deceitful.

The theme of realism in *Quentin Durward* is supported by a style of dialogue which has both an antique and realistic effect. The language of Louis XI, of Quentin's battle-scarred uncle, Le Balafre, and even of Quentin himself at times, sparkles with a sharpness of detail and a reverberation of sound. Le Balafre meets Quentin in a tavern and orders wine for both, "Ho! old Pinch-Measure, our good host, bring us thy best, and that in an instant." When Quentin only sips from his cup because he had been drinking earlier, Le Balafre warns him, "you must fear the wine-pot less, if you would wear beard on your face, and write yourself a soldier. But come—come, unbuckle your Scottish mail-bag—give us the news of Glen Houlakin." He later corrects Quentin's romantic notions of a king feasting "with a great gold crown upon his head, or charging at the head of his troops:"

> Hark in thine ear, man—it is all moonshine in the water. Policy—policy does it all....It is an art this French king of ours has found out, to fight with other men's swords, and to wage his soldiers out of other men's purses. Ah! it is the wisest prince that ever put purple on his back; and yet he

weareth not much of that neither.[37]

Mark Twain appreciated passages like this for their concreteness and resonance as well as their antique flavor. The phrases that he listed from them contain many words which have concrete referents and are monosyllabic and alliterative: *wine-pot, a cup of burnt sack, the foul fiend, I will nail my gauntlet to these gates*.[38] These words are realistic because they give a whole sense impression with each syllable, and their sound patterns reinforce their spoken actuality. Similar stylistic traits appear in the quotations from Shakespeare that Scott uses for epigraphs to various chapters. Le Balafre, for instance, is compared to the "man-at-arms" in *As You Like It*: "Full of strange oaths, and bearded like the pard, / Seeking the bubble reputation / Even in the cannon's mouth" (II, vii, 150, 152-153), and Quentin reflects the cocky ambition of Pistol: "Why then the world is my oyster, which I with sword will open" (*The Merry Wives of Windsor* II, ii, 2-3). Scott found Shakespeare's language a suitable model for realism as well as for historical coloring.

There are indications too that Mark Twain considered Shakespeare a realist. In his preparatory reading for *The Prince and the Pauper* he discovered a conversation in some old book which impressed him because of "the frank indelicacies of speech permissible among ladies and gentlemen in that ancient time." He was impressed "because this conversation seemed real, whereas that kind of talk had not seemed real to me before....It had not seemed to me that the blushful passages in Shakespeare were of a sort which Shakespeare had actually heard people use[,] but were inventions of his own....But here at last was one of those dreadful conversations which commended itself to me as being absolutely real, as being the kind of talk which ladies and gentlemen did actually indulge in in those pleasant and lamented ancient days now gone from us forever."[39] Evidently, Twain found this conversation real because of its subject matter, not just its historical accuracy, and this would make it worthy of imitation as realistic writing even in the present time. Twain practiced writing a conversation of this type in *1601*, with Shakespeare and Queen Elizabeth as participants. Earlier too, when he was courting Livy and trying to convince her and her family of his good breeding, he made himself her cultural advisor. He suggested several books for her to read, but he marked passages that she was to skip because they were too gross, coarse, and indelicate for a virgin reader. Among them were passages from *Don Quixote*, *Gulliver's Travels*, *Tristram Shandy*, *Gil Blas*, and Shakespeare.[40] Although he did not work such passages into *The Prince and the Pauper*, the sources that he consulted for it did contain them, especially the scenes from Shakespeare at the Boar's Head tavern, and he did use the type of language that he found in those passages, with its oaths and curses if not its bawdy details. Also, he stressed other aspects of realism in his novel: low life, squalor, petty crime, satire, and the need for social reform.

It is clear, therefore, that Scott's works helped Twain create an archaic style for *The Prince and the Pauper*, and that they inspired, or at least supported, his recourse to Shakespeare for further help in that style. They could also have suggested and exemplified for him the use of Shakespeare's plots and characters as source material, and, despite their romantic aspects and publication during the romantic era, they could have shown him various traits of realism in style, theme, and character, and caused him to see similar traits in Shakespeare. Scott, along with certain other romantics, however, was only a forerunner of the movement in literary realism that occurred in the latter half of the nineteenth century. A major practitioner, sponsor, and appreciative critic of this movement in America was Twain's closest literary friend and correspondent, William Dean Howells.

After working as a printer and newspaper reporter in Ohio, Howells was chosen to write Lincoln's presidential campaign biography and earned as a result of it the position of American consul in Venice during the Civil War. He then came to Boston as an editor and reviewer for the prestigious *Atlantic Monthly*, where he also published many of his travel sketches, novels, and plays in serial form before they appeared as books. While at the *Atlantic*, and later at *Harpers* in New York, he sought out, published, and wrote favorable reviews for new and experimental authors, especially humorists and realists, who were trying to make a start in the literary profession. Among these was Mark Twain.

Howells wrote detailed and enthusiastic reviews for *Innocents Abroad* and *Roughing It*, and accepted for publication "A True Story," Twain's first piece to appear in the *Atlantic*. True to its title, this black woman's account of losing her family during the Civil War was praised by Howells for its realism. He liked its "rugged truth" and "simple dramatic report of reality," and found it "a study of character as true as life itself, strong, tender, and most movingly pathetic in its fidelity to the tragic fact."[41] In a later essay, "Mark Twain," Howells again applauded Twain's honesty and sincerity, his use of "real types" and "actualities," figures from life rather than from plaster casts. He commended Twain's humor for its lack of artificiality and affectation. It was as simple and direct as Lincoln's statesmanship and Grant's generalship, and furthermore, wrote Howells, "as Shakspere, according to Mr. Lowell's saying, was the first to make poetry all poetical, Mark Twain was the first to make humor all humorous."[42] Howells grouped Twain with Lincoln and Shakespeare again in *My Mark Twain*, a final tribute after Twain's death: "He had the Southwestern, the Lincolnian, the Elizabethan breadth of parlance, which I suppose one ought not to call coarse without calling one's self prudish." Howells hid those letters of Twain "in which he had loosed his bold fancy to stoop on rank suggestion....He was Shakespearean, or if his ghost will not suffer me the word, then he was Baconian."[43] By relating Twain's realism to Shakespeare and the Elizabethans as well as to great men of his own nation and century, Howells must have encouraged Twain to view Shakespeare as a contemporary and compatriot, and to use his works as models of realistic writing.[44]

One close link between Twain's and Howells's use of Shakespeare was *Yorick's Love*, Howells's adaptation of a Spanish drama. Twain saw it performed in March 1880 and wrote Howells that it was "stirring," "charming," and "pathetic." More significantly, he was delighted by its language because it was the same style that he was using in his novel: "The 'thee's' & the 'thou's' had a pleasant sound, since it is the language of the Prince & the Pauper." He included in the letter a plot summary of his novel as if he realized for the first time that he and Howells were working on the same type of thing.[45] *Yorick's Love* does in fact contain the elements that Twain drew from Shakespeare for his novel: archaic language, realism, and models for plot and character.

Since Twain saw *Yorick's Love* only as a play—it was not published until recently—he was not able to study its language closely or take notes on it as he did with Scott's novels. Still, the Elizabethan prose and blank verse which he heard in it must have increased his facility in imitating that style. There are also phrases from Shakespeare in it that Twain would certainly have recognized—*Alas! Poor Yorick, take physic, woe upon your lives*—and these would have supported his own use of Shakespeare for samples of archaic style. However, although the language of *Yorick's Love* is archaic, and poetic in sound and imagery, it does not have the terse realistic thrust that characterizes many of the archaic phrases which Twain recorded in his notes on Scott. Howells's realism is more apparent in his plot and theme.

In *Yorick's Love*, a company of Elizabethan actors find themselves playing roles in a drama that correspond exactly to their positions in a real-life situation. Yorick, a comedian, is married to Alice, a woman half his age, and Alice falls in love with Edmund, his adopted son. In a play within the play, Yorick, Alice, and Edmund play the roles of Octavio, Beatrice, and Manfredo, respectively. Although a comedian, Yorick wanted to play a tragic role, and managed to persuade the director to choose him over Walton, the company's leading tragic actor. Yorick and the other actors perform superbly because they are expressing their real-life experiences. When Walton, angry because of losing the tragic lead, substitutes for a stage letter a real letter from Edmund to Alice plotting an elopement, Yorick, who must read the letter on stage, sees proof of his wife's infidelity and falters in his lines. Disregarding the prompter at first, he speaks in his own words, comparing himself to Count Octavio whom he is playing:

> Thou painted Count!
> Thou poor, unreal thing! Thou effigy!
> Yorick and thou art one in wretchedness!
> Let us be one in language—and speak thou
> For me....

♦   ♦   ♦

> and from this point
> I'll be no longer Yorick but Octavio!

♦   ♦   ♦

> Now, prompter, what was the word?

He then makes Octavio's lines his own, and the stage direction reads, "From this point the dramatic fiction merges into reality...."[46] Realism is therefore demonstrated both by the clash between fiction and reality and the gradual merging of the two.

Although Shakespeare appeared as a character in the original Spanish version of *Yorick's Love*, Howells and Lawrence Barrett, the actor, removed him because they thought the role distracting. Nevertheless, Shakespeare is mentioned in the play, especially as a proponent of realism. He is said to have liked the play that is performed, but also to have wished the speeches reduced, several scenes suppressed, and "some of the highest languaged encounters...resolved to native prose." He derived his own plays from studies of life in the London streets and found a mixture of comedy and tragedy to be the most authentic expression of reality. He also brought reality to art by naming the court jester mentioned in *Hamlet* after his friend, the comedian Yorick.[47]

Although its title refers to a character in *Hamlet, Yorick's Love* follows *Othello* as its paradigm. Yorick is the jealous husband, Othello, and Walton is the equally jealous informer, Iago. Hints are dropped that remind the audience to relate the two plays. The servants joke about Othello's being mismatched because of his age and color, and wonder if Yorick suffers a

similar predicament. When Yorick reads the letter which reveals Edmund's plan to escape with his wife, he first protests
that he will not stab himself as Othello did: "You are thinking
of that blackamoor of Venice / And surely not of this poor merry
Yorick / That never yet was apt for tragedy." Seconds after
saying this, however, he does kill himself. Repetition of key
words from *Othello*—*jealousy* and *proof*—also reinforces the
connection between the two plays.[48] Besides archaic style and
realism, therefore, Twain saw Shakespeare paradigms in
Yorick's Love that could have inspired or confirmed his own
recourse to Shakespeare as a source for plot and character.

Instead of using chapter epigraphs, as Scott did, to draw
attention to his Shakespeare paradigms, Howells used titles.
Many of his plays and novels have phrases from Shakespeare
for titles: *A Foregone Conclusion*, *A Counterfeit Presentment*,
The Undiscovered Country, *A Modern Instance*, *The Quality of
Mercy*, *A Hazard of New Fortunes*, and others. *A Foregone
Conclusion*, for example, follows loosely the plot and themes of
Othello, from which its title is taken (see *Othello* III, iii, 428).
It is set in Venice and describes a romance that develops, not
from an older general telling war stories to a young woman, as
in *Othello*, but from an older Venetian priest teaching a young
American woman Italian. The romance is doomed by misun-
derstanding and cultural differences, and creates jealousy on
the part of the woman's other lover, Ferris, an artist serving as
American consul. Shakespeare is also mentioned in it as a
model of realism. Ferris is working on a portrait of the priest,
but he does not want to decorate it with "tawdry accessories" to
bring out its Venetian qualities: "You all think that there can
be no picture of Venice without a gondola or a Bridge of Sighs
in it. Have you ever read the merchant of Venice, or Othello?
There isn't a boat nor a bridge nor a canal mentioned in either
of them; and yet they breathe and pulsate with the very life of
Venice. I'm going to try to paint a Venetian priest so that you'll
know him without a bit of conventional Venice near him."[49]
Mark Twain read this story when it was being serialized in the
Atlantic in 1874, and he contrasted its genuineness to "old
Walter Scott's artificialities."[50]

Twain saw and enjoyed Howells's play *A Counterfeit Pre-sentment* in January of 1878 when he was writing the early chapters of *The Prince and the Pauper*, and he probably also read it in the *Atlantic* where it ran serially from August to October 1877.[51] The title refers to Hamlet's showing his mother the contrast between pictures of his father and his uncle (see *Hamlet* III, iv, 55), but Howells uses it to describe a physical resemblance between Bartlett, an artist vacationing at a mountain hotel, and the former lover and deserter of Constance, a woman staying at the same hotel who is profoundly affected by the resemblance. Morbid and misanthropic because of a failed romance of his own, and theatrical in temperament, Bartlett, playing Hamlet before his Horatio-like friend, Cummings, addresses Constance's hat as though it were Yorick's skull: "Where be her gibes now, her gambols, her flashes of merriment? Now get you to my lady's chamber, and tell her, let her paint an inch thick, to this favor she must come; make her laugh at that. Dost thou think, Horatio Cummings, Cleopatra looked o' this fashion?   And smelt so—Pah!"[52]   Later in the play, when Bartlett and Constance are unsure about how they should treat one another, Bartlett rejects the brother-sister relationship with more lines from *Hamlet*: "Brother? Forty thousand brothers could not with all their quantity of love make up my sum! You drive me further than your worst enemy from you with that fatal word. Brother? I hate brother! If it had been cousin—and kind? Oh, I would we were 'a little less than kin, and more than kind!'"[53] These Hamlet posturings of Bartlett amplify the themes of madness and ghosts that recur throughout the play. Constance sees in Bartlett the ghost of her former lover, and must grapple with him in order to release herself from the old bond.

In September 1881 Twain suggested to Howells that they collaborate on a play about Colonel Sellers which would be a sequel to Twain's novel, *The Gilded Age*, and to the popular play based on it, *Colonel Sellers*. Two years later, in October 1883, they began work on the play that would eventually be called *Colonel Sellers as a Scientist*.[54] Since Twain's initial conception of this play occurred when Howells was already correcting the proofs of *The Prince and the Pauper*, the play could not have influenced the novel. The eventual collaboration demonstrates, however, that Twain was influenced by Howells to incorporate Shakespeare into his works, since, with this play, Shakespeare references appear in the Sellers story for the first time. They had not been used in either *The Gilded Age* (except for an epigraph written by someone else) or *Colonel Sellers*. It should also be mentioned that, about the same time as this conception for a new play occurred to him, Twain was inspired, by a visit with Howells, to attempt a burlesque *Hamlet*.[55]

The Shakespeare references in *Colonel Sellers as a Scientist* are significant because they appear in an American story, not an old English story, although they do support a theme of English nobility. In a way they recall Twain's earlier comic uses of Shakespeare. When Sellers hears that his distant cousin De Bohun has died in a fire, and realizes that he might inherit the earlship of Dover, he says, "I can at least claim a kinsman's privilege with regard to the—the—mortal coil, so to speak, of this De Bohun." To learn more about the earlship, Sellers tries by spiritualism to materialize the ghost of De Bohun, but when De Bohun shows up alive, Sellers exclaims, "Angels and ministers of gr—show this gentleman in—Daniel!"[56] These two references of Sellers to *Hamlet* (see III, i, 67, and I, iv, 39) concerning the themes of inheritance and ghosts demonstrate Howells's way of using Shakespeare as a paradigm, although the comedy is similar to Twain's. Sellers's later rehearsal of a temperance speech filled with quotes from *Othello*, *Hamlet*, and *Macbeth* follows the tradition of Shakespeare burlesques and resembles the Hamlet soliloquy that Twain wrote earlier that year for *Huckleberry Finn*. Taking a bottle of alcohol, Sellers declaims:

> Oh, that a man should put—put—(*Uncorks the bottle and smells it.*) an enemy in his mouth to steal away his brains! Good Iago—(*Smelling.*) Prythee tell me, (*Smelling.*) I am unused to the soothing mood, (*Smelling.*) and the big wars that make ambition virtue. (*Smelling.*) Be thou a spirit of

health or goblin damned. (*Smelling.*) Out damned spot!
(*Smelling.*) Not all the perfumes of Araby—I've got it! I've
got it![57]

To be authentic, Sellers decides to drink alcohol himself to
show its bad effects. Quoting *Romeo and Juliet* he says, "I
must have a portable spirit—some soon-spreading gear that
quickly as the hasty powder fired, may spread through all the
veins—like brandy, for example."[58] Although this becomes a
typical burlesque of temperance literature and resembles
Twain's earlier comic use of Shakespeare, it relates Shakespeare
to one of Twain's Missouri characters and foreshadows further
relations of this type that will have both a comic and a serious
or tragic effect in *Huckleberry Finn.*

Although *Colonel Sellers as a Scientist* burlesques the
themes of spiritualism and materialization, Howells treated
them seriously in an earlier novel, *The Undiscovered Country.*
The title comes from Hamlet's soliloquy (III, i, 79), which is
discussed briefly in the novel.[59] There is also a tenuous connection between Egeria, the medium in the novel, and Ophelia,
since both are attracted to herbs and wildflowers, although
Egeria cherishes them as part of her recovery from sickness,
while Ophelia's attachment to them is a symptom of her gradual
loss of sanity.[60] Edward Ford, the leading character in the
novel, can be compared to Hamlet because of his general skepticism and his love for Egeria. Twain read and enjoyed the
story when it was being serialized in the *Atlantic* in 1880, so it
could have been another influence on his serious use of
Shakespeare.

What Mark Twain gained, therefore, from reading Howells's
novels and seeing his plays was a way of using Shakespeare
that went beyond comedy and burlesque. He found examples
of archaic language for a historical novel, scenes and characters in Shakespeare that could help him in developing his own
stories—with or without an explicit appeal to Shakespeare as
an authority or paradigm—and a general acceptance of
Shakespeare as a fellow realist. Of course, Twain learned
these things from Scott as well, but Howells added to them the
suitability of Shakespearean material as a source for portray-

ing an American setting. This did not affect *The Prince and the Pauper*, since it was set in the English past, but it would affect Twain's next novel, *Huckleberry Finn*, which was set in nineteenth-century America. As I have shown in my previous chapter, the comic treatment of Shakespeare was already firmly established in American culture, and that itself paved the way for a serious treatment. But Howells's example further convinced Twain that it was not foreign, elitist, or unrealistic to draw elements for an American story from Shakespearean sources. It proved that America and Shakespeare could have some things in common, and that a relation of one to the other was not just comic or ironic.

Renaissance on the Mississippi

Mark Twain spent a major part of his literary career moving back and forth, both physically and creatively, between Europe and America. His first two travel books, *Innocents Abroad* and *Roughing It*, describe expeditions to opposite points of the compass, one to Europe and the Near East and the other to the American West, but they contain matching scenes and patterns. Lake Como is compared to Lake Tahoe, Asiatic beggars resemble American Indians, and the dungeons and crypts of Europe excite the same curiosity as the mines and caves of Nevada. Twain made trips to Europe in 1872, 1873, and 1878. Just as he interrupted work on *Tom Sawyer* to write "Old Times on the Mississippi," so he interrupted *The Prince and the Pauper* to complete *A Tramp Abroad*, and "Old Times" and *Tramp* contain several matching motifs: the river, bloody duels and feuds, swindlers, and beautiful sunsets either observed or missed. Similarly, Tom Canty resembles Tom Sawyer: both read romantic tales and act them out in their play, and dream of participating in glorious adventures. Americans parallel, visit, and disguise as Europeans, and eventually merge into them.

By these constant parallels, crossings, and mixtures Twain used one place to interpret and criticize another. He did the same with time. He explored and expressed his own "gilded age" by comparing it to other ages—Tudor England, the Middle Ages, and especially the antebellum South or Mississippi Valley, which became his primary fictional landscape. He used this setting to escape from, but also to interpret and judge his own time. It might be called his golden age, in contrast to his gilded age. In many ways the novels set in medieval or Tudor England resemble those of the Valley. Twain seemed to see, especially in Tudor England, the England of Shakespeare and the Renaissance, resemblances to the pre-war Mississippi Valley that would turn the personalities, events, and language of the Valley into features of a matching American renaissance.

Twain's first published work situated in the Mississippi Valley was *The Gilded Age*. The story begins before the Civil War and ends in the 1870s. It describes a period of rapid transition and reckless "improvement": Squire Hawkins wants to turn his Tennessee land into coal and copper mines; Sellers wants to change Stone's Landing into a metropolis; Laura achieves riches, status, and political influence in Washington; Philip and Henry jump into profit-making schemes, and Ruth pursues the medical profession. Change and progress fill the atmosphere.

Although Shakespeare references do not appear in the text of *The Gilded Age*, many of the chapter epigraphs, collected by a studious Hartford neighbor of Twain, are quotes from Elizabethan authors and relate the action and characters of the novel to those of the English Renaissance. Ben Jonson's *The Alchemist* and *The Devil is an Ass*, for example, support the themes of trickery, fraud, and smooth talk, as does the Prologue to Shakespeare's *Second Part of King Henry the Fourth* with rumor spreading false reports. In general, the grand speeches and wild schemes of Sellers and others reflect the extravagant language and plots of Elizabethan drama, especially as they concern ambition and advancement. One small reference to Elizabethan England, probably the work of Charles Dudley Warner, Twain's co-author, occurs when Philip and Henry expect to find in the park-like scenery of Missouri "the gables and square windows of an Elizabethan mansion."[61]

Twain's next published work on the Mississippi Valley was

the series of articles which appeared in the *Atlantic* from January to August 1875 under the title, "Old Times on the Mississippi." These articles later became chapters IV to XVII in *Life on the Mississippi*. "Old Times" contains very little Shakespeare, but there are elements in it which Twain would later find and appreciate in Shakespeare. "When I find a well-drawn character in fiction or biography," he wrote, "I generally take a warm personal interest in him, for the reason that I have known him before—met him on the river."[62]

One element in his first "Old Times" article which Twain would later admire in Shakespeare was colorful and explosive language. As a young traveler he was captivated by a shipmate's style of talk: "When he gave even the simplest order, he discharged it like a blast of lightning, and sent a long, reverberating peal of profanity thundering after it." Twain often associated Shakespeare's language with thunder and lightning, from the "thundergust" which he described in *1601* to the thunder and lightning which he remembered in a German production of *King Lear*. He headed a list of resounding German words for thunder and lightning with *Hamlet*'s "ponderous and marble jaws."[63] This is how he was struck by the mate's charge: "Here, now, start that gangplank for'ard! Lively, now! *What*'re you about! Snatch it! *Snatch* it!...*For-ard* with it 'fore I make you swallow it, you dash-dash-dash-*dashed* split between a tired mud turtle and a crippled hearse horse!" The young traveler exclaimed, "I wished I could talk like that."[64] This was the language of the pilots Bixby, Brown, and Ealer, and Twain later remembered Ealer's blending it into recitations of Shakespeare so thoroughly that he could not tell one from the other. The archaic phrases which Twain later listed from Shakespeare and Scott resemble this pilot talk in their curses, metaphors, and alliterative sound patterns.

Then the young traveler was fooled briefly by the sob story of a night watchman who claimed to be the son of an English nobleman. The watchman wove odds and ends of literature into his yarn, including Othello's "hairbreadth escapes." This exposes the ambitious, pretentious, and deceitful qualities that extravagant language can have, and points forward to the King and the Duke in *Huckleberry Finn*, who spout Shakespeare to strengthen their pose as noblemen and renowned tragedians.[65]

After "Old Times" appeared in the *Atlantic*, Twain extended it into *Life on the Mississippi* by adding chapters I to III and XVIII to LX. The new chapters contain several items that associate Shakespeare with the Mississippi. Twain recalled random scows on the river "bearing a humble Hamlet and Co. on an itinerant dramatic trip," and a young apprentice from Hannibal who was enticed to become an actor by two supposed Englishmen playing the swordfight from *Richard the Third*. Twain found him years later standing in a tragic pose on a St. Louis street corner, thinking he was Othello or some such character. Actually, he had a bit part as a soldier in *Julius Caesar*.[66] Two passages which Twain extracted from the book before publication also mention Shakespeare. One is a reprint of Mrs. Trollope's shocked account of Edwin Forrest's *Hamlet* in Cincinnati, where men sat in the theater with their coats off and sleeves rolled up, spitting tobacco and thumping their feet for applause, and interrupting the play with a chorus of Yankee Doodle. The other is an account Twain discovered of a *Hamlet* performance in Pittsburgh which was alternated every other night with a burlesque, and audiences saw no difference between the two.[67] Each of these stories shows an affinity of Shakespeare with the river culture. His characters and lines express the aspirations to greatness, whether tragic or foolhardy, shown on the river frontiers, and his plays, filled with characters from every level of society and directed at an equally diverse audience, gave American pioneers and adventurers the freedom to speak out and behave according to their desires.

Unlike "Old Times," the greater part of *Life on the Mississippi* is not about an apprentice learning the river, but about a retired pilot revisiting the river and regretting the loss of a lively past. The romantic days of steamboat piloting are set in a wider context as just one epoch of the river's history. The first two chapters give a telescopic view of the Mississippi: De Soto discovered the river before Shakespeare was born, and it was not seen again by a white man until after Shakespeare died; its discovery coincided with great events in Europe—the

Renaissance and the Reformation—and with famous art works—
the Sistine Chapel and *Don Quixote*. By associating the discovery of the Mississippi with such names as Martin Luther,
Michelangelo, Henry VIII, Cervantes, and Shakespeare, Twain
seems to prophesy that the river will provide actions, characters, and works of art that match those of the Renaissance and
Reformation, that life on his Mississippi will repeat and resurrect those violent and colorful times.

Viewed in this wider perspective, the history of the Mississippi is divided into three parts: the keelboat era, the steamboat era, and the tugboat and railroad era. In 1882, when
Twain traveled down and up the river and wrote his book, the
steamboat era was over. The wharves of St. Louis had only a
few lifeless steamboats tied to them, and the piles of freight,
crowds of passengers, and cursing dockworkers were replaced
by scattered drunks and sleepers. For Twain, this was melancholy, woeful, and desolate.[68] To dramatize the disappearance
of the old steamboat days, Twain inserted an account of the
Pennsylvania's explosion and his brother Henry's death. This
divides the apprenticeship story from the nostalgic return after
twenty years. Also spaced through the return trip are references to the Civil War, the main event which destroyed the
steamboat and its world. As Twain says, Southerners classify
all events as either before, during, or after the war.

Chapter XXVIII describes the modern improvements made
on the river by West Point engineers. Beacons light up points
and crossings, government boats pull up snags, and dams and
dikes are built to control the river's course. Although Twain
agrees with shipmate Uncle Mumford that no man can tame
the lawless river, he realizes that science has done the impossible before and may do it again. Whether or not control is
possible, however, the sad result is that science has taken the
romance out of piloting. It no longer furnishes exploits and
heroes that are worth writing about. In Chapter LVIII Twain
marvels at how progressive the upper river towns appear with
their colleges, newspapers, libraries, factories, and telephones.
A passing train reminds him of the fall of the steamboat, which
must now go begging for passengers and freight. Lumber rafts

do not have the old "reckless crews of fiddling, song-singing, whiskey-drinking, break-down-dancing rapscallions" any more. Now the crews are "quiet, orderly men, of a sedate business aspect, with not a suggestion of romance about them anywhere."[69] Present times, therefore, do not hold much hope for a storyteller.

Although Twain laments the downfall of romance in the chapters just cited, he seems to celebrate it in Chapter XLII. After *Don Quixote* and the French Revolution destroyed medieval feudalism, Sir Walter Scott brought it back, and the South adopted its slavery, duels, titles, and inflated language. There are signs of realism and progress in the new South—the writings of Joel Chandler Harris and George Washington Cable, and the factories and railroads of Natchez—but sentimentality remains. The people of New Orleans spend more money on the dead than the living, preferring monuments to urns, sentiment to hygiene.[70]

Is Twain then ambiguous toward romance? does he deplore it, yet regret its passing away? are there different kinds of romance? These questions can be answered if history is divided into three eras: medieval, renaissance, and modern. Because the modern era stresses order and sobriety at the expense of heroic deeds, it seems to be inadequate for literature. Some modern writers, therefore, reject their own milieu and resort to earlier times for literary material. Twain seemed to believe that his contemporary scene did not present sufficient material for fiction, but instead of resorting to a romantic past, he tried to create or recreate a renaissance, a time of transition when the old still existed and the new was just beginning to show itself. He saw Shakespeare's England as just such a time, and drew parallels between it and the Mississippi Valley during the steamboat era. A scene originally intended for *Huckleberry Finn*, but withdrawn from it after being published in *Life on the Mississippi*, depicts a keelboatman singing the same ribald ballad that Miles Hendon sang in *The Prince and the Pauper*. It also recounts a battle of exorbitant boasts which resemble in imagery and sound the Middle-Age phrases that Twain collected for his Tudor novel.[71] *The Prince and the Pauper* and *Huckleberry Finn* present two colorful worlds, feudal England and the romantic South, that are about to undergo changes. A new morality is emerging from each of them. Both Edward VI and Huck Finn experience the harshness of a cultural system and do what they can to correct or oppose it.

Walter Blair explains how Twain's reading in the mid-1870s of W. E. H. Lecky's *History of European Morals* influenced parts of *Huckleberry Finn*. He shows how Lecky's treatment of two moralities, one motivated by pure duty and the other by utility, appears in many of Huck's choices.[72] But Lecky does more than contrast the two moralities. He describes their development through history. Primitive peoples usually act on pure duty, stressing zeal, loyalty, heroism, and asceticism. As civilization progresses, morality becomes more utilitarian. More thought is given to intellectual growth, industry, human freedom, and relief of suffering. Moral demands become more amiable and practical.[73] According to Lecky, the Stoics were civilized, or softened, by the Epicureans, the Romans by the Greeks, the Pagans by Christianity, and Christians by the Enlightenment and the Industrial Revolution. Lecky favors the trend toward utility, but believes that duty is distinct from and morally superior to utility and should dominate in moral choices. Without utility, however, duty is inhumane. He permits a person to lie, for example, to save the life of a fugitive.[74]

The problem with the increase in civilization and utility is that it tames and softens reality to such an extent that exciting deeds become rare and literature has nothing to imitate. In *Huckleberry Finn* it is Miss Watson who finally frees Jim, probably for the utilitarian motive of going to heaven, but that would never have made a good story. Tom Sawyer's bold attempts to free him are more exciting and worthy of literature, but they are also unreal, a reversion to the romantic past. Huck enjoys Tom's antics for a while, until he sees through their artificiality and unnecessary trouble, yet he also tries to escape from Miss Watson's "sivilization." Uncomfortable with both Tom's romantic past and Miss Watson's practical modernity, he belongs in a time of transition, or renaissance.

Another book which influenced Twain's view of history was Hippolyte A. Taine's *History of English Literature.* It was published in 1864 and translated into English in 1871. Twain read it in the early 1880s. He later called Taine "The Father of English Literature because he made so many people read serious books which without his advice and encouragement they would never have tackled."[75]

In his introduction Taine insists on a necessary bond between literature and history. Great writers and great books are always products of two things, hereditary racial characteristics and surrounding historical conditions. Both Shakespeare himself, as an author, and the characters that he created, are determined from within by temperament and from without by circumstances. In this sense they resemble machines. According to Taine, Shakespeare's psychology would be: "Man is a nervous machine, governed by a mood, disposed to hallucinations, transported by unbridled passions, essentially unreasoning, a mixture of animal and poet...[having] imagination for prompter and guide, and led at random, by the most determinate and complex circumstances, to pain, crime, madness, and death." Twain too used this "mechanical" philosophy to explain humanity in general and Shakespeare in particular.[76]

In an age when racial temperament and historical circumstances are in accord, great literary triumphs will result. Taine sees the English Renaissance as such an age and Shakespeare as its main product. At that time the spirit of the Pagan Renaissance reigned in England. Its qualities of liberty, sensibility, amusement, splendor, energy, and passion were reflected in English feast days, music, and drama. When these Latin traits mingled with the Saxon ones of melancholy, dreaminess, coarseness, violence, courage, and devotion, the culture was born which finally matured in Shakespeare's works. Before this time, the Saxons were either tied down by a primitive culture and an ascetical religion, or were mere imitators of the superficial refinements of Norman chivalry. For Taine, just as for Twain, Cervantes exposed and destroyed this chivalry in the Renaissance.[77]

The Renaissance, however, did not last. It was a time of transition between the restrictions of Catholic ceremonies and those of Protestant morals, between medieval faith and modern reason, between barbarism and civilization, between Latin romance and German seriousness.[78] Taine sees the Puritan takeover in the 1600s as the beginning of modern culture. From then on England stressed morality, conscience, duty, work, law, science, and philosophy.[79] These new emphases took the power and joy out of the English temperament and therefore hurt its literature. English poetry and fiction became abstract, factual, moral, mechanical, and dogmatic. Sir Walter Scott, along with other Romantics, tried to restore the Renaissance spirit, to become another Shakespeare, but his works were too artificial and respectable, his style diffuse, and he was led astray by the English Puritan traits of "narrow exactitude" and "amelioration of society."[80] American Shakespeare critics explained the English Renaissance in similar terms. Henry N. Hudson quoted the German critic, G. G. Gervinus, who saw it as a period between the primitive crudeness of the Middle Ages and the false civilization of modern times, and Richard Grant White placed Shakespeare between a feudalism that was too rude and a British Empire that was too lettered.[81]

Many of Taine's polarities appear in Twain's works, especially in *Life on the Mississippi*. Taine's Latin traits of gaiety, leisure, elegance, and chivalry existed in the South until the sterner traits of the North, of Taine's German temperament— work, duty, sobriety, and conscience—threatened to replace them. Both Twain and Taine saw Cervantes as the destroyer of chivalry and Scott as its restorer. When Taine describes the people of feudal England as children delighting in dreams and tales of Robin Hood and Guy of Gisborne, it is hard not to think of Twain's medieval tales and of *Tom Sawyer*.[82] Taine's Saxons—coarse, drunk, loud, orgiastic, impulsive, singing, dancing, courageous, affectionate, and imaginative—resemble Twain's keelboat men. Both have a picturesque combination of rudeness and nobility, foulness and honesty.[83] Finally, the idea of conscience appears often in Taine's book as a trait of the modern spirit, the Protestant substitute for Catholic faith. For

Taine, a major conflict in English literature, especially in novels, is whether morality is based on conscience or on instinct, on rule or on liberty. The greatest writers—Shakespeare, Milton, Defoe—base it on instinct.[84] Twain appears to take a similar view in *Huckleberry Finn*.

It is very clear that Taine considers Shakespeare the greatest English writer. What comes before him is preparation, and what comes after is decline. The main feature of Shakespeare's style is pure imagination. Images flow from his mind in profusion and convulsion. They are complex, contorted, and exaggerated, and are not restricted by reason, morality, or practicality. Instead of being selected, restrained, or refined, they move in their natural and primitive power like lightning, waves, whirlwinds, and wild horses. Shakespeare resembles Hamlet in this: "you recognize in him a poet's soul, made not to act, but to dream, which is lost in contemplating the phantoms of its creation, which sees the imaginary world too clearly to play a part in the real world."[85] This is certainly a romantic picture of Shakespeare, but because it treats him as a "machine," or product of his age and race, it fits the deterministic philosophy and history of the later nineteenth century which Twain also accepted. Twain considered Taine a historian and a philosopher, a realist rather than a romantic. He seems to have been influenced both theoretically and creatively by Taine's philosophy and division of history. He chose as his principal literary landscape a period and characters that resemble those of Taine's English Renaissance. As "The Author" of *Huckleberry Finn*, he put his own sharp sensations and vivid imagination into Huck's narrative and point of view just as Shakespeare, according to Taine, put his into Hamlet.

Roger B. Salomon, studying the different stances and shifts in Twain's view of history, found him moving in general from a Whig view, which celebrates a steady material, political, and moral progress, to a modern or cyclic view, which sees decline and return to barbarism. Even when Twain was celebrating progress, however, he realized that the past held more aesthetic appeal than the present. For instance, he found aesthetic wonder and pleasure in the palaces, dungeons, and cathedrals that he described in *Innocents Abroad* even though they reflected a past that was morally and intellectually barbarous.[86] To escape this dilemma, Twain and other Whig historians settled on a "middle state," a peaceful farm life that was democratic and close to nature, and that existed between the aggressive and despotic primitive forest and the overly complex and increasingly despotic modern city. *Tom Sawyer* and the first part of *Life on the Mississippi* are set in this state.[87] It was not long, however, before Twain recognized the injustice and hypocrisy of even this middle state, and this caused him to create an alternate middle state, a dream world of nature, innocence, childhood, beauty, freedom, and instinctive goodness, which was symbolized by life on the river in contrast to the dullness and corruption of the villages and farms on the shores. This state is represented by the happy times that Huck and Jim experience on the raft. It is mythic, idyllic, and romantic, but romantic in a true and profound sense, not like the artificial sentimentality of Southern chivalry or the childish silliness of Tom Sawyer's games.[88] Even though it is not completely historical, this state could gain a bit more foundation in history, and therefore more credibility, I think, by the concept of renaissance that I have been describing. Twain chose the antebellum Mississippi Valley because it provided characters and actions that, no matter how romantic or mythical they seemed, were also real and historical types. The time and place created material worthy of literature. The fact that it was a time of transition or on the verge of transition, and therefore included elements of the past and the future, made it even more comprehensive and exciting. Twain saw resemblances between this time and another historical period, the English Renaissance, and these led him to write a historical novel set in Tudor England and to put renaissance motifs into his writings about the Mississippi Valley. With his concern for history, biography, and realism, he probably would have wanted his main fictional landscape to have some basis in fact.

It is clear, therefore, that Twain used Shakespeare for historical purposes. The language, actions, and characters of Shakespeare's plays helped him recreate Tudor England for

The Prince and the Pauper. Moreover, the literature of the English Renaissance, along with the society that generated it and that it reflected, offered models and subjects for great writing. It had more color, freedom, vigor, honesty, and imagination than Twain found in the progressive and respectable America of his own time. It also reminded Twain of the culture that existed in the Mississippi Valley before the Civil War, and it helped him recreate that culture as his main literary landscape. Finally, the example of Scott and Howells further convinced Twain that Shakespeare's works were valuable sources, not only for historical novels set in the remote past, but also for realistic novels set in nineteenth-century America.

Comedy keeps the heart sweet; but we all know
that there is wholesome refreshment for both mind
and heart in an occasional climb among
the pomps of the intellectual snow-summits
built by Shakespeare and those others.[1]

TRAGEDY

The first extended portrayal of American boyhood, mildly
realistic and partly autobiographical, was Thomas Bailey
Aldrich's *The Story of a Bad Boy.* This 1869 novel set the
standards for many such novels that would follow. It recounted the adventures of a growing boy, stressing the various
rebellions that he felt compelled to raise against the strictures
of family, school, church, and civil authority. It also sanctioned
and universalized these adventures and rebellions by basing
them on models that the boy found in the classic books which
he was given to read. *Robinson Crusoe, The Arabian Nights,
Gulliver's Travels, Don Quixote, Gil Blas, Tristram Shandy,*
and other classics provided actions and sentiments for the boy
to admire and imitate in his own life. In fact, a major theme of
Bad Boy and the novels similar to it was the influence of
literature on the behavior and development of a boy, adolescent, or young man.

Shakespeare is also represented among the literary influences cited in Aldrich's novel. At one point in the story, Tom
Bailey, the main character, organizes his playmates into a
theater company, and they put on plays in the upper room of a
carriage house. During their production of *Hamlet* they need
"the united energies of the Prince of Denmark, the King, and

the Gravedigger, with an occasional hand from 'the fair Ophelia' (Pepper Whitcomb in a low-necked dress)," to raise the cambric curtain. Later in the story, when Tom falls in love with an older girl and loses her to someone else, he considers himself a "blighted being," loiters dejectedly in a graveyard, and patterns his behavior on other suicidal heroes: "I was Hamlet and Werther and the late Lord Byron all in one."[2]

Although they are only cursory and not developed at any length, Aldrich's two references to *Hamlet* admit his novel into a company of books that incorporate motifs from *Hamlet* into stories about the growth and adventures of a boy or young man. Tom, the young hero of *Tom Jones*, attends a performance of *Hamlet* with Mr. Partridge, his mentor and suspected father, and this occurs at a time in the story when Tom is being kept from his beloved Sophia just as Hamlet is kept from Ophelia. Scattered through *Tristram Shandy* are the actions and statements of Parson Yorick, a Cervantean critic of affectation and pretension who is believed to be the descendent of Yorick, the court jester whom Hamlet fondly recalls in the graveyard. An early reference to the ghost in *Hamlet* prepares the reader to see an identification of David Copperfield with Hamlet when David loses his father and is sent away and later mistreated by his step-father. Throughout *David Copperfield* several characters cast reflections of *Hamlet* which relate the problems that these characters have in finding suitable positions in life to the tragic responsibilities thrust upon the young Prince of Denmark. Similarly, in *Great Expectations*, the services that certain characters require of Pip, especially concerning revenge, relate Pip's qualms of conscience and feelings of inadequacy to those of Hamlet, and this relation is made explicit by an early reference to *Hamlet*'s ghost and by Pip's attending a performance of *Hamlet*. Even Boswell, on meeting his mentor Johnson for the first time, felt like Hamlet: Mr. Davis "announced his awful approach to me, somewhat in the manner of an actor in the part of Horatio, when he addresses Hamlet on the appearance of his father's ghost, 'Look, my lord, it comes.'"[3]

The appropriateness of *Hamlet* to these stories of youth,

growth, and education by experience is understandable. Hamlet is comparatively young and a university scholar, and the tragic predicament in which he finds himself causes him to view society and its customs with suspicion, disgust, and rebellion. The death of his father places him in lonely isolation, yet the disclosure and injunction of his father's ghost make him waver between wanting to escape from his father and resolving to carry out his father's command. The conflict between these two urges paralyzes his ability to act and produces habits of speculation and skepticism. Practically all of the boy stories to which I referred above have fathers who are dead, absent, or overbearing in their demands. Aldrich's hero lives apart from his father through most of the story, and finally must confront his father's bankruptcy and death. Aldrich does not relate the father's death directly to *Hamlet*, yet he does position it immediately after Tom's melancholic identification with Hamlet following the departure of his childhood sweetheart. Finally, Hamlet's familiarity with books as a scholar, and the hypersensitivity toward language that he has acquired by his distrust of public discourse and his need to voice dangerous suspicions through irony and equivocation, are only extreme cases of the maturing adolescent's having to choose between living by the book and fashioning new forms of expression. Hamlet's successful use of the play-within-the-play, with his own verses added to it, demonstrates the efficacy of literature and literary composition in fulfilling personal and social demands.

The book that epitomized the use of *Hamlet* in fostering a young man's growth and education, and influenced many books after it in this particular, was *Wilhelm Meister's Apprenticeship* by Johann Wolfgang von Goethe. Although trained by his father for a mercantile position, young Wilhelm feels more attracted to artistic expression in the theater. He wonders to himself, "What mortal in the world, if without inward calling he take up a trade, an art, or any mode of life, will not feel his situation miserable? But he who is born with capacities for any undertaking, finds in executing this the fairest portion of his being." In a juvenile poem he contrasts the urge toward Art that he feels in himself with the obligations of Commerce that

his father imposes on him.[4] When his father sends him on an
extended business trip to collect payments, he falls in with a
traveling drama troupe and soon becomes their benefactor and
playwright, and later he joins another troupe as their principal
actor. During this trip he receives word of his father's death,
and one night, while playing the role of Hamlet, he experiences
real horror in his confrontation with the Ghost because its
voice reminds him of his father.[5] He begins to identify with
Hamlet's predicament. Before his father's death, Hamlet had
inner desires and capacities for honor, courtesy, sentiment,
art, and learning, but after that death, and after the revelation
of it as a murder and the summons to avenge it, Hamlet became solitary, bitter, and morose. He did not have the personal
resources to bear this tragedy and the obligations that came
with it. To Wilhelm, Shakespeare's play represents

> the effects of a great action laid upon a soul unfit for the
> performance of it....There is an oak tree planted in a costly
> jar, which should have borne only pleasant flowers in its
> bosom: the roots expand, the jar is shivered....A lovely,
> pure, noble, and most moral nature, without the strength
> of nerve which forms a hero, sinks beneath a burden it
> cannot bear and must not cast away.[6]

Wilhelm recognizes Hamlet's problem in himself, both in the
conflict between his inner potentials and his father's demands,
and in the need and search for some external action that will
fulfill his inner potentials.

Wilhelm Meister is the leading German *Bildungsroman*, or
narrative of a young man's gradual discovery and cultivation of
his powers by experience, and his eventual choice of a useful
career in the world. Susanne Howe has studied the extensive
influence of Goethe's book on the "apprenticeship novel," its
English equivalent. Such works as Thomas Carlyle's *Sartor
Resartus*, Edward Bulwer-Lytton's *Godolphin* and *Kenelm Chillingly*, novels by Benjamin Disraeli and Charles Kingsley,
Samuel Butler's *The Way of all Flesh* and George Meredith's
The Ordeal of Richard Feverel, all treat a theme similar to

Goethe's, with some variations, and use several of the motifs found in his book: (1) the journey, (2) the absence or antagonism of the father, (3) romantic attachments to various women that represent stages of progression, (4) association with an artist or theater group, and the reading or composing of literature that results from this association and often reflects and interprets the main action, and (5) the choice of an act or occupation that gives the hero a start toward useful living in the real world. Another frequent motif, often related to the theater experience and most likely influenced by Goethe, is the hero's comparing of himself to Hamlet.[7]

In the middle portion of his career, roughly between 1875 and 1885, Mark Twain turned his creative energies not only to culture and seriousness, but also to youth. Besides *The Prince and the Pauper*, which contemporary critics saw as a symbol of his turn to seriousness, Twain recounted the story of a young pilot's apprenticeship in "Old Times on the Mississippi," which subsequently became the first half of *Life on the Mississippi*, and he created his two classics of boyhood, *Tom Sawyer* and *Huckleberry Finn*. Although younger and much less sophisticated than the protagonists of German and English apprenticeship novels, these American boys often experience trials and adventures similar to those of their European counterparts and face comparable dilemmas of truth and goodness. Travel is constantly used by Twain as a source for action and discovery, and books of every kind are scrutinized as possible aids or foils for learning and imitation. The father in his stories is either conspicuously absent or, if present, he provokes moral conflicts and demands. And most important for our purposes, and similar to the apprenticeship novels, *Hamlet* functions for Twain as a literary model against which to measure the thought and behavior of the young heroes.

Mark Twain could have noticed the passing references to *Hamlet* in Aldrich's *Bad Boy*—other features of this novel show up in *Tom Sawyer*, as we shall see—but Twain also read *Tristram Shandy*, *Tom Jones*, *David Copperfield* and other classics that wove threads from *Hamlet* into stories of boyhood adventure. He even read some of the apprenticeship novels in

which Susanne Howe finds the influence of Goethe, for example, *Sartor Resartus* and *Kenelm Chillingly*. Furthermore,
it would not be too farfetched to believe that Twain actually
read *Wilhelm Meister's Apprenticeship*, since he read other
works of Goethe (including *Faust* and *The Sorrows of Young
Werther*) and practically all the works of Thomas Carlyle, relying heavily on them in his own writing. Among Carlyle's works
was an English translation of Goethe's novel.[8] Also, a devotee
and student of German culture, Twain travelled in Germany
and lived there and in Austria for a number of years.

   Whether or not it can be traced to the reading of any one
book, Twain seems to have absorbed the cluster of images and
themes from *Hamlet* that appeared regularly in eighteenth-
and nineteenth-century adventure and apprenticeship novels.
Just as the importance of history in children's stories led him
to consult Shakespeare in preparation for writing *The Prince
and the Pauper*, so the issues and problems of childhood and
adolescence that were unfolding in his conceptions of *Tom
Sawyer* and *Huckleberry Finn* opened to him another vein of
Shakespearean influence, one carrying elements that were
mainly from *Hamlet*. This influence came to him, as other
influences did previously, both directly from Shakespeare's
works and indirectly from the works of other authors who
approached Shakespeare for the same reasons. Moreover, Twain
acknowledged and exploited this influence artistically by leaving references and allusions to Shakespeare in his novels of
American boyhood. His purpose in doing this was not to provide historical accuracy or coloring, since these novels were set
in his own time and country. Rather, it was to reflect, interpret, and universalize the action of his stories. He put
Shakespeare's plays in the background of his stories to uncover
and illuminate the classical themes and tragic situations that
existed in his own time and locality yet may have been too near
at hand to be noticed or understood, or may have seemed too
backward or juvenile to be taken seriously. Shakespeare's
plays furnish a larger perspective from which to analyze and
evaluate the action of Twain's novels, and this enables Twain
to indulge in humor and realism and still achieve a tragic and
universal effect.

Tom Sawyer's Apprenticeship

Besides the frequent occurrences of *Hamlet* in adventure and apprenticeship novels, another likely influence on Mark Twain's use of *Hamlet* in his boyhood classics is his repeated attempts at writing an extended burlesque of *Hamlet* after seeing the play performed in New York. In November 1873, having just returned from a visit to England, Twain stayed in New York long enough to see Edwin Booth in the role of Hamlet. Twain went backstage after the performance and told Booth that he would do a burlesque of the play by adding a character who makes humorous modern comments.[9] For the next ten years he tried various ways of doing this burlesque. Some pieces were evidently written and destroyed, but an unfinished 1881 version survives. Since this version is closer in time to the composition of *Huckleberry Finn*, I shall consider it in my study of that novel. Here, however, I just want to make the point that Twain's plans for a burlesque *Hamlet* were first conceived only a few months before he began writing *Tom Sawyer*.

It is also important to know that Twain first visualized *Tom Sawyer* as a play. Although he began writing it as a novel in the late winter and early spring of 1874, completing about half of it by September of that year, he planned the play as early as 1872. When he finished the novel in July 1875, he sought a copyright for it as a play and included an outline of the projected play in his application. He had written part of the play by August 1876, but did not finish it until February 1884. He also asked William Dean Howells to transform the novel into a play, but Howells declined.[10] This vacillation between novel and play in Twain's conception of *Tom Sawyer* indicates that the story could have been inspired by and modeled after a play, perhaps *Hamlet*.

The only explicit reference to *Hamlet* in *Tom Sawyer* is the phrase "observed of all observers," which appears in one schoolgirl's examination exercise treating the vanities of life. In *Hamlet* Ophelia used the phrase to describe Hamlet before melancholy and madness changed his personality.[11] There are, however, more extensive resemblances in structure and theme between the two works.

At the beginning of each work the hero is restless and disgusted with civilization (Hamlet would use the word *custom*). With his "inky cloak" and "dejected havior" Hamlet spurns the mirth of the court: "How weary, stale, flat, and unprofitable / Seem to me all the uses of this world!" (I, ii, 133-134). When Tom learns that he must work on Saturday, he too indulges in melancholy and sees life as hollow and existence but a burden. After Aunt Polly wrongfully accuses him of spilling sugar, he imagines himself drowned and seeks consolation in desolate places (46, 54-55). Romance is partly the cause of each hero's melancholy. Hamlet is sickened when he discovers that his love letters and courtship are being used for surveillance; and Tom, rejected by Becky Thatcher,

> entered a dense wood ...and sat long with his elbows on his knees and his chin in his hands, meditating. It seemed to him that life was but a trouble, at best, and he more than envied Jimmy Hodges, so lately released; it must be very peaceful, he thought, to lie and slumber and dream forever and ever,...If he only had a clean Sunday-school record he could be willing to go, and be done with it all. (87)

Both Tom and Hamlet long for the sleep of death, but are checked by worries about life after death, Tom by his Sunday-school record and Hamlet by "what dreams may come / When we have shuffled off this mortal coil" (III, i, 66-67).

It is not just the melancholy, but the prolonged meditation on it and dramatic expression of it that make Tom and Hamlet so much alike. Tom's solitary effusions correspond with Hamlet's soliloquies, and in the play *Tom Sawyer* Tom does soliloquize in his first appearance. Dejected because Amy Lawrence did not leave him the promised piece of cake with a love letter in it, he complains:

> Very well, Miss *Amy*, if a person's heart is *nothing* to you, and you can break it and never *care*, and just *gloat* over his sufferings and be *happy*, and him so *miserable*, and rejoice

at seeing him go *down*, and get to be *dissipated* and de-
spised, and fill a drunkard's *grave*—well, let it *be* so, since
it *must* be so—and since you are de*termined* to *have* it so,
and may you always be *happy*, and never come to see and
feel what you've *done*, and how you've blighted a person
that *loved* you so.[12]

Of course Tom is sentimental where Hamlet is reflective, but
they are alike in the frequency and elaborateness of their
interior discourses.

If Twain received help from *Hamlet* in conceiving Tom's
melancholy meditations, he could have been influenced in this
by Aldrich's *Story of a Bad Boy*. Tom Bailey, Aldrich's hero,
patterns his behavior on books just as Tom Sawyer does. He
also feels depressed and confined at Sunday services, takes a
trip to an island where he gets caught in a storm, and falls in
love with a girl who later leaves him, causing him to feel like a
"blighted being." In the midst of his gloom he compares himself to Hamlet, entering graveyards and contemplating suicide,
although, as Tom Sawyer would later do, he wishes that he
could commit suicide without killing himself.[13] In this instance Shakespeare could have come to Twain, if not directly,
at least indirectly through the influence of another author.

As *Hamlet* and *Tom Sawyer* progress, the two heroes find
deeper reasons for sadness and depression. When sneaking
into a graveyard at midnight in order to have a wart taken
away by the devils who come to get Hoss Williams's soul, Tom
and Huck are aware and afraid of spirits and devils; but what
scares them even more is witnessing Injun Joe kill Doctor
Robinson and arrange it so that Muff Potter thinks that *he* is to
blame. After seeing this crime the boys flee in terror from the
graveyard and swear solemnly (by signing their names in blood)
to "keep mum" about the incident (99-101). This scene reflects
the midnight confrontation of Hamlet with his father's ghost
and the revelation of his father's murder by Claudius. Hamlet
too is shaken by this news and forces his companions three
times to swear an oath of secrecy by putting their hands on his
sword (I, v, 145-181). After this both heroes become more

miserable as a result of their secret knowledge. Hamlet be-
haves in a way that resembles madness, and may really be
madness, and Tom suffers through sleepless nights and night-
mares, and is heard talking in his sleep (107, 169). Each one is
infected from within by his dangerous intelligence to the point
where he is too weak and scared to reveal it or act upon it.

To shake off the burden of their knowledge and of the
demands that it may make on them, both heroes use tactics of
delay and jump at opportunities for distraction. Hamlet becomes an enthusiastic spectator and critic of the theater when
the players arrive, but then discovers how he can use the
players to advance his cause. Tom also avoids his fears, responsibility, and pangs of conscience by escaping with his friends
to Jackson's Island, where they spend their time playing pirate, gangster, and Indian roles from their favorite novels. But
even this escape begins Tom's reformation because after returning from it he finally tells the truth, admitting to his aunt
that he eavesdropped on her and left her a message that he was
alive (150-151). This connection of Hamlet to theater and of
Tom to role-playing, especially for purposes of escape, further
allies the two works and supports the probability that Twain
drew from *Hamlet* in composing his novel. Besides reflecting
the literary digressions of the player scenes in *Hamlet*, the
island episode in *Tom Sawyer* also parallels happenings that
occur toward the end of Shakespeare's play. Both heroes leave
the main locality by boat, deal with pirates, and return to
witness a funeral. Although Hamlet is being taken to England
for execution, he is captured, or rather, rescued by pirates.
Tom plays a pirate on the island, and when he finds out that
the townspeople believe him and his companions to be drowned,
he arranges the spectacle of them showing up alive at their
own funeral. Hamlet is presumed by the king to be dead, and
even though he sends letters announcing his return, the king is
unsure of their truth. So when Hamlet appears at the funeral,
he has in a sense come back from the dead. Of course it is
Ophelia's funeral, not his own, although he does leap into
Ophelia's grave. At any rate, just as Tom is moved to tell the
truth after his imaginary death and playfully miraculous re-

turn, so Hamlet becomes resigned to fate or providence by his accidental rescue—he is even able to joke about death with the gravedigger—and he consents to a duel which precipitates the final showdown.

The melancholy reflections, the shocking disclosure of a crime and the felt responsibility to reveal it and restore justice, the delay in exercising this responsibility, especially through preoccupation with drama or fiction, and finally the real or imaginary triumph over death that changes the outlook of the hero toward his task—these are the major motifs that run through *Hamlet* and *Tom Sawyer*. Both works can be considered apprenticeship stories, since both heroes are students (although at different levels of education) and both mature by learning from life experiences. It is interesting that Hamlet's main problem and task involve the loss of his father, whereas the absence of Tom's father seems to have no importance in the story. Still, the loss or absence of a father, together with the comparative youth of the heroes and Hamlet's being deprived of the throne, isolates both heroes from their societies. This isolation promotes a critical reaction to the ceremonies, customs, and institutions of society. Language, art, clothes, school, politics, and religion are portrayed as human artifacts in contrast to the nature or essence of reality. This basic conflict carries through many of Twain's stories, beginning with his early vernacular tales and burlesques. It certainly exists in *Tom Sawyer*, and as we shall see, in *Huckleberry Finn*. Although it is a major conflict in American literature and culture, and fills Twain's stories primarily because they are the works of an American, it is also heavily represented in Shakespeare's works, especially in *Hamlet*. The hero, isolated by youth, loss and disinheritance, reflects on society from a distance. This may be the main quality that allies Tom Sawyer with Hamlet.

At this stage of Twain's reliance on Shakespeare I am still arguing in favor of influence, but not paradigm. In other words, Twain does not seem to have placed allusions to *Hamlet* in *Tom Sawyer* with the intention of having the reader recognize them and draw continual parallels between the two works. He would later do this in *Huckleberry Finn*, but here, I think, he just wanted to write a novel in the tradition of classic adventure and apprenticeship stories, and since many of these used *Hamlet* as a paradigm for their heroes' experiences, Twain was prompted by them to use themes and structural patterns like those in *Hamlet* to develop his novel. Likewise, since he was working intermittently on a burlesque *Hamlet* during the same time that he was writing *Tom Sawyer*, ideas and scenes from the play were in the back of his mind and therefore available as sources. He might also have realized by working on his burlesque that Shakespeare was integrated into American culture, especially through burlesque, and that motifs of Shakespeare would therefore not be out of place in an American story.

In reading *Tom Sawyer* we know that the narrator who articulates Tom's feelings is someone older and more sophisticated than Tom. The concepts and emotions, as well as the diction and grammar that express them, are not those of a boy Tom's age, even if we assume Tom's familiarity with literature and skill in imitating its actions and style. The literary expressions that appear in Tom's own words are much more rugged and fragmentary than those of the narrator. I would suggest that we think of the narrator, and therefore of a part of Twain himself, as a person who is presently reading *Hamlet* and interpreting Tom's mind and the action of the novel from that perspective. This would help the reader, as it apparently helped Twain, to understand the profundity and universality of Tom's experiences in a way that surpasses Tom's understanding of them, limited as he is to his own mental capacities.

Hamlet and Huckleberry Finn

Because of Mark Twain's method of retelling stories at deeper and deeper levels, some critics consider *Tom Sawyer* a rehearsal for *Huckleberry Finn*. For example, Franklin Rogers relates the two books by his theory of burlesque patterns. Arguing that literary burlesque was an important factor in Twain's becoming a mature and original writer, Rogers distinguishes three stages of burlesque: simple literary burlesque, a mixture of burlesque with original and serious material, and an original work with burlesque patterns but without a burlesque intent. Just as Henry Fielding progressed from the simple burlesque *Shamela*, to the mixed *Joseph Andrews*, to the original *Tom Jones*, so Twain progressed from "The Boy's Manuscript," a burlesque romance with children in the roles of adults, to *Tom Sawyer*, also a burlesque romance and juvenile story, but with original material and an intended effect that goes beyond burlesque, to *Huckleberry Finn*, an original and serious work that is constructed, however, out of patterns commonly used in burlesque.[14] An added feature of Rogers' theory is that it increases the number of different purposes that Twain could have in burlesque writing, or writing based on other works of literature. He might burlesque another work just to be funny, or to criticize the style of its author, or to learn some writing skill by imitating that style.[15] When Twain burlesques a work, therefore, he may be gaining literary devices from it that he will later use with a serious intent. I shall presently consider Twain's burlesque *Hamlet* with this in mind, but first I shall examine what *Tom Sawyer* contributed to the composition of *Huckleberry Finn*.

Since he worked on *Huckleberry Finn* intermittently over a period of seven years, from 1876 to 1883, Mark Twain naturally changed his vision of the novel. Rogers discerns three different models that Twain followed: the first, which governed the twelve or so chapters that were written during the summer of 1876, Rogers thinks was probably autobiography; the second model, which Twain's notes and additions seemed to follow between 1876 and 1880, was a detective story; the third model, which Twain discovered in 1880 and used to finish the book in 1883, was a travelogue or pilgrimage.[16]

In the summer of 1876, just after finishing *Tom Sawyer*, Twain wrote approximately what is contained in the first twelve chapters of *Huckleberry Finn*. Since his story begins, "You don't know about me, without you have read a book by the name of 'The Adventures of Tom Sawyer,'" and continues, "Now the way the book winds up, is this," it is legitimate to think that *Huckleberry Finn* started off as a continuation of *Tom*

Sawyer, or another boyhood adventure story. Twain also described his book to William Dean Howells as "Huck Finn's Autobiography," so fictional autobiography could have been another model for it at this early stage.[17] Furthermore, in light of Rogers' theory of burlesque patterns, if *Tom Sawyer* was developed out of the burlesque "The Boy's Manuscript," and if that was partly a burlesque of *David Copperfield*, as Rogers convincingly shows, then *Huckleberry Finn*, which developed out of *Tom Sawyer*, can be considered to have *David Copperfield* and books like it in its literary genealogy. What this points to is that boyhood adventure stories, fictional autobiographies, and novels of apprenticeship, the kinds of books that often related the experiences of their heroes to *Hamlet*, were in the background of *Huckleberry Finn* and could have inspired Twain to relate Huck to Hamlet. Two other items noted by Rogers which may be applicable here are that Twain meant the death or disappearance of Huck's father to be an important element at this stage of his story, and that Twain was considering a traveling-showmen plot for another autobiography that he was writing at this time.[18] Both of these motifs appear often in connection with references to *Hamlet* in adventure and apprenticeship novels.

Full-play burlesques of *Hamlet* seldom included the whole play but only selected and well known scenes or speeches from it. Twain's use of *Hamlet* to compose *Huckleberry Finn* follows this pattern. The three main parts of the play that he drew from at different periods during the composition of his novel are the ghost scenes at the beginning, the play-within-the-play in the middle (including the soliloquy "To be, or not to be"), and the final duel scene.

The Father's Ghost

It is quite clear that *Tom Sawyer* supplied Twain with material for composing the early parts of *Huckleberry Finn*, and this includes the apparent echoes of Hamlet in Tom's behavior. For just as Tom resorted frequently to solitary and melancholy reflection away from the bothers of life, so Huck, at the beginning of his story, feels restless and confined by civilization. He is cramped up by the clothes that the Widow Douglas and Miss Watson make him wear, and by the forced training that they give him in religion, spelling, and table manners. His predicament is something like that of Hamlet, who is asked by his uncle and mother to conform to the customs of the court, which to him seem "weary, stale, flat, and unprofitable" (I, ii, 133-134). Depression induces suicidal thoughts in Hamlet, and Huck too admits, "I felt so lonesome I most wished I was dead."[19] He sits in his room at night, looking out the window. The rustling of leaves seems mournful to him, and the occasional hoots of an owl and cries of a dog remind him of death. He gets the cold shivers down his spine when he thinks that the wind is trying to tell him something. Then he says, "away out in the woods I heard that kind of a sound that a ghost makes when it wants to tell about something that's on its mind and can't make itself understood, and so can't rest easy in its grave, and has to go about that way every night grieving" (4). Huck's feelings of restlessness and dejection, and his sombre night reflections upon death, suicide, and ghosts, especially on a ghost who is trying to reveal something, show the possible influence of Hamlet on his character and experience.

This influence is further supported by what happens next. That same night, when the clock strikes twelve, Huck's friends summon him to a night meeting at which they discuss ways of revenge and swear a solemn oath with their blood not to tell their gang's secrets. Although Tom Sawyer's insistence that they hack a cross in the breasts of their victims is probably taken from Robert Montgomery Bird's *Nick of the Woods*, a popular novel and play, this other source does not preclude the possible influence of *Hamlet* on the scene as well. After his midnight interview on the platform with the ghost of his father, Hamlet too had thoughts of revenge and forced his companions to swear oaths of secrecy. Recall that Twain also used a scene like this in *Tom Sawyer*. It was Twain's creative habit to repeat and further explore such scenes in his fiction. As we progress we shall see more instances of this in connection with the "swearing" scene and with other scenes. Also illustrated here is another of Twain's creative habits, the construction of a scene out of multiple sources. To derive the swearing scene from both *Hamlet* and *Nick of the Woods* gives it both a classical and a popular parentage. In Twain's complex act of creation he combines a burlesque of Tom's boyish imitation of Bird's novel with an imitation of *Hamlet* to bring out the profundity that he feels should be part of the scene. By using different sources for the same scenes he expects the reader to notice the differences and respond with appropriately mixed emotions.

Whether expressed through literary sources having different degrees of merit or not, Huck's experiences and problems are certainly more profound than Tom's juvenile antics. What Hamlet met in the night was his father's ghost, and Huck's descriptions of Pap come as close to the ghostly as can be expected in a realistic novel. In a sense, Pap is both dead and alive. There was a rumor that Pap had drowned in the river and that his face "had been in the water so long it warn't much like a face at all" (14). This picture of him always makes Huck uncomfortable. Huck first sees evidence of Pap's presence by his tracks in the snow (19). He is identified, like a ghost, by coldness and whiteness. Also, the sight of tracks without a person adds to the ghostly aspect of Pap. It leaves Huck shimming down a hill, looking continually over his shoulder. Pap's presence is also surrounded with spiritualism. He wears a cross on his boot heel to keep off the devil, and Huck attributes his appearance to the bad luck that he incurred by overturning a saltcellar at breakfast. After seeing his father's tracks in the snow, Huck consults Jim with his magic hair-ball to find out what Pap is going to do, and Jim says, "Dey's two angels hovern' roun' 'bout him. One uv 'em is white en shiny, en t'other one is black....A body can't tell yit which one gwyne to fetch him at de las'" (22). This haunting association with black and white angels makes Pap seem only half real and puts him into a purgatorial state. Suddenly finding Pap in his room at night takes Huck's breath away. Pap's hair is black, and his eyes shine through it as though he were behind vines. Huck says, "There warn't no color in his face, where his face showed; it was white; not like another man's white, but a white to make a body sick, a white to make a body's flesh crawl—a tree-toad white, a fish-belly white" (23). When confined by Pap in a cabin in the woods, Huck is startled by Pap's attack of delirium tremens. Pap feels snakes biting him and devils holding him, and thinks the Angel of Death is coming to get him (35-36). Finally, when Jim identifies Pap's body in a floating wreck, he tells Huck not to look at the face because it is "too gashly." He says that it would be bad luck to talk about it because bodies that are not buried are likely to go around haunting people (61, 63). In several ways, therefore, Pap haunts Huck like a ghost, even while he is alive. His presence causes fear, sickness, and confinement, and evokes thoughts of sin, death, hell and devils. So like Hamlet, Huck too is afflicted by a ghostly father. But the ghost of Hamlet's father inspired more than just fear. It came with a revelation and a mission. Huck's father also condemns the evils of society, but in an ironic way. He blasts public education and Negro suffrage, and claims that the law has no right to take children away from their parents. His dissolute life belies his criticisms, however, and the reader is expected to disagree with him. The closest thing to a moral burden that he imposes on Huck is his racial prejudice, but this becomes a moral burden only when Huck later realizes that he is helping Jim to escape from slavery.

To find a moral burden for Huck that is equivalent to the one imposed by Hamlet's father we must switch from Pap to Jim. Kenneth Lynn has argued that Jim can be considered Huck's new father since he gives Huck paternal care and the benefit of adult wisdom. He comes closest to fulfilling Huck's search for a father.[20] Moreover, like Pap, Jim is surrounded by supernatural qualities. He deals with witches, devils, omens, prophecies, dreams, and charms. He even seems ghostly himself at times. Huck stumbles upon the ashes of his campfire on the island in almost the same way that he found Pap's tracks in the snow, and he has the same fearful reaction: "My heart jumped up amongst my lungs...my breath come so hard I couldn't hear nothing else" (48). Huck's first sight of Jim in the early dawn, with his blanket around his head and his head almost in the fire, is so spooky that it gives Huck the "fantods";

and when Jim reveals himself, it is he who thinks that Huck is
a ghost (50-51). The separation of Huck and Jim in the fog also
has spiritual overtones. Huck says that nothing looks or sounds
natural in fog, and he gets Jim to interpret the fog episode as a
dream (104). He is fooling Jim, of course, but Twain seems to
want the dream-like quality there anyway. It occurs too in
other episodes.

Symbolically, therefore, Jim is a father and a ghost, and he
soon imposes a moral burden on Huck. But in this first stage of
Huckleberry Finn's composition, Twain apparently did not plan
to develop the issue of race and the qualms of conscience that
Huck suffers for helping Jim to freedom.[21] So at this point let
us limit the influence that *Hamlet* had on *Huckleberry Finn* to
the image of the father-ghost and the reaction that this produces in the hero. Although the topic of the moral burden will
harmonize well with the father-ghost image and further relate
the two works, it was added at a later stage of composition and
will be considered in connection with that. Also, I am presum-
ing that at this first stage Twain was influenced by *Hamlet*,
but in the same way that he was influenced by it in writing
Tom Sawyer. Although the influence is most likely there,
Twain still did not make it obvious enough for the reader to
recognize it and make constant comparisons between the two
works. That would come later.

In the second stage of his work on *Huckleberry Finn*, Mark
Twain followed, according to Rogers, the model of a detective
story. Rogers bases this theory on working notes that Twain
made in 1879 and 1880, and on other writings of Twain in the
late 1870s. In an attempt to re-create what the novel would
have been as a detective story, Rogers stresses the theme of
murder. Since Huck leaves false evidence of his own murder in
his escape from Pap's cabin, the townspeople believe that he
has in fact been murdered, and they suspect both Pap and Jim
of the crime. When Pap himself disappears, he also is believed
murdered, perhaps by Jim. The story would probably end with
a trial scene at the Grangerfords' plantation where Jim would
be acquitted after his supposed victim or victims showed up
alive.[22]

As further support for this theory, Rogers notes that Twain was writing burlesque detective stories in the late 1870s. In 1877 and 1878 he wrote the play, "Cap'n Simon Wheeler, The Amateur Detective," and then half of a novel based on it, "Simon Wheeler, Detective." Rogers finds enough character and plot correspondences between the Wheeler stories and *Huckleberry Finn*—the family feud, the fake murder, the sentimental poet—to conclude that Twain's novel at this stage grew out of these burlesques of Allan Pinkerton's detective stories.[23] *Ah Sin*, a play which Twain collaborated on with Bret Harte in 1876 and 1877, and which was produced in 1877, might also be added to this list. It too contains aspects of *Huckleberry Finn* and the Wheeler stories: a fake murder, switches in identity, a trial, a supposed murder victim showing up alive, and a lynch mob.

Apparently, *Hamlet* also had some impact on *Huckleberry Finn* in this stage of composition. In a sense, *Hamlet* is a detective story because it deals with a "murder most foul" and with the clues that Hamlet seeks to support the ghost's revelation. Of more immediate relevance, however, are the echoes of *Hamlet* in the Wheeler stories. In the play, Tom Hooker, a newspaper reporter, finds a body at midnight, hides it in the bushes, and forces his roommate, telegraph operator Lem Sackett, to swear solemnly to keep it a secret.[24] This scene, like the oath scenes in *Tom Sawyer* and *Huckleberry Finn*, could well have been influenced by *Hamlet*. The fact that the body which Hooker finds is that of Hugh Burnside, who is not really dead and who later emerges from the bushes, adds a ghostly aspect to the scene. In his working notes for the play Twain wrote, "GHOST of dead man appears to the 2 criminals every now and then."[25] This coupling of a ghost with the swearing motif would reinforce the *Hamlet* connection. Also, Burnside, a poet who thinks that he is better than Shakespeare, contemplates suicide because of rejection in love. He attempts suicide and fails, but since he is believed dead he takes advantage of this mistake by attending his own funeral. This too could relate him to Hamlet, who considers suicide and shows up at a funeral after he is believed by some to be dead.

The Wheeler novel also contains *Hamlet* motifs. Hale Dexter is burdened with a task of revenge by his father, who has died. He must kill Hugh Burnside, but he fears and questions his father's command.[26] He also falls in love with Hugh's sister, Clara, and this too interferes with his revenge. Hugh, the lovesick poet who contemplates suicide, is compared to Hamlet, "the observed of all observers," and Tom Hooker, the reporter, is said to reel in drunkenness as Ophelia did in madness.[27] With his continual snooping and roundabout questioning, Simon Wheeler adds a touch of Polonius, and Twain's plans to have Hugh use Wheeler's show costumes and wax figures as disguises and decoys might form a bridge between Hamlet's mousetrap and the theatricals of the King and the Duke in *Huckleberry Finn*.[28]

This second stage of composition adds the themes of murder and revenge to the first-stage themes of the death or disappearance of the father, the ghost, and the swearing of an oath. Twain planned to develop the murder theme and apparently to relate the revenge or trial themes to the Grangerford-Shepherdson family feud as a stirring finale. As the composition progressed, Twain retained or modified these different themes from Act I of *Hamlet*. He kept the death of the father, the ghost, and the murder—but without developing any search for the killers or trial of a suspect—and he dissolved the revenge theme into the feud. He would later add the moral burden and mission to these first-act themes, but first he introduced the travel motif, and this, I think, either led him to or was prompted by the traveling players in the middle-acts of *Hamlet*.

The Play-within-the-Play

Rogers takes Twain's note, "Back a little, CHANGE—raft only *crippled* by steamer," as an indication that Twain decided sometime in 1879 or 1880 not to end his story with the Grangerfords, but to resurrect the raft, which had been run over by a steamboat at the end of what is now Chapter XVI, and carry Huck and Jim farther down the Mississippi. At the same time he also planned to add the traveling showmen to his

story. Another working note reads, "The two printers deliver
temp. lectures, teach dancing, elocution, feel heads, distribute
tracts, preach, fiddle, doctor (quack)."[29] Other notes that outline this plan are: "The Burning Shame at Napoleon, Ark."
"Rich III—15c—B.S. 50c;" "The scow with theatre aboard."
"Burning Shame * Do the mesmeric foolishness, with Huck (&
the King) for performer(s) Jim sawed in two."[30]

Some critics believe that this travel motif was inspired by
Twain's trip down and up the Mississippi in the spring of 1882,
when he gathered material for his book *Life on the Mississippi*.
Bernard DeVoto, for example, dates from that time period the
notes just quoted.[31] Walter Blair, however, dates them sometime before June 1880 and tries to prove that Twain added the
King and the Duke to his novel before the Mississippi trip.
Nevertheless, he agrees that chapters XX and XXI, where the
two imposters plan their theatrical activities, were probably
written after the trip and influenced by it.[32] In Chapter LI of
Life on the Mississippi, for instance, Twain tells of a young
man who was enticed into the theater business after watching
two Englishmen perform the sword fight from *Richard the
Third*. Also, while in New Orleans, Twain saw the balcony
scene from *Romeo and Juliet* acted by two children.[33] Rogers
also believes that Twain thought of the traveling showmen plot
before his Mississippi trip. As early as 1876, in fact, in planning his *Autobiography of a Damn Fool*, Twain jotted down,
"Listens to the printer-tramp and is charmed. Goes on a months
expedition in summer with him, delivering temperance lectures & sermons & spreeing on the proceeds. BURNING
SHAME." Yet Rogers does not think that Twain applied this
idea to *Huckleberry Finn* until 1879 or 1880.[34]

The traveling-showmen plot, one component of the third
stage of *Huckleberry Finn*'s composition, adds to the resemblances between *Huckleberry Finn* and *Hamlet* and could have
been influenced by the traveling-players scenes in *Hamlet*. Up
to this point we have been considering the similarities and
possible influences of the early parts of *Hamlet* on Twain's
novel: the father, the ghost, the murder, and the revenge.
Here we move to the middle section of each work.

In Act II, scene ii of *Hamlet*, Rosencrantz and Guildenstern appear on the scene, sent for by the king to entertain, divert, and spy on Hamlet. They remain until Act IV, scene iv, when they depart with Hamlet for England, carrying orders for Hamlet's execution there. As it happens, Hamlet finds the orders, changes them to demand the execution of Rosencrantz and Guildenstern, and escapes on a pirate ship. The main diversion that Rosencrantz and Guildenstern introduce is the players, who arrive in Act II and control the action of *Hamlet* until the king halts their court performance by a cry for light in Act III, scene ii. During the time of the players' presence, there is discussion of the theater business, critical theory on the purpose and effect of plays, the rehearsal of a dramatic speech, the choice of a play to be performed, the writing of an extra speech for it, and finally the performance. There is also reference to other works of literature as sources for the plays, the *Aeneid* for the rehearsed speech about Troy and the Italian story "The Murder of Gonzago" for the play that will be performed. In striking similarity to this scene, the King and the Duke are picked up by Huck and Jim in Chapter XIX of *Huckleberry Finn* and dominate the central portion of the novel until they steal and sell Jim, send Huck on a wild goose chase to find him, and are finally tarred, feathered and run out of town in Chapter XXXIII after one of their "Royal Nonesuch" hoaxes. While on the scene, they plan, advertise, and pull off several of their fraudulent and money-making operations, including dramatic performances. They plan, rehearse, criticize, advertise, and perform scenes from *Romeo and Juliet*, *Richard the Third*, and *Hamlet*.

The effects on Huck and Hamlet of these new characters and the theatrical activities that they introduce are almost alike. Both protagonists distrust them at first, but then become enthused with the dramatic presentations. They welcome these plays initially as escapes from their more doubtful and exacting predicaments, but they also learn from them facts about themselves and use them for their advantage. From watching an actor show deep passion in reciting a speech from a play, Hamlet is struck by his own *dull, pigeon-livered* reaction to his father's demand, and he also discovers how he can use a play to "catch the conscience of the king" (II, ii, 533-591). Huck too learns about himself from the King and the Duke. Like them he steals, invents stories about his parentage, and considers returning Jim to slavery. By watching with disgust while they do the things that he has been doing all along and might well do in the future, Huck gains some of the self-knowledge that he will need for an eventual change of heart.

As I have mentioned, another aspect of this middle section of each work is references to literature. In *Hamlet* there is the *Aeneid* and "The Murder of Gonzago," and in *Huckleberry Finn* there is the Shakespearean repertoire of the King and the Duke and the jumble of historical facts about kings that Huck recounts to Jim (199-200). Of course, this is not the first time that books are mentioned in *Huckleberry Finn*. Tom Sawyer used *Don Quixote*, *The Arabian Nights*, and *Nick of the Woods* to authorize his fanciful exploits in the early chapters. Here, however, there seems to be a closer and less artificial relation between the literary works and the original incidents of the story. In his discourse on the purpose of drama, Hamlet calls actors "the abstract and brief chronicles of the time," whose purpose is "to hold, as 'twere, the mirror up to nature, to show virtue her own feature, scorn her own image, and the very age and body of the time his form and pressure" (II, ii, 512; II, ii, 20-23). This is exactly what happens in the play-within-the-play. The portrayal of Claudius's crime on the stage does catch his conscience and gives Hamlet proof of his guilt. The literary references in the middle section of *Huckleberry Finn* also reflect the bizarre and tragic happenings of the plot.

Franklin Rogers believes that when Twain decided to continue *Huckleberry Finn* as a travelogue, he revived two techniques that he used in his earlier travel books, *The Innocents Abroad* and *Roughing It*. Rogers calls one the Mr. Twain-Mr. Brown character axis. In this technique, scenes and incidents are commented on from two points of view, one serious and genteel (Mr. Twain), and the other comic and vernacular (Mr. Brown). In *Huckleberry Finn* this axis applies to various pairings of characters—Tom-Huck, Huck-Jim, Duke-King, and

Duke/King-Huck/Jim—and it changes. While Huck plays Mr. Brown in Tom's early appeals to literary precedent, he plays Mr. Twain in explaining French, history, and royalty to Jim.[35] Since the genteel character often quotes from literature and the vernacular one shows ignorance and lack of respect for it, this is a useful technique for evaluating literary expression.

And it is further supported in this function by Rogers' second technique, which might be called an "episode axis." Real episodes are preceded or followed by literary episodes that reflect them either comically or tragically. For instance, Tom's play based on pirate and robber books prefigures Huck's clash with real robbers on the wrecked *Walter Scott*, and Huck's reading about royal frauds in books salvaged from another wreck anticipates his meeting with real frauds, the King and the Duke. This frequent alternating between real and literary episodes gives both Huck and the reader practice in discerning truth from falsehood and in evaluating, therefore, the reliability of literary expression.[36]

Rogers' episode axis offers the best explanation of how Shakespeare's works, especially *Hamlet*, function in *Huckleberry Finn*. The episodes described in chapters XX to XXIII bounce back and forth between the real and the artistic, Shakespeare's plays being one example of the artistic. After a rehearsal and an advertisement for the sword-fight from *Richard the Third*, a real duel occurs between Boggs and Sherburn, followed by the performance of Shakespeare's scene. Clearly, Shakespeare's scene is used to comment on the duel. Similarly, the gullibility of the Arkansas mob is exposed through a real farce, the attempted lynching of Sherburn, and two artistic farces, the circus rider who fools them into thinking that he is drunk, and "The Royal Nonesuch" staged by the King and the Duke. And, although it occurs a few chapters earlier (XVIII), the Grangerford-Shepherdson feud seems to be reflected in the balcony scene from *Romeo and Juliet*. Both concern a romance between members of rival families and end in a bloodbath.[37]

Since this third stage of composition treats the relation between reality and expression through the device that I have called "episode axis," it is here, I think, that Twain began to use Shakespeare more explicitly. Instead of just being influenced by Shakespeare's plays, he now started to use them as paradigms of his novel, and he put clues into his novel to help the reader recognize this and draw parallels between the plays and the novel. His burlesque handling of Shakespeare through the King and the Duke allowed him to use these paradigms without discarding either his own comic identity as Mark Twain or the realistic identity of his chosen narrator, Huck Finn. Yet these burlesque and bungling versions of Shakespeare still leave readers room to make connections that extend far beyond comedy and realism. I have shown briefly how this is true of *Richard the Third* and *Romeo and Juliet*. Although I intend to examine more deeply the relation between these plays and certain scenes in *Huckleberry Finn*, I shall return first to *Hamlet* because I believe that it lies in the background of Twain's entire novel.

We recall that "Hamlet's Immortal Soliloquy" is also part of the King and the Duke's performance. It is rendered in *Huckleberry Finn* like a typical burlesque of a Shakespeare speech. But this was inserted by Twain rather late during the third stage of composition. Earlier influences on this third stage, and perhaps on the first and second stages too, are Twain's plans, attempts, and unfinished version of a burlesque of the whole play *Hamlet*.

I have already noted that Twain first thought of doing a burlesque *Hamlet* after seeing Edwin Booth play the role in November 1873. In 1881 he wrote to Howells that nine years before [1872?], he tried to add a country cousin to the play but it did not work. The other characters would have to speak to a family member, and Twain was not ready to commit the sacrilege of putting words into Shakespeare's mouth. In 1879, however, he wrote in his notebook: "Try Hamlet again, & make free with Shakspere—let Hamlet and everybody else talk with the fellow & wish he was in Holle as the G's say." At this time he apparently considered adding a brother of Hamlet to the play. Finally, in late August and early September 1881 he bought several paperback editions of *Hamlet* and cut selected passages out of them to paste between his own additions, which were speeches and comments of a comic character, Basil Stockmar, a subscription-book agent, who was to be Hamlet's foster brother. After reaching Act II, scene ii, line 185 of *Hamlet*, however, he discontinued the manuscript.[38]

Twain's burlesque covers the early platform and palace scenes of *Hamlet*, including the ghost, the solemn swearing, and the arrival of Rosencrantz and Guildenstern. Stockmar, the book agent, brings vernacular humor to the play. He carries a satchel and an umbrella, smokes a cigar on the king's throne, and probably dresses in nineteenth-century garb. He is first observed practicing a sales pitch that mixes bourgeois commerce with deference to royalty:

> Sir, the book which I have the honor to offer to your worship's consideration, is a work which—which—O, yes!—is a work which is—is a work which has been commended by the highest authorities as an achievement of transcendent and hitherto unparalleled merit....Sir, it is a work which the family circle cannot afford to be without.

One of his canvassing copies happens to contain a quotation from a book that Hamlet is currently reading: "Old men have gray beards; their faces are wrinkled; their eyes purging thick amber and plum-tree gum."[39] Of course, Hamlet might already be reading Stockmar's book, and that would be a plug for it, but if Hamlet is reading some other book, questions might arise about the originality of the book that Stockmar is trying to sell. Stockmar puts the ghost down for six copies, but when he realizes that the ghost is the late king, he ups it to a hundred, expressing himself in nineteenth-century slang:

> That's *him*—no two ways about that; they've got him down to a spot. So, as sure as guns, it *wasn't* a policeman, after all. No *sir*, it was the king—it was the late Grand Turk himself. Let *him* off with six copies? I think I *see* myself! I'll just chalk him up for a level *hundred*, easy enough— and sue the estate![40]

Stockmar's manner of speech contrasts the classes and the centuries. He parodies the way Shakespeare's characters would order a carriage: "Me lord hath given commandment, sirrah, that the vehicle wherein he doth, of ancient custom, his daily recreation take, shall unto the portal of the palace be straight conveyed." He would prefer, "Fetch the carriage, you duffer, and *hump* yourself!"[41]

Basil Stockmar is relevant to *Huckleberry Finn* because Twain created him about the same time as the King and the Duke and he resembles them in many ways. He is a traveling salesman who mixes trade with Shakespeare and combines in his talk the colloquialism of the King and the pseudo-grandeur of the Duke, and as Hamlet's foster brother he, too, is a claimant to nobility. Since his habits and pursuits are similar to theirs, Mark Twain obviously worked on the "Burlesque *Hamlet*" and the middle section of his novel together, using one to help him with the other, and seeing in the process a resemblance between the two larger stories, *Hamlet* and *Huckleberry Finn*. This would be an extension of Franklin Rogers' theory that Twain drew patterns from his burlesques to advance his more serious works. The "Burlesque *Hamlet*," therefore, contributed plot, character, conflict, and style, along with Shakespeare analogues, to the traveling salesman sections of *Huckleberry Finn*.

Another late component in the third stage of *Huckleberry Finn*'s composition, according to Rogers, is the moral pilgrimage. This motif adds the theme of moral education to the travelogue techniques of burlesque and character/episode axis. Rogers thinks that this motif grew out of Twain's description of Prince Edward's moral education in *The Prince and the Pauper*, which itself was influenced by Twain's earlier mixing of an allegory against slavery into his burlesque of Victor Hugo's *L'Homme Qui Rit*.[42] Like *Tom Sawyer*, therefore, *The Prince and the Pauper* was another medium between earlier burlesque exercises and the classic *Huckleberry Finn*. In the previous chapter I demonstrated how Twain used Shakespeare's language, themes, and plots in composing *The Prince and the Pauper*. Perhaps his drawing from it now for the theme of

moral pilgrimage opened him again to the availability of
Shakespeare's example.

Sometime between the spring and summer of 1883, Twain
introduced as the controlling theme of his novel the moral
dilemma that Huck experiences over helping Jim to freedom.
Each episode of the journey down river awakens Huck to his
growing affection and loyalty toward Jim, which scares Huck
because it leads him to lie about Jim's fugitive status and
refuse to turn him in, defying the laws of his slave-holding
State and resisting the legacy of his racist father. One passage
that Twain inserted at this time into his earlier work was the
internal debate that Huck has with himself when he realizes
that he is helping Jim find Cairo and escape up the Ohio River.
Jim begins to feel "trembly and feverish to be so close to freedom," but Huck reflects:

> Well, I can tell you it made me all trembly and feverish,
> too, to hear him, because I begun to get it through my head
> that he *was* most free—and who was to blame for it? Why
> *me*. I couldn't get that out of my conscience, no how nor no
> way. It got to troubling me so I couldn't rest; I couldn't stay
> still in one place. It hadn't ever come home to me before,
> what this thing was that I was doing. But now it did; and
> it staid with me, and scortched me more and more....I got
> to feeling so mean and so miserable I most wished I was
> dead. (123-124)

When Huck lies just after this to protect Jim from two slave
hunters, he comes back to the raft "feeling bad and low, because I knowed very well I had done wrong..." (127). But then
he says to himself:

> hold on,—s'pose you'd a done right and give Jim up; would
> you felt better than what you do now? No, says I, I'd feel
> bad—I'd feel just the same way I do now. Well, then, says
> I, what's the use you learning to do right, when it's trouble-
> some to do right and ain't no trouble to do wrong, and the
> wages is just the same? (127-128)

In his own way Huck is very sensitive and articulate in describing his mental states. There are several times when he stands back to analyze himself and his actions. His moral dilemma about what he should do, and the introspection that it causes, his hesitation and reluctance to act, and his consequent acting on impulse rather than decision, all lead to another resemblance between him and Hamlet. For Hamlet too steps back to analyze himself in his soliloquies. In these he expresses his doubts about the ghost's story, his misery and disgust over the crimes that it discloses, his recoiling from the task of "setting them right," and his self-accusation for the delays and distractions that he allows to get in the way between his task and its accomplishment. Huck's reflections are like Hamlet's soliloquies both in function and content.

The closest that Huck comes to Hamlet is his rendition of the Immortal Soliloquy, "To be, or not to be," in Chapter XXI. Of course, it is the Duke who recites the speech, but Huck "learned it, easy enough" while the Duke was "learning" it to the King. As it stands, the soliloquy is a hodgepodge of quotes from different parts of *Hamlet, Macbeth*, and *Richard the Third*. Whether the mistakes in it are the Duke's or Huck's is unclear. The Duke usually tries to be faithful to Shakespeare, and hodgepodge is certainly an aspect of Huck's literary mind (see his history lesson to Jim in Chapter XXIII), so the mistakes are likely Huck's. They also reflect the motley nature of the King and the Duke's program, and the collective nature of the novel as a whole. So even though the burlesque soliloquy was apparently added to the novel in March 1883, its style fits the shape of the novel and of Huck's mind.[43] Its location also reinforces the structural parallel between the middle sections of *Hamlet* and *Huckleberry Finn*. It is delivered while the would-be actors, the King and the Duke, are rehearsing for their show. This coordination recalls Act III of *Hamlet* when Hamlet speaks the soliloquy and the players are rehearsing for their court performance.

Despite its mistakes, Huck's soliloquy expresses his dilemmas about existence, justice, action, and life after death.[44] He ruminates on these subjects again and again in order to figure out what to do and to put off doing something that does not seem right or that seems troublesome. Hamlet is burdened with the task of revenge, and Huck's task is the freeing of a slave. Each feels uncertain about the rightness of his task and keeps postponing its fulfillment. Each fears that someone may be hurt by its accomplishment: Hamlet is instructed not to "contrive / Against thy mother aught" (I, v, 85-86), and Huck does not want to deprive Miss Watson of her property (124). Each one too is diverted from his task because he is infected by the ills of his society—Hamlet by the laxity, poisoned rhetoric, and sexual perversion of Denmark, and Huck by the romanticizing, drab humor, and racial prejudice of the South.

Much of this moral dilemma concerns the notion of conscience. It is odd that Twain omitted the line "Thus conscience does make cowards of us all" (III, i, 83) from his rendition of the soliloquy, because conscience plays a key role in this novel, in his other works, and in *Hamlet*. Besides making Huck feel mean and miserable for helping Jim escape (124), and lowdown and ornery for not notifying Miss Watson of Jim's whereabouts (268), conscience even blames Huck for the tar and feathering of the King and the Duke (290); and although the word *conscience* is not used, Huck also feels guilty for leaving robbers on a wreck (87) and for causing the Grangerford-Shepherdson feud (153). For Twain in this novel, conscience seems to be an inner voice that directs a person to follow the laws of society, not an individual ethic that might lead one to oppose these laws. That is called by Twain in a later note (in reference to Huck) "heart," in contrast to "conscience."[45] Critics have shown that Twain developed this notion of conscience from reading W. E. H. Lecky in the mid-1870s and after, but his close reading of *Hamlet* during the same years in preparation for a burlesque also contributed to it.[46]

Although dissuading Hamlet from suicide by "the dread of something after death" (III, i, 78), conscience does not disturb him for plotting the execution of Rosencrantz and Guildenstern (V, ii, 58), and, he argues, should not oppose his killing of Claudius (V, ii, 67). His whole purpose in the play scene is to "catch the conscience of the king" (II, ii, 591). Although Laertes defies conscience and dares damnation to avenge his father's death (IV, v, 132), he likewise has to struggle against conscience when he is about to stab Hamlet with a poisoned foil (V, ii, 285). These repeated references to conscience in *Hamlet* probably reminded Twain of the concept and its function while he was composing *Huckleberry Finn*.

Moreover, Twain's notion of conscience is very much like Shakespeare's. When Hamlet complains, "Thus conscience does make cowards of us all, / And thus the native hue of resolution / Is sicklied o'er with the pale cast of thought" (III, i, 83-85), he says something that Huck too might say in his own idiom, and in fact does say in his garbled rendition of the soliloquy: "And thus the native hue of resolution, like the poor cat i' the adage, / Is sicklied o'er with care" (179). *Hamlet* and *Huckleberry Finn* operate on a basic conflict of nature ("native hue") against custom or civilization. Included under nature are instinct, heart, impulse, feeling, and action, while custom comprises books, education, conscience, laws, and thought. Illustrating this ideological conflict is a conflict between images: nakedness-clothes, night-day, death-life, individual-society. Both stories alternate scenes of night, watching, dreams, and spirits with those of day, which usually signify dullness, meanness and superficiality. Both Hamlet and Huck are obsessed with death and the dead. Huck wishes several times that he were dead, fakes his own murder, and usually kills off his family in the stories that he tells to escape from tight situations. Both Hamlet and Huck also choose loneliness over society and thereby become critics of society. To them society means trouble, confinement, sickness, artificiality, and evil. Since conscience for both is connected with custom and society, they reject it in favor of nature and instinct.

One scene in *Huckleberry Finn* that combines the sensitivity and self-disclosure of soliloquy with the conflict between nature and civilization is Huck's attempt at prayer in Chapter XXXI. Undecided about whether to write to Miss Watson about Jim, and torn inside between conscience and heart, education and instinct, Huck finds that he cannot pray:

> It was because my heart warn't right; it was because I
> warn't square; it was because I was playing double. I was
> letting *on* to give up sin, but away inside of me I was
> holding on to the biggest one of all. I was trying to make
> my mouth *say* I would do the right thing and the clean
> thing,...but deep down in me I knowed it was a lie, and He
> knowed it. You can't pray a lie—I found that out. (269)

This scene and speech resemble Claudius's troubled attempt at
prayer in *Hamlet*. Huck's words and concepts echo his:

> Pray can I not,
> Though inclination be as sharp as will.
> My stronger guilt defeats my strong intent,
> And like a man to double business bound
> I stand in pause where I shall first begin,
> And both neglect.
>
> ♦ ♦ ♦
>
> My words fly up, my thoughts remain below.
> Words without thoughts never to heaven go.
> *(III, iii, 38-43, 97-98)*

Both of these scenes occur in spots where key practical deci-
sions are made. Hamlet decides not to kill Claudius while at
prayer because he wants to send him to hell. Huck decides not
to report Jim and expects to go to hell as a result. Both scenes
also express the disharmony between words and feelings, custom and nature, that Hamlet and Huck—and, in this instance,
Claudius—experience. It may be significant too that both
Hamlet and Huck begin their approaches to a showdown by
dealing with letters, Hamlet by substituting one and Huck by
tearing one up.

   Therefore, two components of the third stage of *Huckleberry Finn*'s composition, the traveling showmen and the moral
reflections, connect the middle section of Twain's novel with
the players and soliloquy in the middle of *Hamlet*. Since Twain
refers explicitly to Shakespeare in the plays and to *Hamlet* by

the soliloquy, and since the plays reflect other events in the novel, it is quite clear that Twain intended, at least from this point on in his composition, that the Shakespeare scenes function as paradigms to the action of his story. Some of the Shakespeare scenes reflect just one episode—I have shown this in connection with *Richard the Third* and *Romeo and Juliet*—but the *Hamlet* speech, besides reflecting the moral dilemmas of Huck, also illuminates the images and ideas from *Hamlet* that appear in the early chapters of the novel and makes explicit a relation between the two works that has up to this point been only a conscious or unconscious influence. From here on, Twain expects the reader to notice the relation and make continual comparisons between the two works.

The Final Duel

In addition to the early ghost and father scenes, and the middle play and soliloquy scenes, the final episodes of *Huckleberry Finn* at the Phelps farm seem again to parallel *Hamlet*. In each story an earlier character returns to precipitate the action. Tom Sawyer shows up with the same spirit as Laertes. Each faces his task, freeing a slave in one case and revenge for a father's murder in the other, with the same resolution and display, while the main characters, Huck and Hamlet, who all along have delayed and pondered over their tasks, allow themselves to be led to a showdown. Both the duel between Hamlet and Laertes and Tom Sawyer's evasion plot are inflated by excessive verbiage and ceremony. They are games played for show, even though violence is planned and done in each case. As a result, the primary task in each story is accomplished, Jim is freed and Claudius is killed, but not by the plan of the main character, and this fact introduces a common theme of "divine providence" in both stories.

When Hamlet is challenged to a duel with Laertes, a duel which he realizes may involve a plot against his life, he accepts the challenge against Horatio's warning by saying, "There is a special providence in the fall of a sparrow. If it be now, 'tis not to come; if it be not to come, it will be now; if it be not now, yet it will come" (V, ii, 208-211). He also attributes to providence, although he does not use the word, his finding the orders for his execution in the baggage of Rosencrantz and Guildenstern—"There's a divinity that shapes our ends, / Rough-hew them how we will" (V, ii, 10-11)—and his having his father's signet with him so he can change the orders and make it look official (V, ii, 48). Huck too trusts in providence when he first arrives at the Phelps farm: "I went right along, not fixing up any particular plan, but just trusting to Providence to put the right words in my mouth when the time come" (277). When he starts to fear that providence has let him down and that he will have to tell the truth, Mrs. Phelps identifies him to her husband as Tom Sawyer and he has a ready-made story to tell (280, 282). In a sense it is really providence that frees Jim because Miss Watson, who believed in a terrifying and demanding providence, felt ashamed for planning to sell Jim down the river and probably freed him in her will in hope of being admitted into the good place (14, 357).

Moreover, as in other instances of Twain's use of Shakespeare, these direct influences of *Hamlet* on the final episodes of *Huckleberry Finn* are also supported by indirect ones. In March 1883 Twain received from his old *Territorial Enterprise* editor, Joseph T. Goodman, the rough copy of a play, "Hamlet's Brother," which he was expected to revise and complete. Like Twain's earlier burlesque of *Hamlet*, Goodman's play mixes select clippings from the text of *Hamlet* with original speeches of an added comic character. Here the character is Bill, Hamlet's brother, who has a sprightly and playful temperament and who tries by several tricks to cure Hamlet of his morbid, dreamy, and verbose habits. He disguises as the ghost of Hamlet's father, revises the speech that Hamlet wrote for the play-within-the-play, gets Polonius and Ophelia to play dead and to endure mock obsequies and Laertes to fake revenge, and finally disarms Hamlet in a duel while the supposed dead show up alive.[47] Apparently Twain did some work on this burlesque. Following Goodman's suggestion, he wrote a speech for Bill to give in the ghost disguise. He also claimed to have found a letter stating that Bill received a pair of boxing gloves from a Tom Sayers.[48] *Sayers* was the name of a nineteenth-century British prize fighter, but it comes close enough to *Sawyer* for one to see a correspondence between Bill and Tom. Both characters are lively and enjoy doing things with a grand style, and they both use theatrical games based on literary classics to bring rousing finales to their stories, one to "Hamlet's Brother" and the other to *Huckleberry Finn*. The fact that Twain received and worked on this play in the spring of 1883, when he was planning how to end *Huckleberry Finn*, indicates that both the play itself, and the original that it burlesques, could have influenced the final episodes of his novel. Just as Twain's earlier burlesque of *Hamlet* may have contributed the traveling showmen plot to the middle section of his novel, so Goodman's burlesque could have supplied the theatrical antics of an energetic boy to the final section.

These parallels with *Hamlet*, both direct and indirect, add one more literary source to the Phelps farm episode. Tom Sawyer bases his evasion plot on the works of Scott, Dumas, Baron Trenck, Casanova, and Benvenuto Cellini, but his romantic exploits strike Huck as foolish, troublesome, and unnecessary. They result in Tom's being shot and almost get Jim hanged. They represent a misuse of literary sources and parody both the works on which they are based and the act of freeing Jim. By way of contrast, the parallels with *Hamlet* are toned down, just like the behavior of Hamlet and Huck toward the end of their stories. They cause the reader to reject Tom's foolishness and take a serious view of the situation. They carry the episode beyond comedy by setting it in the context of Shakespeare's classic tragedy, and this setting evokes a deeper interpretation of the action and provides a more solemn reconciliation to the trouble and absurdity.

The *Hamlet* parallels also help defend Twain against the critics who charge him with losing control of his novel in the Phelps farm episode. Franklin Rogers, for example, blames the final section for damaging the structure and coherence of the novel. He argues that this section does not provide an adequate conclusion to the story that comes before it: "Huck fails to act in accordance with the instinctive humanity which characterizes his relations with Jim during the journey."[49] If, however, the final episode is related to the *Hamlet* influences in the early chapters of the novel and to the *Hamlet* paradigms in the middle chapters, completing a story that has developed gradually along lines parallel with *Hamlet*, then the novel as a whole does have a unified plan, albeit one that evolved over time in increasing degrees of explicitness. Considered from this perspective, Huck's passivity in the final episode can be compared to the similar state of Hamlet near the end of his story and can contribute to the theme of providence that is common to both works.

From his attempts to write a burlesque *Hamlet* and his weaving of motifs from *Hamlet* into his major and minor compositions during the years when he was working on *Huckleberry Finn*, Mark Twain clearly had a deep desire to write his own *Hamlet*. He found in that play the structure, the conflicts, the characters, and the themes which stimulated his creative talents. The father's loss yet lingering presence and demand, the resulting melancholy and introspection of the son, the escape from these burdens through art and entertainment, and the final resolution by providence, burlesque, or both—these are the features of *Hamlet* that most affect *Huckleberry Finn*. Twain began his classic with influences from *Hamlet*, both direct and indirect, perhaps unconscious, but he gradually became more aware of the correspondences between the two works and left explicit signs of this recognition in his text so that his readers could enjoy an added depth and richness in his novel and feel more at home in an integrated literary tradition.

The King and the Duke

Of course *Hamlet* is not the only play of Shakespeare cited in *Huckleberry Finn*, nor the only literary classic. In fact, there are so many references and allusions to other works that the novel may be considered a journey through literature. Aside from the books that Tom Sawyer appeals to as authorities for his adventures—*Don Quixote*, *The Arabian Nights*, *The Count of Monte Cristo*, and others—there are more subtle associations made with the Bible, *Pilgrim's Progress*, and *Robinson*

Crusoe. This plurality of literary models allows Twain to show different reactions to literature among his characters and elicit the same from his readers. It also supports the travel and education motifs of his novel. Just as the action moves from place to place, so literary descriptions and paradigms of the action move from book to book, and the characters and readers learn how to manage and interpret their lives by measuring events against different forms of literary expression. The Shakespeare plays that are mentioned fit this pattern well by their plurality, by the conflict of reactions that they produce when tragic scenes are performed in comic fashion, and by their paradigmatic connection with other scenes in the novel. It is significant too that Shakespeare is fragmented into brief scenes from different plays, much like the lines from different plays that appear in the Duke's rendition of Hamlet's soliloquy. This referential admixture mirrors the episodic quality of the novel as a whole and the hodgepodge of information that exists in Huck's adolescent mind, simultaneously reflecting the divisions of section, class, race, and generation that create the plot and conflicts of the story. There is even historical precedent for it since theatrical troupes in nineteenth-century America, especially those that traveled through the West and on the rivers, often performed famous scenes from different Shakespeare plays and followed them with a burlesque or minstrel show.

The main focus of Shakespearean references in *Huckleberry Finn* is the motley program of the King and the Duke in the middle of the novel, chapters XX to XXIII. Scenes from three different plays are performed—*Richard the Third, Romeo and Juliet*, and, of course, *Hamlet*—and they demonstrate a variety of approaches and reactions to literature. On the one hand, they are scenes from tragedies put on by "world renowned tragedians," yet the actors are frauds, and the quality of their performance, if the rehearsal gives any indication, must have been particularly low. Still, the Duke aims for excellence. Even though the bald and bearded King plays Juliet, the Duke instructs him to recite his lines "soft and sick and languishy," and not to "bray like a jackass." In practicing the sword-fight, the Duke prances about the raft in grand style, but the King trips and falls overboard (177). If the Duke's efforts at delicacy and finesse do not give much hope of a decent performance, they at least remind the reader that Shakespeare's plays are sublime when they are done with discretion. Ironically, even the inept performance of the King and the Duke seems to go over the heads of the Arkansas audience. Since Shakespeare proves too much for them, the Duke resorts to "The Royal Nonesuch" farce, yet calls it a "Thrilling Tragedy." This alternation or mixture of comic and tragic features in Shakespeare scenes elicits a variety of reactions from the reader. The farcical rendition of a Shakespeare tragedy stresses the inability of literature to reflect reality adequately, or it exposes reality in its absurd aspects, which might also be tragic. Finally, it reminds the reader of the serious play behind the farcical performance, adding a broader tragic perspective to help interpret and alleviate the sadness and horror of life.

The Shakespeare scenes in the program of the King and the Duke also serve as paradigms for other events in the novel. The sword-fight from *Richard the Third* is rehearsed and advertised just before the Boggs-Sherburn duel, and since the actual performance of the fight is mentioned but not described, the duel itself becomes the performance, thus blending the theatrical scene with an actual event. Although the fight is merely a stage direction in Shakespeare's text—"Enter Richard and Richmond; they fight. Richard is slain" (V, v), theater groups in the nineteenth century usually performed Colley Cibber's version of the play, which includes twenty lines of dialogue between the two combatants.[50] Boggs resembles Richard in several ways. He staggers around ranting and raving and keeps challenging Sherburn to come out. He leaves his horse and is being rescued and supported by two of his followers when Sherburn appears (184-185; see *Richard III*, V, iv). Association with Shakespeare's play brings out the pathetic contrast in the duel between a victim who is drunkenly raging and gesturing, and a killer who is quiet, sober, and methodic.

Richard the Third was a popular hit in nineteenth-century America, partly because of its portrayal of a scheming, violent, and defeated monarch. Huck reflects this interest in his tirade against the King and the Duke after they collect almost five hundred dollars from their show. He denounces them as typical kings, or "regular rapscallions," and he includes Richard III in his list of royal villains. He also accuses Henry VIII of drowning his father, the Duke of Wellington, in a butt of mamsey, confusing (among other things) Henry with Richard III, who had Clarence stabbed and drowned in a malmsey butt (199; *Richard III*, I, iv, 265). The Duke's rendition of Hamlet's soliloquy also contains a slightly misquoted verse from *Richard*: "And all the clouds that lowered o'er our housetops" (I, i, 3). Evidently both Huck and Twain see Shakespeare's kings as models of those who fleece and defraud the common people.

Just as the sword-fight from *Richard the Third* parallels the Boggs-Sherburn duel, so the balcony scene from *Romeo and Juliet* parallels the Grangerford-Shepherdson feud. Both stories describe romances between members of rival families. Each couple receives help from the church: Friar Laurence brings Romeo and Juliet together, and Harney Shepherdson informs Sophia of the time for their elopement by leaving a note in her Bible. Both stories also end with bloodbaths, although Twain's lovers escape unharmed.

Twain had previously treated the theme of love between members of rival families in the novel "Simon Wheeler, Detective," which he wrote in late 1877 and early 1878, about a year and a half before composing the feud chapters in *Huckleberry Finn*. I find no specific references to *Romeo and Juliet* in "Simon Wheeler." However, Walter Blair notes that novels about Southern feuds often compared the rival families to the Capulets and the Montagues. For example, John William DeForest's *Kate Beaumont*, which Twain listed in his notebook after its serialization in the *Atlantic Monthly* in 1871, compares its McAlister-Beaumont feud to that in Shakespeare's play.[51] Also, George Washington Cable's *The Grandissimes* opens with a masked ball at which lovers of rival families meet, an obvious allusion to *Romeo and Juliet*. Twain read and enjoyed the book, and he heard Cable read from it during his visit to New Orleans in 1882.[52] This is another instance of Twain's receiving Shakespeare from other authors who were using him for the same reasons.

The slapdash rendition of the balcony scene—especially with the bald and white-bearded King playing Juliet—provides a fitting comment on the contradictions of Southern gentility exposed in the Grangerford-Shepherdson feud. The myths of chivalry and romance, expressed by the sentimental paintings, poetry, and sheet music in the Grangerford house, and the men's spotless linen suits and stilted speech, are exploded by the violence, irrationality, and cowardice displayed in the killings of the feud, especially in the final skirmish. As presented by the King and the Duke, Shakespeare's play reflects the absurdity of this situation, but as remembered by the reader, it also brings out the tragedy of the feud and offers some relief by its classic stature and universal applicability.

I have already explained in the previous section of this chapter how the Duke's rendition of Hamlet's soliloquy and the context in which it occurs create correspondences between Huck's and Hamlet's extended reflections on their moral dilemmas and between their ways of avoiding these dilemmas by preoccupation with drama. Moreover, the explicitness of this reference to *Hamlet* in the middle of the novel clarifies and supports the subtler influences of *Hamlet* on the earlier and later sections, so that Shakespeare's play can be considered a paradigm for the novel as a whole. This *Hamlet* paradigm is the most sustained and developed of the Shakespeare parallels in *Huckleberry Finn*.

Another play, which is not part of the program presented by the King and the Duke but is in their repertoire, since they have a costume for it, is *King Lear*. Just before the King and the Duke land to prepare for their activities at the Wilks funeral, they dress Jim in a Lear costume and paint him up as a sick Arab in order to scare suspicious eavesdroppers away from the raft (203). When Huck returns to the raft again after the Wilks episode, he is so frightened by Jim's disguise that he falls overboard (259). This placement of the Lear costume both right before and right after the Wilks episode (chapters XXIV to XXIX) invites the reader to compare the episode to the action of *King Lear*. There are, indeed, parallels. In each story an inheritance is to be divided among three sisters, and the dividing itself is done in a ceremonial whose real purpose is to bring glory to the bestowers, that is, to Lear and to the King and the Duke, and this ceremonial creates an atmosphere in both stories of flattery and false rhetoric. In each story, too, there is a character who sees through the falsehood, Kent in *Lear* and Dr. Robinson in *Huckleberry Finn*, and one of the sisters, Cordelia and Mary Jane, leaves the main locale of the action. Then, during a storm, truth and goodness are disentangled from falsehood and greed. Since the King takes most of the initiative in the episode, he could represent Lear. He certainly indulges in inflated language, although his motive is greed rather than Lear's desire for filial homage. He is, however, only a burlesque Lear because he gains none of the self-knowledge that Lear does after his ordeal.[53] The fact that one of the Wilks sisters, Joanna, has a harelip, a defect believed in *Lear* to be caused by a fiend, further connects the scene with Shakespeare's play (206; *Lear* III, iv, 110).

Jim might also be considered a Lear figure since he actually wears the costume. He certainly is abused by society—about to be sold by his owner and hunted as a runaway slave—and in his attempt to escape from this he exposes himself to the rage of the elements.[54] However, rather than isolate Jim as a Lear figure, it would be better to view him as part of a character axis. We recall that Franklin Rogers found a character axis to be one of the burlesque patterns used by Twain in the travel sections of *Huckleberry Finn*. Following this pattern, a genteel-vernacular contrast is acted out between the King and the Duke on the one hand and Huck and Jim on the other. Thus, the King and the Duke are burlesques of Lear, since the costume is theirs, and Jim in turn is a burlesque of them, since he wears the costume.

The King and the Duke claim to be disinherited nobles, and they find themselves left out in a storm, like Lear. Interestingly, during the storms Lear invites his fool and his supposed servant Kent to take shelter in a hovel, while the King and the

Duke seize the wigwam on the raft for themselves and leave
Huck and Jim out in the rain (167-168; *Lear* III, iv, 23-27).
During a second storm, the King and the Duke escape from the
Wilkses after being exposed and "disinherited" again. They
return to the raft, accuse one another of blundering and be-
trayal, and fall asleep in the wigwam (257-264). They thus
prove themselves to be merely burlesque Lears since they experience none of the profound inner changes that Lear does
while suffering on the heath.

It is Huck, ironically, who does experience such changes.
By braving the elements with Jim on the raft, by listening to
his stories, and by noticing how Jim takes both watches at
night and lets him sleep, Huck begins to understand Jim as a
fellow human being and to feel a closeness that will later
prevent him from reporting Jim to slave hunters (168, 201).
These sentiments of warmth toward a social inferior yet fellow
sufferer resemble those felt by Lear on the heath. Although
the King and the Duke cheapen and distort the values and
sentiments of *King Lear*, Huck and Jim seem to revive and
reflect them. It may also be significant that Twain's original
title for the King and the Duke's farce was "The Burning
Shame," a phrase from *Lear*, although there it refers not to
something farcical and obscene but to Lear's remorse for what
he did to Cordelia.[55]

There are several storms in *Huckleberry Finn*, and Huck
describes them in vivid onomatopoeic language:

> My souls, how the wind did scream along! And every
> second or two there'd come a glare that lit up the white-
> caps for a half a mile around, and you'd see the islands
> looking dusty through the rain, and the trees thrashing
> around in the wind; then comes a *h-wack!*—bum! bum!
> bumble-umble-um-bum-bum-bum-bum—and the thunder
> would go rumbling and grumbling away, and quit—and
> then *rip* comes another flash and another sockdolager. (167-
> 168; see also 59-60, 257-258)

Lear too gives a vivid description of the storm he sees:

Blow, winds, and crack your cheeks. Rage, blow.
You cataracts and hurracanoes, spout
Till you have drenched our steeples, drowned
    the cocks.
You sulph'rous and thought-executing fires,
Vaunt-couriers of oak-cleaving thunderbolts,
Singe my white head. And thou, all-shaking thunder,
Strike flat the thick rotundity o' th' world,
Crack Nature's molds, all germains spill at once,
That make ingrateful man.

♦   ♦   ♦

Rumble thy bellyfill. Spit, fire. Spout, rain.

(III, ii, 1-9, 14)

Twain was mightily impressed by the storm in a German production of *King Lear* and drew up a list of words to describe
it.[56] Evidently, the storms in his fictional landscape, including
the ones in *Huckleberry Finn*, were influenced in part by *King
Lear*. In a sense, the river in *Huckleberry Finn*, where all of
the storms occur, functions like the heath in *King Lear*. Both
places receive refugees from civilization and expose their false-
hoods and pretensions. They show wanderers and escapees
lying about their past and inventing stories to fool supposedly
civilized people, and they use these petty crimes and frauds to
reveal and criticize the greater crimes and stupidities of those
who become their victims. The events on the river satirize
those on the shore just as the relationships on the heath do
those in the castles. The river and the heath, and the storms
that occur on them, strip away artificiality and bring the indi-
viduals who endure them closer to nature and human kindness.

Another fact that supports the influence of *King Lear* on
Huckleberry Finn is Twain's simultaneous work on *The Prince
and the Pauper*. He began *The Prince* in the fall of 1877, a little
over a year after he had begun *Huckleberry Finn*, worked on

both novels during 1880, and wrote parts of *Huckleberry Finn* while he was reading the proofs for *The Prince* in 1881. The chapters in which the King and the Duke are introduced were composed at this time. We recall that Franklin Rogers believes *The Prince* to have influenced Twain's continuation of *Huckleberry Finn* as a moral pilgrimage.[57] In my study of *The Prince* in Chapter III I demonstrated how Prince Edward's wanderings, hardships, and consolations contained allusions to Lear's experience on the heath during the storm. Apparently Twain's treatment of fallen grandeur on the raft came from the same source of inspiration. The storm scenes in *Lear* helped him express many of his dominant themes: flight from the artificialities of society and civilization, contact with reality and goodness through exposure to natural forces, and forced association with outcasts, rogues, and fugitives on the way toward building a more just and sympathetic community.

Another play that deserves some mention as a possible influence on *Huckleberry Finn*, although there are no explicit references to it, is *Othello*. It was very popular in nineteenth-century America, its title role made famous by Edwin Forrest, whose Othello Twain had seen more than once. It was also frequently burlesqued—by Artemus Ward, by Twain himself, and by the minstrel companies, especially since it easily lent itself to comment on the Negro question during the eras of abolition and Reconstruction. Because Jim is a leading character and slavery an important issue in *Huckleberry Finn*, and because other Shakespeare tragedies figure so prominently in the story, it is probable that Twain thought of *Othello* while composing his novel. There are resemblances between Jim and Othello, although they are literary stereotypes of Negro character: both were slaves at one time, and both are skilled at story-telling and magic arts. Jim once struck his daughter for not obeying him, but felt deep remorse when he realized that his daughter had become deaf from scarlet fever and did not hear his command (201-202). Othello is a classic case of a man's misjudgment of a woman. He falsely accused Desdemona of infidelity, struck her at one point, and later killed her and suffered a remorse that led to his own suicide.

In a way, Huck could be considered an Iago to Jim's Othello. He fools Jim into believing at first a story that he tells after their separation in the fog (103-105), and he plans to turn Jim in as an escaped slave. Yet he repents of his fog story and tells most of his lies to hide and protect Jim. An article by Shakespeare scholar Richard Grant White was published in the *Atlantic Monthly* while Twain was working on the middle chapters of *Huckleberry Finn* and could have contributed to an association of Huck with Iago. White argues that Iago had honesty, bravery, and compassion, but used them always for his own self-interest, that selfishness was the guiding principle of his life. He had no moral sense: "If by doing right he could have prospered as well as by doing wrong, he would have done right, because right doing is more respectable and popular and less troublesome than wrongdoing."[58] These are some of the same concepts and words that Huck uses in his moral reflections (124-125, 127-128). He lies and flatters others in order to save himself, and the criteria of his moral choices are usually comfort and lack of trouble. What makes him honest is that he admits acting from a selfish motive, and as he grows closer and closer to Jim, his comforts become bound and identified with Jim's, so that his selfish motives gradually become communal.

The varied Shakespeare associations in *Huckleberry Finn*, whether they come directly from Shakespeare or indirectly from another author, and whether they are conscious references or unconscious influences on Twain's part, reinforce the novel as a travelogue, especially a travelogue through literature. Although they add to the humor of the novel, since laughter is caused both by their incompetent production and their apparent unsuitability for reflecting the events and characters of the Mississippi, they still enhance the seriousness of the novel and give its local events and characters a tragic and epic proportion. They extend its horizons in space and time, and stretch the concrete into the universal. By incorporating material from Shakespeare, Twain makes *Huckleberry Finn* not just a Southern, or American, or nineteenth-century novel, but a work that embraces a long tradition and follows the precedents of classic literature. It represents the apex of his relation to Shakespeare since it contains a rich variety of uses and integrates them into a unified whole. After *Huckleberry Finn* his uses of Shakespeare continue, but they lose some of their richness because they do not appear on the American scene and so do not exploit the contrasts between serious drama and comic burlesque that marked Shakespeare performances in the American tradition. Rather, they revert to Twain's earlier use of Shakespeare for historical coloring, since they appear in novels set in the actual or imaginative past. They do, however, include scenic and thematic parallels with Shakespeare that give these novels greater depth and universality.

The Yankee, the Maid, and the Stranger

Although *A Connecticut Yankee in King Arthur's Court* is based loosely on scenes from Sir Thomas Malory's *Le Morte D'Arthur* and contains both extended passages and occasional words and phrases from that book, it also relies substantially on Shakespeare for scenic and stylistic effects. Its treatment of Shakespeare resembles that in *The Prince and the Pauper*. Both novels contrast an archaic and ornate style of dialogue, either taken from Shakespeare or generally influenced by his works, with a modern literary style of narrative. *A Connecticut Yankee* adds further contrast, however, by juxtaposing this archaic style with the modern slang of business and advertising. Traveling as a knight errant with his Demoiselle "Sandy," Hank Morgan wins a skirmish and becomes "proprietor" of some knights. Counting his "assets" and considering it a "good haul," he asks Sandy who they are and where they "hang out." When Hank has to explain that he wants to know where they live, Sandy, relishing his phrase, replies:

> "Hang they out—hang they out—where hang—where do they hang out; eh, right so; where do they hang out. Of a truth the phrase hath a fair and winsome grace, and it is prettily worded withal. I will repeat it anon and anon in mine idlesse, whereby I may peradventure learn it. Where

do they hang out. Even so! already it falleth trippingly from my tongue...[59]

Howard Baetzhold noticed the echo here of Hamlet's advice to the players, "Speak the speech...trippingly on the tongue."[60] Baetzhold also believes that Hank's description of Clarence the page as a "forked carrot" was influenced by Falstaff's reference to man as a "forked radish," and that the "vanities laced with his golden blood," which refers to a page who was stabbed by Morgan Le Fay, is an echo of Duncan's "silver skin lac'd with his golden blood" in *Macbeth*.[61] There are, in fact, several words and phrases in *A Connecticut Yankee* that are common in Shakespeare: *haste thee, compass thee about, twixt sun and sun, go to, perdition catch, give commandment, sup in hell.* Twain used these to create an aura of antiquity and a contrast with modernity in his novel.

Besides this contrast in style between antique expression and modern slang, Twain specified a second contrast in the antique style itself. On the one hand it is described as gracious, courtly, gentle, and stately. When Hank had grown accustomed to its atmosphere of reverence, respect, and deference, he was shocked by the discordant and flippant tone of Clarence's modern newspaper (66, 303-304). On the other hand, however, Hank found indelicacies in the conversation of gentlemen and ladies at Camelot that "would have made a Comanche blush." At Morgan Le Fay's supper table, ladies told anecdotes that would have made "even the great Elizabeth of England hide behind a handkerchief" (78, 197). This combination of stateliness and coarseness in language is exactly what Twain liked about Shakespeare's style, and he practiced imitating it in the ribald conversation of Queen Elizabeth, Shakespeare, and other nobles and commoners in *1601*. He did not, however, give any concrete examples of the coarseness in *A Connecticut Yankee*.

Parallel with this language play, there are scenes in *A Connecticut Yankee* which seem to have been patterned after scenes in Shakespeare. Clarence describes the events that happened while Hank was in France as acts of a drama, and

Hank calls the flooding of the ditches during the Battle of the Sand-belt the "last act of the tragedy" (459, 486). The tragedy most pertinent to the events that happen toward the end of *A Connecticut Yankee* is *Hamlet*. Doctors conspire to send Hank away from England just as Claudius arranges to have Hamlet taken to England from Denmark. Hank and Hamlet return alone from their absences and witness abbreviated funerals (456, *Hamlet* V, i, 205 ff). Twain wrote in his notebook that Ophelia's burial influenced his account of the effects of excommunication in the "Smallpox Hut" episode in Chapter XXIX of his novel.[62] It is possible, therefore, that Ophelia's burial and the events after it also influenced the action in Chapter XLI. After the funerals, both Hank and Hamlet return to their castles, meet their friends Clarence and Horatio, and exchange stories of the events that occurred during their absences. The tragic situations in both kingdoms result from the suspicions that nephews of both kings have of adulterous relationships with the queen, Hamlet's in one case and Mordred's and Agravaine's in the other (459). Finally, tragic bloodbaths occur, and the friends, Horatio and Clarence, live to tell the stories after the heroes' deaths. These connections with *Hamlet* intensify the tragic nature of *A Connecticut Yankee*, especially in the final chapters, and turn Hank into a tragic hero. Through most of the story he acts more like a clown, which may be the result of Twain's early conception of the novel as a burlesque. It may also result from the possible influence of Twain's burlesque *Hamlet* on *A Connecticut Yankee*.[63] In both instances a nineteenth-century figure enters a world of the past and produces comic incongruities in language and action by introducing business, advertising, and technology. In both instances too the references to Shakespeare seem to provoke ridicule for the bourgeois blandness and complacency of the modern figures rather than suffering ridicule themselves as specimens of an antiquated world in an ancient-modern contrast. The difference is that in *A Connecticut Yankee* what begins as burlesque and comedy ends as tragedy, and the *Hamlet* paradigms foster this transition.

Another scene in *A Connecticut Yankee*, a key scene in the

section which deals with moral and social reform, has close parallels with scenes in *King Lear*. In my discussions of *The Prince and the Pauper* and *Huckleberry Finn* I demonstrated how Twain used the scenes of Lear's education on the heath, in the storm, and in the hovel to reflect the moral education of his own heroes. The same scenes from *Lear* are influential here also. King Arthur and Hank roam through the countryside as Lear and his fool do over the heath. In both cases the kings gain sympathy and mercy by associating with the poor and the sick. While he travels with Arthur, Hank utters prophecies and compares them to Merlin's prophecies just as Lear's fool does (314-315; *King Lear* III, ii, 80, 95). This parallel supports a general comparison of Arthur and Hank with Lear and his fool. At the Smallpox Hut Arthur learns about poverty and oppression from the sick peasant woman just as Lear at the hovel learns from Edgar in the disguise of Tom o' Bedlam. When Lear is shown into the hovel, he asks, "Wilt break my heart?" and Hank rushes Arthur away from the hut with the words, "then will follow that which it would break your heart to hear," as the brothers return free to find their family dead (337, *Lear* III, iv, 4). Like Lear, Arthur also suffers the elements of darkness, lightning, and rain until he finds shelter in another peasant's hut (339-341).

In my first chapter I explained Delia Bacon's theory that Shakespeare hid ideas for social reform in his plays, most notably in the scenes describing Lear's experiences on the heath. I also noted that in 1887, when he was working on *A Connecticut Yankee*, Twain read Ignatius Donnelly's *The Great Cryptogram*, which argued a point similar to Bacon's. At this time too he did a comic exercise on Milton to burlesque Donnelly's study of Shakespeare, proving that just as Shakespeare concealed his ideas for social reform in plays, so Milton planned to conceal his in an Arthurian epic.[64] Inspired by his theory about Milton, Twain put ideas for social reform into his own Arthurian tale, and in doing this he might have thought that he was also imitating Shakespeare's strategy as argued by Donnelly and Bacon. This thought on Twain's part could explain why he incorporated references to Lear on the

heath into Arthur's moral pilgrimage.   Unless Twain read
Shakespeare's texts very creatively himself, Bacon's and
Donnelly's books were the only sources from which he could
have drawn comprehensive arguments for the presence of social reform ideas in Shakespeare's plays.

Another play in which Delia Bacon saw overtures toward
social reform was *The Tempest*, and this play also has echoes in
A Connecticut Yankee.   Like Prospero, Hank is both a social
reformer and a magician.   He tries to save himself from being
burned at the stake by pretending to cause a solar eclipse.
When he manages by this trick to instill fear into the hearts of
the people and leaders of Camelot, he solemnly dismisses the
eclipse: "Let the enchantment dissolve and pass harmless away"
(96).   Later, when Morgan le Fay is about to seize and burn an
old woman who curses her for murdering her grandson, Sandy
gets the nod from Hank to exclaim, "Recall the commandment,
or he will dissolve the castle and it shall vanish away like the
instable fabric of a dream" (198).   Both of these statements
reflect the famous speech by which Prospero dismisses the
magic banquet and masque:

> Our revels now are ended. These our actors,
> As I foretold you, were all spirits and
> Are melted into air, into thin air;
> And like the baseless fabric of this vision,
> The cloud-capped towers, the gorgeous palaces,
> The solemn temples, the great globe itself,
> Yea, all which it inherit, shall dissolve,
> And, like this insubstantial pageant faded,
> Leave not a rack behind. We are such stuff
> As dreams are made on, and our little life
> Is rounded with a sleep.
>
> *(IV, i, 148-158)*

Where Prospero says "like the baseless fabric of this vision,"
Sandy says "like the instable fabric of a dream."   Mark Twain
was fond of this speech and quoted it in both "A Memorable
Midnight Experience" and *Is Shakespeare Dead?*   Besides the

theme of magic, he could also have derived the dream imagery
for his novel from it. Hank often refers to his experience in
Camelot as a dream, from the first moments when he awakens
there, through his imprisonment and the eclipse, to his last
words before his death (492). Dreams play an important role in
Twain's later works, and they could have been influenced partly
by *The Tempest*. Twain knew that this was believed to be
Shakespeare's last play, and in a letter to Howells he called *A
Connecticut Yankee* "my swan-song, my retirement from literature permanently."[65] Following Shakespeare's example, therefore, he expressed his farewell to literature through Prospero's
abjuration of his magic: "I'll break my staff, / Bury it certain
fathoms in the earth, / And deeper than did ever plummet
sound / I'll drown my book" (V, i, 61-64).

Yet Twain did not retire at this time. He had to continue
writing in order to recover himself from severe financial problems in the 1890s. He also carried on his quest and exploration
of the dream, which usually involved a creative journey back to
the remote past. In *Personal Recollections of Joan of Arc*
(1896), the visions and voices experienced by Joan are the
equivalents to the dream, although they are carefully distinguished from actual dreams.[66] Twain read extensively to prepare himself for writing this book, and he listed his principal
sources. Although not appearing on this list, Shakespeare was
also a source, yet his works influenced the history and realism
of the book rather than its visionary motifs.

One obvious play of Shakespeare that could have influenced Twain's *Joan of Arc* is *The First Part of King Henry the
Sixth*, in which Joan appears as a character. The scene in
which Joan recognizes the Dauphin, even though he has someone else stand in his place to test her, appears in both works, as
do suspicions about Joan's being a devil or witch.[67] Yet
Shakespeare's Joan is a sorcerer and libertine instead of a
saint. The influence of this play on Twain, therefore, would
have to be minimal. Rather, it is the *Henry the Fourth* plays,
which Twain had used previously as sources for *The Prince and
the Pauper*, that contribute most to his novel.

Twain seems to compare the rise of the Dauphin, crowned

Charles VII of France, to that of Prince Hal, who became Henry
V. Henry and his famous victory at Agincourt are referred to
several times in *Joan of Arc*. Like Henry, when he was carous-
ing in Eastcheap with Falstaff and other low types, the Dauphin must be rescued from evil companions who keep him "idle
and in bondage to his sports and follies." He must learn to
"assert himself and rise and strike for crown and country like a
man."[68] Yet this comparison is not developed any further in
the novel. Rather, the influence of the *Henry the Fourth* plays
focuses on the character and shenanigans of Falstaff. Baetzhold
has demonstrated how Twain's character, Edmond Aubrey, or
The Paladin, is modeled on Shakespeare's Falstaff. The tavern
and party scenes described in chapters V, VII, and XV of Book
II of *Joan of Arc*, with their exaggerated brags and practical
jokes, reflect the Boar's Head Tavern scenes of the *Henry* plays.
As Falstaff does in those plays, Aubrey exaggerates and multi-
plies his daring exploits, and on one occasion, Louis de Conte
and Noel Rainguesson enter a tavern in disguise to hear him
expound in detail on Joan's audience with the Dauphin even
though he had not been present at the event. This is exactly
what Prince Hal and Poins do to Falstaff. They bait and
encourage him to tell stories so they can enjoy the performance
and catch him in his lies.[69] Both Falstaff and Aubrey attack
corpses during a battle and carry off captives. Aubrey delivers
a speech on "merit" like Falstaff's on "honor," and both of them
hold forth on "discretion."[70] Finally, unlike Prince Hal, Joan
does not abandon her amusing companions when she comes to
power. She gives them positions of authority and they die
fighting bravely at her side. On the contrary, when hailed by
Falstaff during the coronation procession, Prince Hal, now
King Henry V, exclaims, "I know thee not, old man."[71] Although both Falstaff and Aubrey play comic and earthy roles in
their stories, Falstaff is left behind as Prince Hal progresses
toward maturity and responsibility, while Aubrey remains with
Joan to keep her in touch with human nature and folly. As he
had done in previous works, therefore, Twain again made use
of Shakespeare's characters for realistic and vernacular effect.
They balance Joan's innocence and spirituality with their earthy

and delinquent behavior. Baetzhold points out that Twain celebrated them and their ilk in "Queen Victoria's Jubilee," a piece written the year after *Joan* was published. Inspired by the procession on the Queen's jubilee day, Twain imagines the victory parade after the battle of Agincourt with Sir John Oldcastle, or Falstaff, come back from the dead to march with his motley crew. Oldcastle is "fat-faced, purple with the spirit of bygone and lamented drink,...leering at the women,...proclaiming his valorous deeds as fast as he could lie,...a living, breathing outrage, a slander upon the human race." After him come his paladins, "the mangiest lot of starvlings and cowards that was ever littered."[72] This mingling of high and low, of serious and comic, was one of the qualities that Twain admired in Shakespeare and translated into his own books.

After *A Connecticut Yankee* and *Joan of Arc*, Twain apparently had recourse to Shakespeare once again in *The Mysterious Stranger*, a story which he neither finished nor published, but which critics see as his potential farewell piece. As such, it is often compared to *The Tempest*, which is believed to be Shakespeare's final play. After enumerating several possible sources for the concept that life is a dream, which appears in the story through the name Philip Traum and through Traum's final speech, Coleman Parsons suggests that the central source of Twain's dream musings is Prospero's speech: "We are such stuff / As dreams are made on...."[73] John Tuckey adds to the likelihood of this influence by finding that while Twain was working on Traum's final speech he wrote to his daughter Clara that he had broken his bow and burned his arrows, a probable allusion to Prospero's breaking his staff and drowning his book.[74] Although William Gibson proves that the dream speech belongs to a different version of the story from the one which Albert Bigelow Paine edited and published, he still sees common traits between the mysterious characters of both versions of the story (Philip Traum and No. 44) and Shakespeare's spirit (Ariel). Both have "the ability to enchant with music, the globe-girdling swiftness, the antic and mercurial moods (untroubled by any Moral Sense), and the power of melting 'into

air, into thin air'..."[75] In the version of the story that Twain
had originally called "The Chronicle of Young Satan," Traum is
often referred to as an angel, and he has the power to create
and destroy. The boys who admire him pity those lost in one of
his storms just as Miranda does those lost in Ariel's storm at
sea.[76] There are also enchanted banquet scenes in both stories.[77] Chess games are played by lovers in both stories, and
clothes are miraculously either not wet or not stained after
being soaked with water.[78] Each story too criticizes the wrongs
of society, although Twain's assault is much more general and
severe, and does not offer the correction and reconciliation that
are the result of Shakespeare's play. In the version entitled
"No. 44, The Mysterious Stranger," elements common to *The
Tempest* include dreams, spirits, music, and magic, one of the
tricks being a miraculous banquet.[79] The master of the print
shop is a man absorbed in his books like Prospero, and No. 44
must begin his apprenticeship by performing the menial task
of carrying logs as Ferdinand does toward his rehabilitation.[80]
The spirits here, however, are not under the control of humans
as they are in *The Tempest*. The magician may threaten and
even burn No. 44, but he has no real power over him like that of
Prospero over Ariel and the sprites. The dream selves operate
without the consent of their human doubles.

Mark Twain resorted to dream imagery in *The Mysterious
Stranger* not just because he thought that it might be his last
book and that he was putting his artistic talents to rest as
Shakespeare seemed to be doing in *The Tempest*, but also
because he was suffering through a period of private and public
tragedy. While he was working on the different versions of his
story, he lost his favorite daughter, Susy, and his wife. He was
also distressed at the wars, imperialism, thoughtless acts of
mankind through history and in his own time, and at the
apparent incapability of God or religious belief to correct or
dispel these evils. In fact, over the centuries religion seemed to
support and enhance the powers of evil. The only way that
Twain was able to manage these tragedies at this time in his
life was consciously or unconsciously to deny their existence, to
place them somewhere in a dream world of unreality. He likely

received confirmation in this method of dealing with evil through psychological concepts that were current at this time and by the denial of evil that is part of the belief in Christian Science. His interest in the dream was an effect of real tragedies and an attempt to transcend them.

The book that turned out to be Mark Twain's last was *Is Shakespeare Dead?*, his comic-serious reaction to the Shakespeare-Bacon controversy, and this book bears resemblances to both *The Tempest* and *The Mysterious Stranger*. As I have previously noted, a traditional view of *The Tempest* is that Shakespeare portrayed himself in the role of Prospero to give a final tribute and farewell to his theatrical career before retirement. Twain associated his book with Shakespeare's play by quoting in it the famous speech of Prospero, "We are such stuff / As dreams are made on."[81] He also projected himself on to Shakespeare as Shakespeare is supposed to have done with Prospero. By subtitling his book "From my Autobiography," he clearly wanted its subject and main character to serve as a foil, if not a model, for himself. He called Shakespeare a "Claimant," which is close enough to *Clemens* to be a clue; he referred to the name *Shakespeare* as a *nom de plume* (like *Mark Twain*), and he contrasted Shakespeare's technical knowledge and hometown reputation with his own. He found in the Shakespeare of the Shakespeare-Bacon controversy a shady character that brought out the always complex, sometimes contradictory, and often dubious roles that he himself had to play all through his career as Mark Twain, the humorist, storyteller, and social critic. He could easily see himself as both Shakespeare (or Bacon) the poet and Shakespeare the imposter, the illiterate, and the businessman. Each of these personas contributed to art. It is also interesting that what revived his interest in the Shakespeare-Bacon controversy and led to his writing the book was the discovery by William Stone Booth of Francis Bacon's signature in ciphers in Prospero's epilogue to *The Tempest*.

The mystery and imposture surrounding Shakespeare that were supposedly revealed in the controversy also led Mark Twain to associate him with Satan, and this created another link between himself and Shakespeare, since he was himself currently speaking in the character of Satan in such works as *The Mysterious Stranger* and "Letters from the Earth." In his book Twain finds the parallel between Satan and Shakespeare curious and romantic. Both are supreme, illustrious, sublime, yet historically unknown. Both are mysterious strangers, and both are claimants (Clemenses).[82] Of course, Twain is again portraying himself as both Satan and Shakespeare. He is especially devilish in recalling a desire that he had as a boy in Sunday-school for gathering facts about Satan's life in order to produce a biography of him: "I was anxious to be praised for turning my thoughts to serious subjects, [but the teacher] rebuked me for inquiring into matters above my age and comprehension." Following Satan's temptation and example, he wanted to eat from the Tree of Knowledge, but this was considered irreverent and sinful. The teacher prohibited him from writing the life of Satan "because, as he said, he had suspicions— suspicions that my attitude in this matter was not reverent, and that a person must be reverent when writing about the sacred characters. He said that anyone who spoke flippantly of Satan would be frowned upon by the religious world and also be brought to account." Then the boy Sam Clemens replied in an ostensibly innocent, yet ironic and diabolic way:

> I assured him, in earnest and sincere words, that he had wholly misconceived my attitude; that I had the highest respect for Satan, and that my reverence for him equaled, and possibly even exceeded, that of any member of any church. I said it wounded me deeply to perceive by his words that he thought I would make fun of Satan, and deride him, laugh at him, scoff at him;

He explained that he really wanted to make fun of the conjecturers who made up facts about Satan. The shocked teacher told him that the conjecturers themselves were so sacred "that whoso ventured to mock them or make fun of their work, could not afterward enter any respectable house, even by the back door." Then the elderly Twain reflects back after almost seventy years:

> How true were his words, and how wise! How fortunate it
> would have been for me if I had heeded them. But I was
> young, I was but seven years of age, and vain, foolish, and
> anxious to attract attention. I wrote the biography, and
> have never been in a respectable house since.[83]

Twain treated Shakespeare in the same way that he claimed
to treat Satan. He aimed his scoffing not at Shakespeare
himself, but at the idolators who tried to extol Shakespeare by
conjectures and assumptions about his life. Yet Twain's treatment of Shakespeare, as we have seen, reached far beyond the
Shakespeare-Bacon controversy. He exercised his irreverence
also by burlesquing Shakespeare, although here too the mock-
ery was usually directed, not at Shakespeare's lofty passages,
but at those who affected a false eloquence and grandeur in
reciting them. In his historical novels he used Shakespeare to
develop a period style of language that seemed both colorful
and realistic, and he drew scenes and ideas from Shakekspeare
that reinforced his efforts at social criticism and reform. Finally, with Shakespeare as his guide and model, he explored
the depths of human tragedy, evil, fate, and suffering in his
most mature works. From Shakespeare, and Satan, therefore,
he received both comic and tragic inspiration.

With Mark Twain's last book we have come full circle.
Although Twain read and saw Shakespeare's plays in his early
years as a schoolboy, printer's apprentice, and printer, and
even dabbled in Shakespeare burlesque as an occasional correspondent, he seems, from his own recollection of it, to have first
discussed Shakespeare at length, taking sides for and against
him, in the arguments that he had about the Shakespeare-
Bacon controversy with his pilot-instructor, George Ealer. It is
then that he came to realize the mysteries and contrasts surrounding Shakespeare—the magnificence of the works, yet the
obscurity and doubts about the person—and these led him
later to see Shakespeare as an image and model of himself.
They also concurred well with the lively mixture of homage and

ridicule that Shakespeare received in American popular culture of his time. In his last book he recalled and analyzed this special relation between himself and Shakespeare. It came to him on the river, like the subjects of his major writing, and it finally found expression in the first and only installment of his formidable autobiography to be published during his lifetime.

Notes

Introduction

[1] Nancy Webb and Jean Francis Webb, *Will Shakespeare and His America* (New York: Viking Press, 1964), pp. 98, 106, 213-214; Esther C. Dunn described Shakespeare's conquest of the same territories, with added discussion of his prominence in American education, literary criticism, and research, in *Shakespeare in America* (New York: Macmillan, 1939); for more particularized studies, see Charles H. Shattuck, *Shakespeare on the American Stage*, Vols. I and II (Washington: Folger Shakespeare Library, 1976, 1987); *Shakespeare in the South: Essays on Performance*, ed. Philip C. Kolin (Jackson: University Press of Mississippi, 1983); Lawrence W. Levine, *Highbrow/Lowbrow: The Emergence of Cultural Hierarchy in America* (Cambridge: Harvard University Press, 1988).

[2] *Shakespeare's America, America's Shakespeare* (London and New York: Routledge, 1990), pp. 51, 59.

[3] "Is Shakespeare Dead?" in *What Is Man?*, *The Complete Works of Mark Twain*, Volume XII, Authorized Edition (New York: Harper and Brothers, 1917), pp. 297-298; this edition of Mark Twain's works will be referred to as *Complete Works*.

[4] "Hawthorne and his Mosses," *Herman Melville*, ed. Willard Thorp (New York: American Book Company, 1938), pp. 333-336.

[5] "Shakespeare; or, the Poet," in *Representative Men*.

[6] Thomas J. Richardson, "Is Shakespeare Dead? Mark Twain's Irreverent Question," in *Shakespeare and Southern Writers: A Study*

in Influence, ed. Philip C, Kolin (Oxford: University Press of Mississippi, 1985), pp. 63-82, esp. pp. 66, 70. For references to Twain's general reading and use of Shakespeare, see Howard G. Baetzhold, *Mark Twain and John Bull* (Bloomington: Indiana University Press, 1970), pp. 255-262, 371-374; and Alan Gribben, *Mark Twain's Library: A Reconstruction* (Boston: G. K. Hall, 1980), pp. 623-636.

⁷ See S. Schoenbaum, *Shakespeare's Lives* (New York: Oxford University Press, 1970), p. 484; see also the chapter progression in Edward Dowden's *Shakspere: A Critical Study of his Mind and Art* (New York: Harper and Brothers, 1897; first publ. 1875).

⁸ "Unconscious Plagiarism," *Mark Twain's Speeches, Complete Works* XXIV (1923), pp. 78, 79.

⁹ "Mental Telegraphy" and "Mental Telegraphy Again," *In Defense of Harriet Shelley, Complete Works* XVI (1918), pp. 116-122, 129-130.

¹⁰ *Modern English Literature: Its Blemishes and Defects* (London: Longman, Brown, Green, & Longmans, 1857), pp. 218-219; see Walter Blair, *Mark Twain & Huck Finn* (Berkeley and Los Angeles: University of California Press, 1960), pp. 59-60.

¹¹ *The Anxiety of Influence: A Theory of Poetry* (New York: Oxford University Press, 1973), pp. 66-69.

¹² Ibid., pp. 120-126.

Biography

¹ A note that Mark Twain wrote in his copy of George Greenwood, *The Shakespeare Problem Restated* (London and New York: John Lane Company, 1908), p. 81. Twain's copy is in the Henry W. and Albert A. Berg Collection of the New York Public Library, Astor, Lenox and Tilden Foundations.

² John Payne Collier, *New Facts Regarding the Life of Shakespeare* (New York: AMS Press, 1970), pp. 5, 38. For background on Collier see S. Schoenbaum, *Shakespeare's Lives* (New York: Oxford University Press, 1970), especially pp. 335-341.

³ Collier, pp. 10-11, 31-33, 40-44.

⁴ *Mark Twain's Autobiography*, ed. Albert Bigelow Paine, *The Complete Works of Mark Twain*, Authorized Edition (New York: Harper and Brothers, 1924), Vol. I, pp. 2, 193, 269, 283, 326-328; Vol. II, pp. 245, 311-312. This edition of Mark Twain's works will be referred to as *Complete Works*.

⁵ Autobiographical Dictation, 11 January 1909, Mark Twain Papers, Bancroft Library, University of California at Berkeley. See Albert Bigelow Paine, *Mark Twain: A Biography* (New York: Harper and Brothers, 1912), chs. 276, 277.

[6] William Stone Booth, *Some Acrostic Signatures of Francis Bacon* (Boston and New York: Houghton Mifflin, 1909), pp. 60-61; *The Tempest*, Epilogue, 1-20; Shakespeare quotations will be taken from *William Shakespeare: The Complete Works*, The Pelican Text Revised, ed. Alfred Harbage (Baltimore: Penguin Books, 1969); see also Booth's study of acrostics in *Hamlet*, pp. 422-423, 490-491.

[7] Autobiographical Dictation, 11 January 1909.

[8] Greenwood, pp. 54, 174-190; "Is Shakespeare Dead?" is in *What Is Man?*, *Complete Works* XII (1917).

[9] See Greenwood, pp. 48, 181, and "Is Shakespeare Dead?" pp. 317-323.

[10] Greenwood, pp. 55, 64, 81.

[11] Ibid., p. 75.

[12] Ibid., p. 56.

[13] "Is Shakespeare Dead?" pp. 299-305.

[14] Ibid., p. 304.

[15] *Autobiography*, ed. Paine, Vol. II, p. 312.

[16] *The Autobiography of Mark Twain*, ed. Charles Neider (New York: Harper and Brothers, 1959), p. 16.

[17] "Is Shakespeare Dead?" pp. 331, 373.

[18] For studies of Twain's double persona see Kenneth S. Lynn, *Mark Twain and Southwestern Humor* (Boston: Little, Brown and Company, 1959), pp. 144-173; Justin Kaplan, *Mr. Clemens and Mark Twain: A Biography* (New York: Simon and Schuster, 1966), pp. 17-18, 67, 101-102; James M. Cox, *Mark Twain: The Fate of Humor* (Princeton: Princeton University Press, 1966), pp. 18-24, 39-44, 90-94; and "*Life on the Mississippi* Revisited," in *The Mythologizing of Mark Twain*, ed. Sara de Saussure Davis and Philip D. Beidler (University of Alabama Press, 1984), pp. 99-115.

[19] "Is Shakespeare Dead?" pp. 298-304.

[20] Edgar M. Branch, "A Proposed Calendar of Samuel Clemens's Steamboats, 15 April 1857 to 8 May 1861, with Commentary," *Mark Twain Journal* 24 (Fall, 1986), pp. 3, 12-14.

[21] *Life on the Mississippi*, *Complete Works* VII (1911), p. 176.

[22] Vivian Constance Hopkins, *Prodigal Puritan: A Life of Delia Bacon* (Cambridge: Harvard University Press, 1959), especially ch. 5.

[23] *Putnam's Monthly*, VII (January, 1856), pp. 7-10.

[24] Hopkins, pp. 197-198.

[25] Ibid., pp. 203, 225-226.

[26] *Philosophy of the Plays of Shakspere Unfolded* (New York: AMS Press, 1970), "Introduction," chs. 1, 2.

[27] Ibid., pp. 13, 24, 32, 35.

[28] Ibid., pp. lv, lxvi, lxxi.

[29] Ibid., pp. lxxiii-lxxv.

[30] Ibid., pp. 70, 75, 87-88.

[31] Ibid., pp. lxxxvii-lxxxix.

[32] Ibid., pp. 194-197; see *The Second Part of King Henry the Fourth*, III, i, 4-31, and *King Henry the Fifth*, IV, i, 97-108, 224-270.

[33] Bacon, pp. 222, 224, 225; see also pp. 208-209; see *King Lear*, III, iv, 1-36.

[34] *Life on the Mississippi*, pp. 172-173.

[35] *The Daily Picayune* (Morning, June 11, 1857), p. 4.

[36] *Picayune* (Afternoon, June 16, 1857), p. 1, from the Boston *Courier*; see also *Picayune* (Afternoon, October 12, 1857), p. 1, from the *North American Review*.

[37] *Mark Twain, Business Man*, ed. Samuel C. Webster (Boston: Little, Brown and Company, 1946), p. 384; *Mark Twain's Letters to his Publishers*, ed. Hamlin Hill (Berkeley and Los Angeles: University of California Press, 1967), p. 230.

[38] See Martin Ridge, *Ignatius Donnelly: The Portrait of a Politician* (Chicago: University of Chicago Press, 1962).

[39] *The Great Cryptogram* (London: Sampson Low, Marston, Searle & Rivington, 1888), Vol. II, Bk. II, Pt. I, chs. 2, 3.

[40] Ibid., Vol. II, Bk. II, Pt. II, summary p. 620, narrative and computations pp. 655-888.

[41] Ibid., pp. 802-803, 812-816, 833-838.

[42] *Mark Twain's Notebooks and Journals* Vol. III, ed. Robert Pack Browning, Michael B. Frank, Lin Salamo (Berkeley and Los Angeles: University of California Press, 1979), pp. 324-328.

[43] Ibid., p. 239.

[44] *Life on the Mississippi*, p. 185.

[45] *Autobiography*, ed. Paine, Vol. I, pp. 354-355.

[46] Ibid., Vol. I, pp. 355-360.

[47] *Roughing It*, ed. Franklin Rogers and Paul Baender, *The Works of Mark Twain* 2 (Berkeley and Los Angeles: University of California Press, 1972), pp. 356-359. This edition of Twain's works will be referred to as *Works*.

[48] *Europe and Elsewhere, Complete Works* XX (1923), xxxi, xxxii.

[49] Ibid., pp. 1-13.

[50] *Mark Twain's Notebooks and Journals* Vol. I, ed. Frederick Anderson et al. (Berkeley and Los Angeles: University of California Press, 1975), pp. 562-568.

[51] *Mark Twain to Mrs. Fairbanks*, ed. Dixon Wecter (Los Angeles: Plantin Press, 1949), p. 168.

[52] *1601: A Tudor Fireside Conversation* (Gloucester, Va.: Land's End Press, 1969), n.p.

[53] *Mark Twain to Mrs. Fairbanks*, p. 217.

[54] Samuel Taylor Coleridge, *Shakespearean Criticism*, ed. Tho-

mas Middleton Raysor (New York: Dutton, 1960), p. 180; see also pp. 171-176, 194-197.

55 See August Wilhelm Schlegel, *Lectures on Dramatic Art and Literature*, trans. John Black (New York: George Bell and Sons, 1892), Lecture XXII, pp. 342-344, Lecture XXIII, pp. 369-371, 374-375.

56 *Kenilworth, Waverley Novels* 21, Parker's Edition (Philadelphia: Desilver, Thomas, and Company, 1836), Vol. I, pp. 223, 230, 237-238, 241.

57 *William Shakespeare: A Biography* (London: R. Clay, 1843), pp. 48, 51.

58 Ibid., pp. 234, 285, 356-357.

59 *Memoirs of the Life of William Shakespeare* (Boston: Little, Brown, and Company, 1866), pp. 198-199, 206.

60 Ibid., pp. 110-111; see also pp. 38, 43, and 82 on Shakespeare's other labors.

61 *Shakespeare: His Life, Art, and Characters* (Boston: Ginn and Company, 1872), Vol. I, p. 187; see pp. 153 (on the era), 34 and 181-182 (on genius and study), 184 (on borrowing and originality), 198 (on styles), and 184-187 (on tragedy and comedy).

62 Ibid., p. 51; see also p. 45.

Comedy

1 From a letter of Samuel Clemens to his mother, January 30, 1862, *Mark Twain's Letters*, Vol. I, ed. Edgar M. Branch, Michael B. Frank, Kenneth M. Sanderson (Berkeley and Los Angeles: University of California Press, 1988), pp. 146-147.

2 *Domestic Manners of the Americans*, ed. Donald Smalley (New York: Alfred A. Knopf, 1949; first publ. 1832), pp. lxxvii-lxxviii, 44-47.

3 Ibid., pp. 133-134, 270-271, 340.

4 Lawrence W. Levine, *Highbrow/Lowbrow: The Emergence of Cultural Hierarchy in America* (Cambridge: Harvard University Press, 1988), pp. 21-30, 56.

5 *Life on the Mississippi*, ed. Edward Wagenknecht (New York: Heritage Press, 1944), pp. 393, 404-405.

6 Hannibal *Tri-Weekly Messenger* (August 24, 1852); *Mark Twain, Early Tales and Sketches*, Vol. I, ed. Edgar M. Branch and Robert H. Hirst (Berkeley and Los Angeles: University of California Press, 1979), pp. 72-74; Minnie Brashear, *Mark Twain, Son of Missouri* (Chapel Hill: University of North Carolina Press, 1934), pp. 109-116.

7 *Messenger* (August 26, 1852); Shakespeare quotations will be taken from *William Shakespeare: The Complete Works*, The Pelican

Text Revised, ed. Alfred Harbage (Baltimore: Penguin Books, 1969).

[8] Hannibal *Journal* (September 16, 1852); see also *Early Tales and Sketches*, pp. 75-77, and Mark Twain, "My First Literary Venture," in *Sketches New and Old, Complete Works* XIX (1917), pp. 95-98.

[9] For a description of the contrast between vernacular and genteel, see Henry Nash Smith, *Mark Twain: The Development of a Writer* (Cambridge: Harvard University Press, 1962), pp. 1-21.

[10] *Messenger* (September 16, 18, 23); *Early Tales and Sketches*, p. 73.

[11] *Early Tales and Sketches*, pp. 86-87.

[12] Shelley Fisher Fishkin, *From Fact to Fiction: Journalism and Imaginative Writing in America* (Baltimore: Johns Hopkins University Press, 1985), pp. 63, 65-68.

[13] *Messenger* (November 23, September 28, and November 23, 1852).

[14] Edgar M. Branch, "A Chronological Bibliography of the Writings of Samuel Clemens to June 8, 1867," *American Literature* XVIII (1946), p. 114.

[15] *Carpet-bag* Vol. I: No. 34, p. 6, No. 35, p. 7 (see also No. 26, p. 7, No. 31, p. 3); No. 41, p. 7, No. 44, p. 4; Vol. II: No. 5, pp. 1, 3. The "literary burlesques" published in the *Carpet-bag* will be treated in the second part of this chapter.

[16] *The Adventures of Thomas Jefferson Snodgrass*, ed. Charles Honce (Chicago: Pascal Covici, 1928), p. 37.

[17] *Roughing It, Works* 2 (Berkeley and Los Angeles: University of California Press, 1972), pp. 297-305.

[18] *Early Tales and Sketches* I, pp. 173, 242, 355.

[19] *Mark Twain of the Enterprise*, ed. Henry Nash Smith (Berkeley and Los Angeles: University of California Press, 1957), p. 94.

[20] Ibid., pp. 102, 108.

[21] Don C. Seitz, *Artemus Ward* (New York: Harper and Brothers, 1919), p. 312. See *Hamlet* III, i, 136-137.

[22] See Edward P. Hingston, *The Genial Showman* (London: Chatto and Windus, 1881), pp. 2, 95, 104.

[23] *Artemus Ward, His Book* (London: Chatto and Windus, 1887), pp. 84, 65, 118, 119, 104, 94.

[24] Hingston, pp. 293-296.

[25] Ivan Benson, *Mark Twain's Western Years* (Palo Alto: Stanford University Press, 1938), p. 97. For more on Ward's influence on Twain see David E. E. Sloane, *Mark Twain as Literary Comedian* (Baton Rouge: Louisiana State University Press, 1979). "First Interview with Artemus Ward" is in *Sketches New and Old*.

[26] Paul Fatout, *Mark Twain on the Lecture Circuit* (Bloomington: Indiana University Press, 1960), p. 46.

27 *Mark Twain of the Enterprise*, p. 199.

28 *Tri-Weekly Messenger* (March 3, 1853), p. 3.

29 *Carpet-bag*, Vol. I: No. 40, p. 7, No. 33, p. 6; Vol. II: No. 5, p. 3, No. 20, p. 3.

30 *Adventures of Thomas Jefferson Snodgrass,* pp. 3-16.

31 *Mark Twain as Literary Comedian*, pp. 1-3, 14, 45.

32 *Artemus Ward, His Book*, pp. 80-83.

33 Franklin Walker, *San Francisco's Literary Frontier* (Seattle: University of Washington Press, 1969), pp. 132-133, 178-184. See also Franklin Rogers, *Mark Twain's Burlesque Patterns* (Dallas: Southern Methodist University Press, 1960), pp. 14-25.

34 Letter quoted in Walker, op. cit., p. 179.

35 *His Book*, p. 86.

36 *Sketches New and Old*, p. 355.

37 *The Celebrated Jumping Frog of Calaveras County and Other Sketches*, ed. John Paul (New York, C. H. Webb, 1867), "Advertisement."

38 Buffalo *Express* (May 21, 1870), p. 2; also in *The Forgotten Writings of Mark Twain*, ed. Henry Duskis (New York: Philosophical Library, 1963), pp. 249-255.

39 *The Autobiography of Mark Twain*, ed. Charles Neider (New York: Harper and Brothers, 1959), pp. 58-59.

40 *Autobiography*, ed. Neider, pp. 59-60.

41 *Nineteenth Century Shakespeare Burlesques*, ed. William Stanley Wells (Wilmington, Delaware: M. Glazier, 1978), Vol. V, pp. 129, 130; 143, 144. For a class interpretation of minstrel shows, see Robert C. Toll, *Blacking Up: The Minstrel Show in Nineteenth-Century America* (New York: Oxford University Press, 1974), pp. 51-53, 70-75.

42 *Dar's De Money* (New York: Samuel French, n.d.), *The Darkey Tragedian* (New York, 1874), *The Actor and the Singer* (New York: Samuel French, n.d.); other minstrel burlesques can be found in *This Grotesque Essence: Plays from the American Minstrel Stage*, ed. Gary D. Engle (Baton Rouge: Louisiana State University Press, 1978); see also Ray B. Brown, "Shakespeare in American Vaudeville and Negro Minstrelsy," *American Quarterly* 12 (Fall 1960), pp. 374-391; and Charles Haywood, "Negro Minstrelsy and Shakespearean Burlesque," in *Folklore & Society*, ed. Bruce Jackson (Hatboro: Folklore Associates, 1966), pp. 77-92.

43 Edgar M. Branch, *The Literary Apprenticeship of Mark Twain* (Urbana: University of Illinois Press, 1950), pp. 4, 5, 35. Smith's books were *The Theatrical Apprenticeship of Sol Smith* and *The Theatrical Journey-Work* (Philadelphia: T. B. Peterson, 1854), and *Theatrical Management in the West and South* (New York: Harper and Brothers, 1868).

[44] *Apprenticeship*, ch. 5; *Journey-Work*, chs. 20, 22; *Management*, Act V, ch. 1, Act IV, ch. 7.

[45] *On the Poetry of Mark Twain: With Selections from his Verse*, ed. Arthur L. Scott (Urbana: University of Illinois Press, 1966), p. 56. See also *Mark Twain's Letters from Hawaii*, ed. A. Grove Day (London: Chatto and Windus, 1967), pp. 198-201.

[46] *Adventures of Huckleberry Finn*, ed. Walter Blair and Victor Fischer (Berkeley and Los Angeles: University of California Press, 1985), p. 179; see *Hamlet* (III, i, 56, 69, 76, 78), and *Macbeth* (II, ii, 35, 38; V, v, 44-45).

[47] *Punch*, Vol. 44 (March 14, 1863), p. 105.

[48] For example, the soliloquy from Arthur Clement Hilton's *Hamlet; or Not Such a Fool as He Looks* was published in W. A. Clouston's *Literary Curiosities and Eccentricities* (1875). Other such anthologies are R. W. Criswell's *The New Shakespeare and Other Travesties* (1882), *Burdett's Book of Comic Parodies* (1883), and Walter Hamilton's *Parodies of the Works of English and American Authors* (1885).

[49] *Nineteenth Century Shakespeare Burlesques*, Vol. I, p. xxi, Vol. V, p. xi; Charles Shattuck, *The Hamlet of Edwin Booth* (Urbana: University of Illinois Press, 1969), p. 68.

[50] *Nineteenth Century Shakespeare Burlesques*, Vol. I, p. 24.

[51] Ibid., Vol. V, p. 26.

[52] Albert Bigelow Paine, *Mark Twain, A Biography* (New York: Harper and Brothers, 1912), Vol. I, p. 495. See also *Mark Twain's Satires and Burlesques*, pp. 49-50.

[53] *Satires and Burlesques*, pp. 69-70.

[54] "Twain's Version of Hamlet," *The Twainian* II, No. 9 (June, 1943), pp. 4-6.

[55] *Satires and Burlesques*, pp. 51-53.

[56] "Twain's Version of Hamlet," pp. 5-6.

[57] "Hamlet's Brother," p. 22. The original manuscript is no. DV 320a, in the Mark Twain Papers, The Bancroft Library, University of California at Berkeley.

History

[1] *Mark Twain in Eruption*, ed. Bernard De Voto (New York: Harper and Brothers, 1922), p. 206; a comma has been inserted after *use* for clarity.

[2] Catharine Morris Wright, *Lady of the Silver Skates: The Life and Correspondence of Mary Mapes Dodge, 1830-1905* (Jamestown, R.I.: Clingstone Press, 1979), pp. 14-17, 23-26.

[3] From a letter and article quoted in Wright, pp. 69-70.

4 *Hans Brinker or, The Silver Skates* (New York: Charles Scribner's Sons, 1958), p. 10.

5 Wright, pp. 11, 29-31, 79; *Hans Brinker*, pp. 10-11.

6 *Hans Brinker*, pp. 189, 206.

7 *St. Nicholas*, III, no. 7 (May 1876), p. 441; III, nos. 5-10 (March - October 1876); VI, no. 9 (July 1879), pp. 581ff; V, no. 1 (November 1879), pp. 1ff; I, no. 3 (January 1874), pp. 146-147.

8 *Life on the Mississippi, Complete Works* VII (1911), p. 185.

9 *Mark Twain and Southwestern Humor* (Boston: Little, Brown and Company, 1959), pp. 157-159.

10 *Innocents Abroad, Complete Works* II (1911), Vol. II, pp. 1-5.

11 *Innocents Abroad*, Vol. I, pp. 223, 217.

12 See *Traveling with the Innocents Abroad*, ed. David Morley McKeitham (Norman: University of Oklahoma Press, 1958), p. 60. See also Henry Nash Smith, *Mark Twain: The Development of a Writer* (Cambridge: Harvard University Press, 1962), pp. 24-25.

13 See Kenneth R. Andrews, *Nook Farm: Mark Twain's Hartford Circle* (Cambridge: Harvard University Press, 1950), pp. 190-193.

14 *Mark Twain in Eruption*, p. 206.

15 See Albert E. Stone, Jr., *The Innocent Eye: Childhood in Mark Twain's Imagination* (Hamden, Conn.: Archon Books, 1970), pp. 112-116; Howard G. Baetzhold, *Mark Twain and John Bull* (Bloomington: Indiana University Press, 1970), pp. 51-54; *The Prince and the Pauper*, ed. Victor Fischer and Lin Salamo, *Works* 6 (1979), pp. 19-25; this will be abbreviated to *P&P*.

16 *Mark Twain in Eruption*, p. 206.

17 *P&P*, Appendix A, pp. 351-361.

18 *Mark Twain in Eruption*, pp. 204-205.

19 Citations are to *William Shakespeare: The Complete Works*, ed. Alfred Harbage (Baltimore: Penguin Books, 1969).

20 *P&P*, p. 134.

21 Compare *I Henry IV*: I, i, and III, ii, and *II Henry IV*: IV, iv with *P&P* ch. 5.

22 Compare *I Henry IV*: II, ii and iv, and *II Henry IV*: I, ii, 52-53 and V, ii, 70-71 with *P&P* chs. 18, 22 and 23.

23 See *P&P*, Appendix A, pp. 354, 357.

24 Robert L. Gale, "The Prince and the Pauper and King Lear," *Mark Twain Journal* XII (Spring 1963), pp. 14-17.

25 See Baetzhold, pp. 59-62, for the influence of Lecky on this theme.

26 See *Life on the Mississippi*, pp. 332-333, 369-370, 375-376. For Twain's mixed reaction to Scott see Sidney J. Krause, *Mark Twain as Critic* (Baltimore: Johns Hopkins University Press, 1967), pp. 148-189.

²⁷ *Ivanhoe; A Romance. Waverley Novels* 15, Parker's Edition (Philadelphia: Desilver, Thomas, and Company, 1836), Vol. I, pp. iv-v, 10-11; see Baetzhold, p. 50.

²⁸ *Ivanhoe*, Vol. I, pp. 23-24, 48-49, 62; see *P&P*, Appendix A, p. 353.

²⁹ *P&P*, p. 237.

³⁰ *Ivanhoe*, Vol. I, pp. 131, 237; see *The Merchant of Venice*, II, viii, 15-17.

³¹ *Kenilworth. Waverley Novels* 21, Vol. I, chs. I-III, especially II, p. 24; see *King Lear* I, iv, 190 and *Romeo and Juliet* III, v, 150; and *P&P*, Appendix A, p. 357.

³² *Kenilworth*, Vol. II, p. 138.

³³ Ibid., Vol. I, pp. 237-240.

³⁴ See Krause, pp. 158-160, and Baetzhold, pp. 94-97.

³⁵ *P&P*, pp. 56, 84, 155-157.

³⁶ *P&P*, pp. 117-118, 145.

³⁷ *Quentin Durward, Waverley Novels* 29, Vol. I, pp. 79-80, 85.

³⁸ *P&P*, Appendix A, pp. 362-364.

³⁹ *Mark Twain in Eruption*, p. 206.

⁴⁰ *The Love Letters of Mark Twain*, ed. Dixon Wecter (New York: Harper and Brothers, 1949), p. 76; see also pp. 34, 126, 132.

⁴¹ *Mark Twain: The Critical Heritage*, ed. Frederick Anderson (New York: Barnes & Noble, 1971), pp. 54-55; original in *Atlantic Monthly* (December 1875).

⁴² Ibid., pp. 99, 102; original in *Century Magazine* (September 1882).

⁴³ *My Mark Twain*, ed. Marilyn Austin Baldwin (Baton Rouge: Louisiana State University Press, 1967), pp. 5, 6.

⁴⁴ Henry N. Hudson, an American Shakespeare critic, also saw Shakespeare as a realist. See *Shakespeare: His Life, Art, and Characters* (Boston: Ginn and Company, 1872), Vol. I, pp. 166f.

⁴⁵ *Mark Twain-Howells Letters*, ed. Henry Nash Smith and William M. Gibson (Cambridge: Harvard University Press, 1960), Vol. I, pp. 291-292.

⁴⁶ *Yorick's Love*, in *The Complete Plays of W. D. Howells*, ed. Walter J. Meserve (New York: New York University Press, 1960), p. 136.

⁴⁷ Ibid., pp. 118-120.

⁴⁸ Ibid., pp. 126, 138; see demands for proof, pp. 132, 134, and compare with *Othello* III, iii, 359-386.

⁴⁹ *A Foregone Conclusion* (Boston: James R. Osgood and Company, 1875), p. 75.

⁵⁰ *Mark Twain-Howells Letters*, Vol. I, p. 21; see also pp. 17-18, 48.

51 Ibid., Vol. I, pp. 180, 216.

52 *A Counterfeit Presentment*, in *Complete Plays*, p. 75; see *Hamlet* V, i, 177-182.

53 Ibid., p. 99; see *Hamlet* V, i, 256, and I, ii, 65.

54 *Mark Twain-Howells Letters*, pp. 372-373; see also *My Mark Twain*, ch. VI.

55 *Mark Twain-Howells Letters*, pp. 369-370.

56 *Colonel Sellers as a Scientist*, *Complete Plays*, pp. 220, 221.

57 Ibid., p. 227; see *Othello*, II, iii, 277-279; V, ii, 349; III, iii, 350; *Hamlet*, I, iv, 40; *Macbeth*, V, i, 32, 47-49.

58 Ibid. p. 228; see *Romeo and Juliet* V, i, 59-65.

59 *The Undiscovered Country* (Boston: Houghton, Mifflin and Company, 1880), p. 373.

60 Ibid., pp. 186-202, 203-204, 292, 300; see *Hamlet*, IV, v, 174-184, vii, 165-182.

61 *The Gilded Age*, *Complete Works* X (1915), Vol. I, p. 163.

62 *Life on the Mississippi*, p. 163.

63 *Mark Twain's Notebooks and Journals*, Vol. II, ed. Frederick Anderson (Berkeley and Los Angeles: University of California Press, 1975), pp. 85, 100.

64 *Life on the Mississippi*, p. 41; see "Old Times on the Mississippi," *Atlantic Monthly* XXXV (January 1975), p. 73.

65 *Life on the Mississippi*, p. 43.

66 Ibid., pp. 176, 231, 409-411.

67 *Life on the Mississippi*, ed. Edward Wagenknecht (New York: Heritage Press, 1944), pp. 393, 404-405.

68 *Life on the Mississippi*, *Complete Works*, pp. 193-195.

69 Ibid., p. 476.

70 Ibid., pp. 345-346.

71 Ibid., p. 20, and *P&P*, pp. 148-150.

72 *Mark Twain and Huck Finn* (Berkeley: University of California Press, 1960), p. 136.

73 *History of European Morals from Augustus to Charlemagne* (New York: D. Appleton and Co., 1908), Vol. I, pp. 126-131, 257.

74 Ibid., Vol. I, p. 118.

75 Henry Fisher, *Abroad with Mark Twain and Eugene Field* (New York: N. L. Brown, 1922), p. 138.

76 Hippolyte A. Taine, *History of English Literature*, trans. H. Van Laun (London: Chatto and Windus, 1871), Vol. I, p. 340; for Twain's philosophy see *What is Man?*, *Complete Works* XII (1917), pp. 8-9, and "Joan of Arc," in *In Defense of Harriet Shelley*, *Complete Works* XVI (1925), pp. 376-377; Twain delivered a paper "What is Happiness?" to the Monday Evening Club in February, 1883, which is an early version of *What is Man?*.

[77] *History of English Literature*, Vol. I, pp. 83, 187.

[78] Ibid., Vol. I, pp. 225ff.

[79] Ibid., Vol. I, pp. 356ff.

[80] Ibid., Vol. II, pp. 254-259; Henry N. Hudson also places Shakespeare in an age of transition between "primitive crudeness" and "vitiated taste," *Shakespeare: His Life, Art, and Characters*, Vol. I, pp. 153ff.

[81] See Hudson, *Shakespeare: His Life, Art, and Characters*, Vol. I, p. 153, and White, *Memoirs of the Life of William Shakespeare* (Boston: Little, Brown, and Company, 1866), pp. 199, 206.

[82] Taine, Vol. I, pp. 83-84, 90-93.

[83] Compare Ibid., Vol. I, ch. I, parts 2 and 3 with *Life on the Mississippi*, ch. III.

[84] Ibid., Vol. II, p. 159.

[85] Ibid., Vol. I, p. 340.

[86] *Twain and the Image of History* (New Haven: Yale University Press, 1961), pp. 59-67.

[87] Ibid., pp. 13-14, 49, 69-70.

[88] Ibid., pp. 86-87, 155, 160-166.

Tragedy

[1] "About Play Acting," *The Man That Corrupted Hadleyburg, The Complete Works of Mark Twain*, Volume XV (New York: Harper and Brothers, 1902), p. 225; this will be cited hereafter as *Complete Works*.

[2] Thomas Bailey Aldrich, *The Story of a Bad Boy* (New York: J. H. Sears and Company, 1928; first pub. 1869), pp. 53, 216.

[3] See Henry Fielding, *Tom Jones*, Bk. XVI, ch. 5; Laurence Sterne, *Tristram Shandy*, Bk. I, chs. 10-12, Bk. II, ch. 17, Bk. IV, ch. 27, Bk. V, ch. 31, Bk. VI, ch. 11; Charles Dickens, *David Copperfield*, chs. 1, 25; *Great Expectations*, chs. 4, 31; James Boswell, *Life of Johnson*, 1763, age 54; also see Robert F. Fleissner, *Dickens and Shakespeare: A Study in Histrionic Contrasts* (New York: Haskell House, 1965), pp. 149-184, 185-207.

[4] *Wilhelm Meister's Apprenticeship*, trans. Thomas Carlyle (New York: The Heritage Press, 1959; first pub. 1795, trans. by Carlyle 1824), Bk. I, pp. 48, 26.

[5] Bk. V, pp. 307-308.

[6] Bk. VI, pp. 206-207, 233-234.

[7] Susanne Howe, *Wilhelm Meister and his English Kinsmen* (New York: AMS Press, 1966; first pub. 1930); Howe notes references to *Hamlet* in *Wilhelm Meister*, pp. 50, 54, in *Godolphin*, p. 158, and in John Sterling's *Arthur Coningsby*, p. 218; see also *Kenelm Chillingly*, Bk. IV, ch. 2.

⁸ See Alan Gribben, *Mark Twain's Library: A Reconstruction* (Boston: G. K. Hall, 1980) for Twain's reading of Carlyle, pp. 127-130, Goethe, pp. 263-265, and others.

⁹ Albert Bigelow Paine, *Mark Twain: A Biography* (New York: Harper and Brothers, 1912), Vol. II, p. 495.

¹⁰ *Mark Twain's Hannibal, Huck and Tom*, ed. Walter Blair (Berkeley and Los Angeles: University of California Press, 1969), pp. 243-252.

¹¹ *The Adventures of Tom Sawyer, Works* 4, ed. John Gerber, Paul Baender, and Terry Firkins (Berkeley and Los Angeles: University of California Press, 1980), p. 160; further page references to this edition will appear in the text; see *Hamlet* III, i, 154. Phrases in *Tom Sawyer* that show the influence of other Shakespeare plays are "whistle her down the wind," p. 109 (see *Othello* III, iii, 262), and "homeless heads," p. 137 (see "houseless heads" in *King Lear* III, iv, 30), and "old humpbacked Richard" is mentioned on pp. 176-177. Citations to Shakespeare are from *William Shakespeare: The Complete Works*, ed. Alfred Harbage (Baltimore: Penguin Books, 1969).

¹² "Tom Sawyer: A Play in Four Acts," *Mark Twain's Hannibal, Huck & Tom*, p. 269.

¹³ *The Story of a Bad Boy*, pp. 213, 216; see *Tom Sawyer*, p. 55; on the influence of *Bad Boy* on *Tom Sawyer* see Walter Blair, *Mark Twain and Huck Finn* (Berkeley: University of California Press, 1960), p. 64.

¹⁴ *Mark Twain's Burlesque Patterns* (Dallas: Southern Methodist University Press, 1960), pp. 11, 97-98, 106-109.

¹⁵ Ibid., p. 10.

¹⁶ Ibid., pp. 127-128.

¹⁷ *Mark Twain-Howells Letters*, ed. Henry Nash Smith and William M. Gibson (Cambridge: Harvard University Press, 1960), p. 144.

¹⁸ See Rogers, pp. 128, 136.

¹⁹ *Adventures of Huckleberry Finn*, ed. Walter Blair and Victor Fisher (Berkeley and Los Angeles: University of California Press, 1985), p. 4; further page references to this edition will appear in the text. I am grateful to Victor Doyno for making sure that the passages on which I base my argument exist also in the recently discovered 1876 manuscript of *Huckleberry Finn*.

²⁰ "Huck and Jim," *Yale Review* 47 (May 1958), p. 428; see also Lynn's *Mark Twain and Southwestern Humor* (Boston: Little, Brown, and Company, 1959), pp. 215, 240-241.

²¹ See Rogers, pp. 136-138.

²² Rogers, pp. 130-132, 135.

²³ Ibid., pp. 132-135.

²⁴ "Cap'n Simon Wheeler, The Amateur Detective," *Mark Twain's*

Satires & Burlesques, ed. Franklin Rogers (Berkeley and Los Angeles: University of California Press, 1968), pp. 236-237.

[25] Ibid., p. 291.

[26] "Simon Wheeler, Detective," *Satires & Burlesques*, pp. 335-336, 339.

[27] Ibid., pp. 378, 391.

[28] Ibid., p. 453.

[29] Rogers, pp. 135-136.

[30] Bernard DeVoto, *Mark Twain at Work* (Boston: Houghton Mifflin, 1967), pp. 64-67.

[31] DeVoto, pp. 63, 67.

[32] Walter Blair, "When was *Huckleberry Finn* Written?" *American Literature* XXX (March 1958), pp. 7-10; see also Blair, *Mark Twain and Huck Finn*, pp. 199f.

[33] *Life on the Mississippi*, p. 409; *The Love Letters of Mark Twain*, ed. Dixon Wecter (New York: Harper and Brothers, 1949), p. 212.

[34] Rogers, pp. 128, 136.

[35] Rogers, pp. 139-144.

[36] Rogers, pp. 144-148.

[37] Other critics who associate the feud with *Romeo and Juliet* are Howard Baetzhold, *Mark Twain and John Bull: The British Connection* (Bloomington: Indiana University Press, 1970), p. 258; Edward Mendelsohn, "Mark Twain Confronts the Shakespeareans," *Mark Twain Journal*, 17 (Winter 1973-1974), p. 20; and Victor Doyno, who also relates *Richard the Third* to the killing of Buck Grangerford, *Writing Huck Finn: Mark Twain's Creative Process* (Philadelphia: University of Pennsylvania Press, 1991), pp. 120-123.

[38] See Editor's Note, "Burlesque *Hamlet*," in *Satires & Burlesques*, pp. 49-54.

[39] *Satires & Burlesques*, p. 56; see *Hamlet*, II, ii, 196-198.

[40] *Satires & Burlesques*, p. 68.

[41] Ibid., pp. 69-70.

[42] Rogers, p. 138; see also pp. 113-127.

[43] Blair, *Mark Twain and Huck Finn*, p. 302.

[44] For a study linking the themes of the soliloquy and the novel, see E. Bruce Kirkham, "Huck and Hamlet," *Mark Twain Journal* XIV (Summer 1969), pp. 17-19.

[45] Rogers, pp. 138, 176 n.46; see a similar contrast between conscience and heart in *Tom Sawyer*, p. 40.

[46] See Blair, *Mark Twain and Huck Finn*, pp. 139-142; also see Twain's essay on conscience, "Facts Concerning the Recent Carnival of Crime in Connecticut," in *Tom Sawyer Abroad*, *Complete Works* XIV (1917), pp. 302-325.

[47] "Hamlet's Brother," DV 320a, Mark Twain Papers. The Bancroft Library, University of California at Berkeley.

[48] "Twain's Version of Hamlet," *The Twainian*, 2, No. 9 (June 1943), pp. 4-6.

[49] Rogers, p. 148.

[50] "The Tragical History of King Richard III," in *Five Restoration Adaptations of Shakespeare*, ed. Christopher Spencer (Urbana: University of Illinois Press, 1965), pp. 342-343.

[51] Blair, *Mark Twain and Huck Finn*, pp. 218-219; see *Kate Beaumont*, ch. vii.

[52] Gribben, *Mark Twain's Library*, I, p. 123; see *The Grandissimes*, chs. i, xxxvi.

[53] Victor Doyno argues the connection between *Lear* and the Wilks episode in *Writing* Huck Finn, p. 123.

[54] Doyno relates Jim's remorse over hurting his deaf daughter, which is described just before the Wilks episode, to Lear's remorse over mistreating Cordelia, Ibid., p. 122; see *Huckleberry Finn*, pp. 201-202, and *Lear* V, iii, 258-275.

[55] See *Lear* IV, iii, 46; Paul Schacht studies imagery of nature and mistreatment of the daughter in *Lear* and in *Huckleberry Finn* in "The Lonesomeness of Huckleberry Finn," *American Literature* LIII (May 1981), pp. 193-196.

[56] *Notebooks and Journals*, Vol. II, pp. 100-101; Schacht notes this, and also compares passages describing storms in *Lear* and *Huckleberry Finn*.

[57] *Mark Twain's Burlesque Patterns*, pp. 128, 138.

[58] "On the Acting of Iago," *Atlantic Monthly* XLVIII (August 1881), pp. 209-211.

[59] *A Connecticut Yankee in King Arthur's Court*, ed. Bernard L. Stein, *Works* 9 (1979), pp. 172-173; page numbers to this edition will henceforth be given in the text.

[60] *Mark Twain and John Bull*, p. 257; see *Hamlet* III, ii, 1-2.

[61] Ibid., pp. 372, 373; see *Connecticut Yankee*, pp. 61, 208, *II Henry IV*, III, ii, 289, and *Macbeth* II, iii, 108.

[62] *Mark Twain's Notebooks and Journals* Vol. III, ed. Robert Pack Browning, Michael B. Frank, Lin Salamo (Berkeley and Los Angeles: University of California Press, 1979), pp. 502, 506.

[63] Both Baetzhold, op. cit. p. 257, and Rogers, *Mark Twain's Satires & Burlesques*, Introduction, p. 8, see this influence.

[64] *Mark Twain's Notebooks and Journals* III, p. 239.

[65] A letter of August 24, 1889, *Mark Twain-Howells Letters*, pp. 610-611.

[66] *Personal Recollections of Joan of Arc*, *Complete Works* XVII (1924), Vol. I, pp. 61, 69, 70-72.

[67] Ibid., I, pp. 141, 251; see *Henry VI Part I*, I, ii, 60-72 and V, iii, 30-35.

[68] *Joan of Arc* I, p. 126.

[69] Baetzhold, *Mark Twain and John Bull*, p. 259; compare *Joan of Arc* I, pp. 149-156 with *Henry IV Part II*, II, iv.

[70] Baetzhold, p. 260; compare *Joan of Arc* I, 123 and II, 82 with *Henry IV Part I* V, iv, 127; *Joan* I, 121-122 with *Henry V*, iv, 118; *Joan* I, 286 with *Henry V*, i, 129-139.

[71] *Henry IV Part II* V, v, 48; see Baetzhold p. 261.

[72] *Europe and Elsewhere, Complete Works* XX (1923), pp. 201-202; see Baetzhold p. 259.

[73] "The Background of *The Mysterious Stranger*," *American Literature* XXXII (March 1960), pp. 71-72.

[74] *Mark Twain and Little Satan: The Writing of "The Mysterious Stranger"* (West Lafayette, Indiana: Purdue University Studies, 1963), p. 69.

[75] *The Mysterious Stranger*, ed. William M. Gibson (Berkeley and Los Angeles: University of California Press, 1970), pp. 2-3, 31-33.

[76] *The Mysterious Stranger*, pp. 51-52; see *The Tempest* I, ii, 1-13.

[77] *The Mysterious Stranger*, pp. 71, 84; *The Tempest* III, iii, 17-52.

[78] *The Mysterious Stranger*, pp. 91-92, 102; *The Tempest* V, i, 171, II, i, 60-63.

[79] *The Mysterious Stranger*, pp. 329-330.

[80] Ibid., pp. 230, 237, 240; see *The Tempest*, III, i, 1-17.

[81] "Is Shakespeare Dead?" in *What is Man?*, *Complete Works* XII, p. 362.

[82] Ibid., pp. 297, 311.

[83] Ibid., pp. 307-310.

BIBLIOGRAPHY

Aldrich, Thomas Bailey. *The Story of a Bad Boy*. New York: J. H. Sears, 1928.

Andrews, Kenneth R. *Nook Farm: Mark Twain's Hartford Circle*. Cambridge: Harvard University Press, 1950.

Bacon, Delia. *Philosophy of the Plays of Shakspere Unfolded*. New York: AMS Press, 1970.

— "William Shakespeare and his Plays: An Inquiry Concerning Them." *Putnam's Monthly* VII (January 1856), pp. 1-19.

Baetzhold, Howard G. *Mark Twain and John Bull: The British Connection*. Bloomington: Indiana University Press, 1970.

Benson, Ivan. *Mark Twain's Western Years*. Palo Alto: Stanford University Press, 1938.

Blair, Walter. *Mark Twain and Huck Finn*. Berkeley: University of California Press, 1960.

— "When Was *Huckleberry Finn* Written?" *American Literature* XXX (March 1958), pp. 1-25.

Bloom, Harold. *The Anxiety of Influence: A Theory of Poetry*. New York: Oxford University Press, 1973.

Booth, William Stone. *Some Acrostic Signatures of Francis Bacon*. Boston: Houghton Mifflin, 1909.

Branch, Edgar M. "A Chronological Bibliography of the Writings of Samuel Clemens to June 8, 1867." *American Literature*, XVIII (1946-7), pp. 109-159.

— *The Literary Apprenticeship of Mark Twain*. Urbana: University of Illinois Press, 1950.

— "A Proposed Calendar of Samuel Clemens's Steamboats, 15 April 1857 to 8 May 1861, with Commentary." *Mark Twain Journal* 24 (Fall 1986), pp. 2-34.

Brashear, Minnie. *Mark Twain: Son of Missouri*. Chapel Hill: University of North Carolina Press, 1934.

Bristol, Michael D. *Shakespeare's America, America's Shakespeare*. New York: Routledge, 1990.

Browne, Charles F. *Artemus Ward, His Book*. London: Chatto and Windus, 1887.

Browne, Ray B. "Shakespeare in American Vaudeville and Negro Minstrelsy." *American Quarterly* XII (Fall 1960), pp. 374-91.

— "Shakespeare in the Nineteenth-Century Songsters." *Shakespeare Quarterly* VIII (1957), pp. 207-18.

Brownell, George Hiram. "Twain's Version of Hamlet." *The Twainian* II (June 1943), pp. 4-6.

The Carpet-bag. Boston (1851-1853).

Clemens, Samuel L. *Adventures of Huckleberry Finn*. Ed. Walter Blair and Victor Fischer. Berkeley: University of California Press, 1985.

— *The Adventures of Tom Sawyer*. Ed. John Gerber, Paul Baender, Terry Firkins. Berkeley: University of California Press, 1980.

— *The Adventures of Thomas Jefferson Snodgrass*. Ed. Charles Honce. Chicago: Pascal Covici, 1928.

— *The Autobiography of Mark Twain*. Ed. Charles Neider. New York: Harper and Brothers, 1959.

— *The Celebrated Jumping Frog of Calaveras County and Other Sketches*. Ed. John Paul. New York: C. H. Webb, 1867.

— *The Complete Works of Mark Twain*, Authorized Edition. 26 Vols. New York: Harper and Brothers, 1907-1935.

— *A Connecticut Yankee in King Arthur's Court*. Ed. Bernard L. Stein. Berkeley: University of California Press, 1979.

— *The Forgotten Writings of Mark Twain*. Ed. Henry Duskis. New York: Philosophical Library, 1963.

— *Life on the Mississippi*. Ed. Edward Wagenknecht. New York: Heritage Press, 1944.

— *The Love Letters of Mark Twain*. Ed. Dixon Wecter. New York: Harper and Brothers, 1949.

— *Mark Twain, Business Man*. Ed. Samuel C. Webster. Boston: Little, Brown, 1946.

— *Mark Twain: Early Tales and Sketches* Vol I. Ed. Edgar M. Branch and Robert H. Hirst. Berkeley: University of California Press, 1979.

— *Mark Twain-Howells Letters*. Ed. Henry Nash Smith and William Gibson. Cambridge: Harvard University Press, 1960.

— *Mark Twain in Eruption*. Ed. Bernard De Voto. New York: Harper and Brothers, 1940.

— *Mark Twain of the Enterprise*. Ed. Henry Nash Smith. Berkeley: University of California Press, 1957.

— *Mark Twain to Mrs. Fairbanks*. Ed. Dixon Wecter. Los Angeles: Plantin Press, 1949.

— *Mark Twain's Hannibal, Huck, and Tom*. Ed. Walter Blair. Berkeley: University of California Press, 1969.
— *Mark Twain's Letters* Vol. I. Ed. Edgar M. Branch, Michael B. Frank, and Kenneth M. Sanderson. Berkeley: University of California Press, 1988.
— *Mark Twain's Letters from Hawaii*. Ed. A. Grove Day. London: Chatto and Windus, 1966.
— *Mark Twain's Letters to his Publishers*. Ed. Hamlin Hill. Berkeley: University of California Press, 1967.
— *Mark Twain's Notebooks and Journals* Vols. I and II. Ed. Frederick Anderson, Michael B. Frank, and Kenneth M. Sanderson. Berkeley: University of California Press, 1975.
— *Mark Twain's Notebooks and Journals* Vol. III. Ed. Robert Pack Browning, Michael B. Frank, and Lin Salamo. Berkeley: University of California Press, 1979.
— *Mark Twain's Satires and Burlesques*. Ed. Franklin Rogers. Berkeley: University of California Press, 1968.
— *The Mysterious Stranger*. Ed. William Gibson. Berkeley: University of California Press, 1970.
— *On the Poetry of Mark Twain*. Ed. Arthur L. Scott. Urbana: University of Illinois Press, 1966.
— *The Prince and the Pauper*. Ed. Victor Fisher and Lin Salamo. Berkeley: University of California Press, 1979.
— *Roughing It*. Ed. Franklin Rogers and Paul Baender. Berkeley: University of California Press, 1972.
— *1601: A Tudor Fireside Conversation*. Gloucester, Virginia: Land's End Press, 1969.
— *Traveling with the Innocents Abroad*. Ed. David Morley McKeitham. Norman: University of Oklahoma Press, 1958.
Coleridge, Samuel Taylor. *Shakespearean Criticism*. Ed. Thomas Middleton Rayson. New York: Dutton, 1960.
Collier, John Payne. *New Facts Regarding the Life of Shakespeare*. New York: AMS Press, 1970.
Cox, James M. "*Life on the Mississippi* Revisited." *The Mythologizing of Mark Twain*. Ed. Sara de Saussure Davis and Philip D. Beidler. Tuscaloosa: University of Alabama Press, 1984.
— *Mark Twain: The Fate of Humor*. Princeton University Press, 1966.
The Daily Picayune. New Orleans, 1857.
The Darkey Tragedian. New York, 1874.
Dar's De Money. New York: Samuel French, n.d.
Desdemonum. New York, 1874.
De Voto, Bernard. *Mark Twain at Work*. Boston: Houghton, Mifflin, 1967.
— *Mark Twain's America*. Boston: Little, Brown, 1932.
Dodge, Mary Mapes. *Hans Brinker or, The Silver Skates*. New York: Charles Scribner's Sons, 1958.

Donnelly, Ignatius. *The Great Cryptogram*. London: Samson Low, Marston, Searle, Rivington, 1888.

Dowden, Edward. *Shakspere: A Critical Study of His Mind and Art*. New York: Harper and Brothers, 1897.

Doyno, Victor. *Writing* Huck Finn: *Mark Twain's Creative Process*. Philadelphia: University of Pennsylvania Press, 1991.

Dunn, Esther C. *Shakespeare in America*. New York: Macmillan, 1939.

Express. Buffalo, New York, 1870.

Fatout, Paul. *Mark Twain on the Lecture Circuit*. Bloomington: Indiana University Press, 1960.

Fisher, Henry. *Abroad with Mark Twain and Eugene Field*. New York: N. L. Brown, 1922.

Fishkin, Shelley Fisher. *From Fact to Fiction: Journalism and Imaginative Writing in America*. Baltimore: Johns Hopkins University Press, 1985.

Five Restoration Adaptations of Shakespeare. Ed. Christopher Spencer. Urbana: University of Illinois Press, 1965.

Fleissner, Robert F. *Dickens and Shakespeare: A Study in Histrionic Contrasts*. New York: Haskell House, 1965.

Gale, Robert L. "The Prince and the Pauper and King Lear." *Mark Twain Journal* XII (Spring 1963), pp. 14-17.

Goethe, Johann Wolfgang von. *Wilhelm Meister's Apprenticeship*. Trans. Thomas Carlyle. New York: Heritage Press, 1959.

Goodman, Joseph T. "Hamlet's Brother." Unpublished manuscript in Mark Twain Papers, Bancroft Library, University of California at Berkeley.

Greenwood, George. *The Shakespeare Problem Restated*. London: John Lane, 1908.

Gribben, Alan. *Mark Twain's Library: A Reconstruction*. Boston: G. K. Hall & Company, 1980.

Griffin, G. W. H. *The Actor and the Singer*. New York: Samuel French, n.d.

Haywood, Charles. "Negro Minstrelsy and Shakespearean Burlesque." *Folklore and Society*. Ed. Bruce Jackson. Hatboro, Pennsylvania: Folklore Associates, 1966.

Hingston, Edward P. *The Genial Showman*. London: Chatto and Windus, 1881.

Hopkins, Vivian Constance. *Prodigal Puritan: A Life of Delia Bacon*. Cambridge: Harvard University Press, 1959.

Howe, Susanne. *Wilhelm Meister and his English Kinsmen*. New York: AMS Press, 1966.

Howells, William Dean. *The Complete Plays of W. D. Howells*. Ed. Walter J. Meserve. New York: New York University Press, 1960.

— *A Foregone Conclusion*. Boston: James R. Osgood and Company, 1875.

— *My Mark Twain*. Ed. Marilyn Austin Baldwin. Baton Rouge: Louisiana State University Press, 1967.

— *The Undiscovered Country*. Boston: Houghton, Mifflin, 1880.

Hudson, Henry N. *Shakespeare: His Life, Art, and Characters*. Boston: Ginn and Company, 1872.

Journal. Hannibal, Missouri, 1852.

Kaplan, Justin. *Mr. Clemens and Mark Twain: A Biography*. New York: Simon & Schuster, 1966.

Kirkham, E. Bruce. "Huck and Hamlet." *Mark Twain Journal* XIV (Summer 1969), pp. 17-19.

Knight, Charles. *William Shakespeare: A Biography*. London: R. Clay, 1843.

Krause, Sidney. *Mark Twain As Critic*. Baltimore: Johns Hopkins University Press, 1967.

Lecky, W. E. H. *History of European Morals from Augustus to Charlemagne*. New York: D. Appleton and Company, 1908.

Levine, Lawrence W. *Highbrow / Lowbrow: The Emergence of Cultural Hierarchy in America*. Cambridge: Harvard University Press, 1988.

Lynn, Kenneth. "Huck and Jim." *Yale Review* 47 (May 1958), pp. 421-31.

— *Mark Twain and Southwestern Humor*. Boston: Little, Brown, 1959.

Mark Twain: The Critical Heritage. Ed. Frederick Anderson. New York: Barnes and Noble, 1971.

Mendelsohn, Edward. "Mark Twain Confronts the Shakespeareans." *Mark Twain Journal* 17 (Winter 1973-1974), pp. 20-21.

Nineteenth Century Shakespeare Burlesques. Ed. William Stanley Wells. Wilmington, Delaware: M. Glazier, 1978.

Paine, Albert Bigelow. *Mark Twain, A Biography*. New York: Harper and Brothers, 1912.

Parsons, Coleman. "The Background of *The Mysterious Stranger*." *American Literature* XXXII (March 1960), pp. 55-74.

Richardson, Thomas J. "Is Shakespeare Dead? Mark Twain's Irreverent Question." *Shakespeare and Southern Writers: A Study in Influence*. Ed. Philip C. Kolin. Oxford: University Press of Mississippi, 1985.

Ridge, Martin. *Ignatius Donnelly: The Portrait of a Politician*. University of Chicago Press, 1962.

Rogers, Franklin. *Mark Twain's Burlesque Patterns*. Dallas: Southern Methodist University Press, 1960.

Salomon, Roger. *Twain and the Image of History*. New Haven: Yale University Press, 1961.

Schacht, Paul. "The Lonesomeness of Huckleberry Finn." *American Literature* LIII (May 1981), pp. 189-201.

Schlegel, August Wilhelm. *Lectures on Dramatic Art and Literature*. Trans. John Black. New York: George Bell and Sons, 1892.

Schoenbaum, S. *Shakespeare's Lives*. New York: Oxford University Press, 1970.

Scott, Sir Walter. *Waverly Novels*. Parker's Edition. Philadelphia: Desilver, Thomas, and Company, 1836.

Seitz, Dan C. *Artemus Ward*. New York: Harper and Brothers, 1919.

Shakespeare, William. *William Shakespeare: The Complete Works*. The Pelican Text Revised. Ed. Alfred Harbage. Baltimore: Penguin Books, 1969.

Shakespeare in the South: Essays on Performance. Ed. Philip C. Kolin. Jackson: University Press of Mississippi, 1983.

Shattuck, Charles H. *The Hamlet of Edwin Booth*. Urbana: University of Illinois Press, 1969.

— *Shakespeare on the American Stage*. Washington: Folger, 1976.

Sloane, David E. *Mark Twain as Literary Comedian*. Baton Rouge: Louisiana State University Press, 1979.

Smith, Henry Nash. *Mark Twain: The Development of a Writer*. Cambridge: Harvard University Press, 1962.

Smith, Sol. *The Theatrical Apprenticeship of Sol Smith*. Philadelphia: T. B. Peterson, 1854.

— *The Theatrical Journey-Work of Sol Smith*. Philadelphia: T. B. Peterson, 1854.

— *Theatrical Management in the West and South*. New York: Harper and Brothers, 1868.

Stone, Albert. *The Innocent Eye*. Hamden, Connecticut: Archon Books, 1970.

Taine, Hippolyte A. *History of English Literature*. Trans. H. Van Laun. London: Chatto and Windus, 1871.

Tenney, Thomas A. *Mark Twain: A Reference Guide*. Boston: G. K. Hall & Company, 1977. Supplements in *American Literary Realism*.

This Grotesque Essence: Plays from the American Minstrel Stage. Ed. Gary D. Engle. Baton Rouge: Louisiana State University Press, 1978.

Toll, Robert C. *Blacking Up: The Minstrel Show in Nineteenth-Century America*. New York: Oxford University Press, 1974.

Tri-Weekly Messenger. Hannibal, Missouri, 1852.

Trollope, Frances. *Domestic Manners of the Americans*. Ed. Donald Smalley. New York: Alfred A. Knopf, 1949.

Tuckey, John. *Mark Twain and Little Satan*. West Lafayette, Indiana: Purdue University Press, 1963.

Walker, Franklin. *San Francisco's Literary Frontier*. Seattle: University of Washington Press, 1969.

Webb, Nancy and Jean Francis. *Will Shakespeare and his America*. New York: Viking, 1964.

White, Richard Grant. "The Bacon-Shakespeare Craze." *Atlantic Monthly* LI (April 1883), pp. 507-521.

— *Memoirs of the Life of William Shakespeare*. Boston: Little, Brown, 1865.

— "On the Acting of Iago." *Atlantic Monthly* XLVIII (August 1881), pp. 203-212.

Wright, Catharine Morris. *Lady of the Silver Skates: The Life and Correspondence of Mary Mapes Dodge, 1830-1905*. Jamestown, Rhode Island: Clingstone Press, 1979.

INDEX